CHARISMATISM
Awakening or Apostasy?
by O. Talmadge Spence

*from
Leo C. Davis
1982*

BOB JONES UNIVERSITY PRESS, INC.
GREENVILLE, SOUTH CAROLINA 29614

© 1978 Bob Jones University Press, Inc.
Greenville, South Carolina 29614

ISBN: 0-89084-065-2

Printed in the United States of America

TABLE OF CONTENTS

Sound of the Sirens
Old and New Enemies
Sounds at Corinth
Sin: Species and Mutation
Neo-Christianity and Neo-Ecumenism

PART ONE
THE FALLACY OF
INTERPRETIVE HISTORY

Heilsgeschichte Versus Neo-Pentecostalism
The Present Ecumenical Pentecostal Movement
The Classical Pentecostal
The Historical Presupposition of the Classical Pentecostal
A Personal Conclusion
Dangers Involved in Interpretive History
Possible Views of History

The Trinity Versus a Schizophrenic Godhead
Another Perspective in History Leading to Modern
    Pentecostalism
What Does This Mean?

Another View of the Former and Latter Rain
The Rains
Another Presupposition
Another View of the Book of Acts
Another View of the Corinthian Catastrophe

PART TWO
THE WEAKNESS OF HUMAN EXPERIENCE

PART THREE
THE INFALLIBILITY OF
DIVINE REVELATION

Foreword

It is amazing how relatively little public controversy has been engendered by the modern so-called "charismatic movement." It is true that sermons have been preached showing from the Scriptures the fallacies and errors of the movement. Occasional critical articles have been written; but, for the most part, people have either been captured by this new cult (and cult it is beyond a shadow of a doubt) or have more or less ignored it or tolerated it. Some Roman Catholic prelates tried to ignore it. Others, more self-seeking and clever, have realized this is something all organized apostasy can use and have embraced it, promoted it, and let it run like wildfire through the Roman church. Opportunists like Jerry Falwell speak well of it and welcome the support of its followers while privately professing to oppose it. For example, speaking at the Southwide Baptist Fellowship on October 5, 1977, he said, "I want to tell you, I love charismatics. Do you know there are many charismatics in America who know that we are just like this who support us regularly, and I have never sent a dime back. I love them and they love me." Yet he has privately declared, "As a matter of fact, we take a very strong stand against the charismatic movement. For example, we will not accept a student into Liberty Baptist College who either has spoken in tongues or believes that tongues is for today."[1]

Many preachers have chosen to ignore the whole affair—either out of fear of offending some of their people who have become involved in the modern charismatic movement or, in some cases, of grieving the Holy Spirit by criticizing something that might be of God; but this is a Scriptural perversion which must be faced and dealt with. Ignoring it or remaining silent concerning it will not cause it to go away. All too few are aware of its dangers or recognize its true nature. It will destroy Biblical faith, undermine the doctrine of the inspiration of Scripture, substitute emotionalism for the Gospel and a sensual experience for sound doctrine. Follies and immorality attend upon it. The charismatic movement is the handmaiden of apostasy and the servant of Antichrist. It is as deceptive as its father the Devil, as dangerous as death itself, as much to be dreaded as leprosy and corruption. It perverts Biblical separation and Scriptural Christian living, preferring Satanic prophecies to the infallible proofs of the Word of God and demonic revelations to the words of the Holy Spirit given us through holy men of old who "spake as they were moved" by Him.

This, therefore, is a book that *had* to be written. No man is better qualified to write it than Dr. O. Talmadge Spence, who comes out of the historic Pentecostal movement. He is well acquainted with the leaders of traditional Pentecostalism and ably contrasts their attitudes, doctrines, outlooks, and purposes with those of the charismatics today and draws a sharp distinction between sincerity of the traditional Pentecostal leaders and the trickery and dishonesty of the clowns performing in the present charismatic circus. The reader need not hold to the historic Pentecostal doctrines and traditions any more than I do in order to benefit from this book, for this book is not written to promote Pentecostalism or argue its theological tenets. This book is both an

[1]Personal letter from Falwell to Jack Van Impe, March 8, 1978.

historical analysis of the tradition and an exposé of the current emphases.

Any sincere Christian, certainly any Bible-believing, Fundamental Christian, must judge any religious phenomena on the basis of Biblical teaching and Scriptural truth. This is Dr. Spence's standard of judgment. Fundamental Christians will not always agree on matters of doctrinal interpretation; but we must all agree on the infallibility, inspiration, and divine authority of the Book as our standard for faith and practice. I am confident that Dr. Spence has been raised up by God to save many from the insidious and Satanic aberration of the charismatic movement and to warn God's people against it. This book will be bitterly attacked, but not with logic or the Word of God. Charismatics are incapable of logic and too incapacitated by their emotionalism and spiritual blindness to handle the Word of God honestly and effectively. The charismatic leadership, composed not only of deceived people but of deceivers as well, if they determine not to be helped by Dr. Spence's volume, would be well advised to ignore it altogether, for they cannot answer its argument or dull its edge.

Bob Jones

Preface

Born as the son of a preacher, Bishop Hubert T. Spence of the Pentecostal Holiness Church, I grew up under the influence of spiritual Christianity. My mother and father were Godly, the family altar was important, the Lord's Day was sacred, discipline was regular, and the Bible was the pattern.

Every now and then a circus would come to town, and quite naturally, as a boy, I wanted to attend. I would approach my mother, and by evening my father would hear of my desire. He would proceed to admonish me of the world, the flesh, and the Devil, making a clear distinction between the character of a Christian and the phoniness of a clown. He made it clear that one could not mix Christ and His Christian with the circus and its clown.

Some years later, after I had returned from service in the United States Navy and was attending Bob Jones College, I was gloriously saved; and Biblical Christianity became a living reality in my life.

In the thirty years that have intervened, I have seen the face of popular Christianity greatly change in its testimony to the world. Whereas formerly there was a distinction between the world and the institutional church, sin and the saint, there is now, in many places, an admixture of all these antitheses.

In fact, the deeper spiritual concepts of the Bible have been brought into an integration of worldly and carnal unities. Individuals and movements speak of "glossolalia," "Charismatics," "miracles," and "gifts" from God, but there is not the transformation of life that formerly accompanied the practices and habits of the Christian. One of the loftiest truths in Pauline theology involves "spiritual" (*pneumatikon*) and "gifts" (*charismaton*), and we are hearing from many quarters of the world about certain "Spirit-filled" Christians.

The word *charisma* is popularly used in connection with football players, presidents, Hollywood stars, and evangelists. Webster's two definitions of this word reveal the "Heinz' 57 varieties" and the many "Duke's mixtures" in contemporary Christendom: "Charisma is an extraordinary power (as of healing) given a Christian by the Holy Spirit for the good of the church," or "a personal magic of leadership arousing special popular loyalty or enthusiasm."

In reality, these definitions are opposite; and when they are integrated with Biblical spirituality into worldly ways, the Church goes to the circus and the Christian becomes a clown—a Charismatic clown, if you please.

A few years ago, at a youth convention at Raleigh, North Carolina, a notable Charismatic Pentecostal evangelist called Jesus a "hippy," the three Hebrew Children "hippies," and God, the Father, "the granddaddy rabbit of them all."

Over and over again we hear such blasphemous remarks as, "God is a cool cat"; "Jesus is a living doll"; "the Holy Spirit is a trip to blow your mind."

In view of my personal background—having been born in a Pentecostal home and denomination in the third generation—and in view of the confrontations and controversies I have received from my own ministry, Foundations Bible College was born in April 1974. As founder and president of this non-denominational institution through these years, I have witnessed great blessing from the Lord through His providence behind the scenes and His direct guidance of the Holy Spirit. And as the days have come and gone since my childhood, I have found that the things that are labeled "Charismatic," "spiritual," and even "Biblical," have changed among the Pentecostals. They have moved away from the Biblical base of truth, and have become weak and less meaningful in the matter of true spirituality.

Spiritually speaking, every now and then a circus comes to town with its sideshow, its three-ring features, and its clamor for the worldling. And usually it is led in the personality of a Charismatic Clown.

January 23, 1978
O. Talmadge Spence

Introduction

In many small towns of America there is a particular practice to which people have become accustomed in their daily lives. This practice involves the sound of the town whistle announcing the midday break from the discipline and duty of labor. It is also a reminder that the workday is half over. When this whistle is heard, people move from the work area to a place of conversation and refreshment. Some even scurry home in their automobiles for a more private repose.

Sound of the Sirens

The midday sound used to be that of a steam whistle. Today it is the shrill sound of the siren. This is something *new* in our time, and sometimes it presents a problem. When the siren of a firetruck or police car is heard near the usual time of the lunch whistle, care must be exercised to be sure that one is following the sound of refreshment and not the sound of tragedy. This problem brings to mind the "Sirens" of ancient Greek mythology. These sea nymphs, with their trap of sound and song, lured sailors to their island and to destruction.

In these late seventies we are hearing a *new* sound in the Protestant and Roman Catholic churches of the world, and we need to discern whether it is the joyous sound of spiritual refreshment or the sad sound of a

tinkling spiritual tragedy. The sound to which I refer is
the sound of the reputed "glossolalia" among the Neo-
Pentecostals and Roman Catholic Charismatics. Is it the
sign of spiritual refreshment, renewal, and reform? Or is
it the sign and sound of another spiritual tragedy,
tangent, and error in church history? Is it a Godly spirit, a
seducing spirit, or an erroneous spirit? Is it an awakening
or an apostasy? We have come to a time when the siren
and the whistle are being sounded during the high-noon
babel of Neo-Christianity, and there is a neo-ecumenism
in the air.

Old and New Enemies

Many Christians are fighting old enemies who are
either too weak to hurt us or who have already died and
left us. Consider this: it is always the "new" and the
"change" that plagues the soldier of the Cross of Calvary,
and this demands that we keep in spiritual touch with
God, as well as with Scriptural truth in God's Word. The
enemy is no longer simply "snuff"; it has mutated to a
complicated system of "drugs." To the Christian, it is no
longer old Modernism or "Liberalism" leading an old
ecumenism; it is now an entirely new vogue—the "Neo-
Christianity" leading into a new ecumenism.

To any age, the foe is relatively *new* in his manner of
presentation; but he is always *old* in his relationships to
sin and Satan by origin. Some people have misunderstood this problem and falsely concluded that the
Bible has to be made relevant and relative to each changing age. This assumption is neither possible nor necessary. The Word of God is sufficient and effective, and It
remains alive and timely through all the vicissitudes of
time and the erroneous mutations of the ages. We do not
need to make the Bible relevant through some new
interpretation or translation; we need to preach the One
Word of God applicable, on target, through each
succeeding change in each succeeding generation.

In our present time we are not only passing through a
new age; it also ends in the Apostasy. This adds another
question to our already growing list: Are we presently

living in a spiritual awakening from God? Or are we living in a spiritual apostasy from Satan?

The "Liberals" and the Modernists of the old time are about gone, as to their former appearance. But the old ecumenism has merely shifted; it is not dead. Too many Fundamentalists and Evangelicals are reloading old shells that have already been shot at enemies who no longer exist. Quite often the Christians who know the Cure and are able to do something about the plague, live behind the times. Slow to do their spiritual homework, they lack the spiritual discernment to see the truth of the matter.

Almost everyone in this day talks a conservative, evangelical language. The Bible and being "born again" have become quite popular. In a recent election three presidential candidates spoke of having been "born again." Around the world the siren sounds and noon whistles are being heard. The old ecumenism has shifted to a new ecumenism that sounds somewhat like the old-time religion of our forefathers. This brings before us two questions: What should we do if it is refreshment and renewal time? What *must* we do if these sounds announce a Christian tragedy or a demonical seduction?

Sounds at Corinth

It is appropriate at this point to set forth Paul's words concerning the sounds of the "Corinthian catastrophe."[1] Paul maintains his Biblical position concerning the "glossolalia" by reminding his readers that he could say, "I thank my God, I speak with tongues more than ye all" (I Corinthians 14:18) and "forbid not to speak with tongues" (v. 39b). Yet Paul *warns* them as well. He personally wishes that "all spake with tongues" (v. 5a). However, between Paul and the Corinthians in general we readily see two different definitions and understandings of the gifts of the Holy Spirit. Therefore the Apostle, under the immediate revelation and inspiration of the Holy Spirit, sets forth certain restraints. He announces the superiority of the gift of prophesying above the gift of tongues (I Corinthians 12:28;

14:1-5, 19, 39a). He counsels that when the gift of tongues is manifested, the gift of interpretation must be exacted (I Corinthians 14:27, 28). And he cites women, in particular, as a threat to this gift and use of tongues in public services (I Corinthians 14:34, 35). Paul's implication is that the Corinthians were *volitionally* speaking in tongues, rather than allowing the Holy Spirit to speak under His own volition (I Corinthians 14:26; cf. Acts 2:4), thus interrupting the Spirit in His sovereign leadership. Paul argues that if there is no interpretation, there must be rebuke or silence in the church in this matter of tongues. Then he adds, "and let him speak to himself, and to God" (v. 28).

There were other problems, of course, that surrounded this false manifestation of the gift of tongues. These problems included a general disorder in the services, the outspeaking disorder of certain women (vv. 29-35), and the "present distress" of at least seven heresies in the church. These heresies involved divisions (1:10-4:16), immorality (4:17-6:20), practices pertaining to marriage (ch. 7), Christian liberties (chs. 8-11), Spiritualities (including the gifts, chs. 12-14), teachings concerning the Resurrection (ch. 15), and matters concerning the Collections (ch. 16).

The greater emphasis in the church should have been upon love (*agape*), which could be entitled, "The More Excellent Road" (Greek: *hodos*). In other words, instead of Charismatics it was to be character. This love (I Corinthians 13) was not *eros* (physical love), *sterkein* (kindred love), or *philein* (emotional and responsive love); it was *agapein* (divine and devotional love). This divine love did not originate in any earthly human experience of love; it was from above and was shed abroad in the heart by the Holy Spirit (Romans 5:5). It was unlike any kind of natural love.

Let us note the heartbeat sound of Paul's instruction as distinguished from the other sounds of Corinth:

Now, brethren, if I come unto you speaking with tongues, what shall I profit you, except I shall speak to you either by revelation, or by knowledge, or by prophesying, or by doctrine? And even things without life giving sound, whether pipe or harp, except they give a distinction in the sounds, how shall it be known what is piped or harped? For if the trumpet give an uncertain sound, who shall prepare himself to the battle? So likewise ye, except ye utter by the tongue words easy to be understood, how shall it be known what is spoken? for ye shall speak into the air. There are, it may be, so many kinds of voices in the world, and none of them is without signification. Therefore if I know not the meaning of the voice, I shall be unto him that speaketh a barbarian, and he that speaketh shall be a barbarian unto me. Even so ye, forasmuch as ye are zealous of spiritual gifts, seek that ye may excel to the edifying of the church (I Corinthians 14:6-12).

The Corinthian catastrophe, aside from its other schisms, divisions, and heresies, was rooted in the duplicity of definitions with regard to the gifts of the Holy Spirit in the New Testament church, as well as in the abuses and excesses of genuine gifts placed in the Body of Christ and operated by the sovereignty of God rather than by the volition of men. This duplicity is noted in many ways in this section of Paul's Letter, but a particular metaphor involves the sounds of certain musical instruments. They are "pipe" (*aulos*), "harp" (*kithara*), and "trumpet" (*salpigx*). The Apostle makes it clear that a "distinction" (*diastolein*) must be made in these sounds and instruments so that there might be no "uncertain" (*adeilon*) understanding of that which the sound represents. In other words, we must be able to discriminate between the pipe, as a wind instrument; an harp, as a stringed instrument; and the trumpet, as a warrior's instrument. We must recognize not only the difference in the sounds of the instrument, but also the message which the sound conveys. I repeat: there was to be a recognized, distinguished message to which the sound pointed in these matters. As the instruments vary from the ecstasy of dance and delight to duty, discipline, and war, so the message, in the final analysis, could be as wide as ecstatic song to that of prepared warfare. That

wide difference lies in the word "distinction," which
derives from a compound Greek word meaning "to set,
place, arrange asunder" (Vine). Thus, the sounds of the
various sirens of life must be distinguished. There is a
Biblical message which we must accept and a barbarian
jargon which we must reject.

Sin: Species and Mutation

It remains ever true that we must not believe the *errors*
that result from the constant mutation of sin, throughout
the centuries, in its new and sundry varieties. Yet we must
not fight the *truths* that emerge from the constant actions
of our sovereign God throughout the centuries in His
preservation of certain fundamental principles of the
Bible and His will that marks the consummation to which
He leads us.

Somewhere in this matter we are taught that every
Christian must make *progress* in keeping up with the
mutations of sin in his own age; yet he must retain a
changeless Biblical integrity against the *change* that
leads to a compromise of the Word of God in any age. It is
really something to manage, if we will dare to stand,
prepared to meet the age as a soldier of Christ.

This is a delicate balance of position between progress
without Biblical change, and change—often honorable
within itself—without compromise. We believe in
progress because we believe that God is moving with His
will through history. However, that progress must be
made on the Biblical base of God's changeless Word, for
we also believe that men are moving, with Satan and
their wills, through this same history. John says:
"Hereby know we the spirit of truth, and the spirit of
error" (I John 4:6b). True Bible believers have been able,
always, to know or recognize the *species* of sin. But we are
also called upon to know the changing *mutations* of that
original species of sin, as it is manifested in each
generation. The species of sin is constant; the mutations
of sin are never the same or duplicated again, exactly, in
any ongoing age.

Standing supreme and beyond all recognitions of sin—error: its species and its mutations—are Jesus Christ—the Truth, the Changeless Lord Jesus—and His Word. He stands "towering over the wrecks of time" and over all the changes produced by compromise and sin. To know error without knowing truth is to know the disease without the cure. But to be content to know truth without a recognition of the various manifestations of the errors of our time is to be subjects of naiveté and deception as well.

We would not have guessed—and certainly we would not have desired—that in the last days we would meet a final test such as knowing the true Christ in the great flourishing of a Neo-Christianity. It has come upon us, however, and we must make a decision. There is no turning back. We must meet the "new" foe victoriously!

Neo-Christianity and Neo-Ecumenism

The shift from the old ecumenism, promulgated by the old Modernism, has been a shift to a new quarter of authority, fostering new ecumenism. The same point that Satan made in the *old* ecumenism will now be made through the new ecumenism, but with a new emphasis. This brings before us several questions:

Is Neo-Orthodoxy the same as the original Palestinian and/or Hellenistic consciousness of the Lord Jesus Christ in the first century?

Are existentialism and the dialectical principles, after all, the true key to Biblical interpretation and the New Testament "crisis" which was received in the New Birth? Is the modern teaching of "Easter-Faith" the same as that which our forefathers—from Paul to Luther, Calvin, and Wesley—received through early, Biblical faith?

Is the methodology of Neo-Evangelicalism and its practice of an unseparated pew and platform, as well as the emphasis placed upon intellectualism in the license of dialogue with false faiths identical with the practices given by Christ and the Holy Spirit in the evangelistic crusades of the early Apostles?

Is Neo-Morality and its emphasis upon love as the supreme quest and motive in the various situational ethics of the twentieth century the same as the Biblical *Agape* of Christ and the Biblical truths heartily set forth in Holy Scripture?

Is the proliferation of Charismatic claims by Neo-Pentecostalism in Protestantism and Roman Catholicism the same truth and spirit as that which was manifested in the Upper Room on the Day of Pentecost, and later spilled into other incidents recorded in the Book of Acts?

Are we living in an outpouring of the Holy Spirit comparable to the early days of the New Testament, which were *fresh* and *new* (Greek: *kainos*)? Or are we actually witnessing in the twentieth century a *new* (Greek: *neos*) and erroneous teaching and demonstration of the doctrine of the Holy Spirit?

Neo-Orthodoxy, Neo-Evangelicalism, Neo-Morality, and Neo-Pentecostalism represent, respectively, a new teaching of the mode of Biblical hermeneutics, a new teaching on Biblical methodology, a new teaching of Biblical love, and a new teaching on the baptism of the Holy Spirit and the gifts and glossolalia attending that baptism. The *Neo* is manifested in all of these new movements of our century, and it is my opinion that they are here to stay as a part of the End-time influence. During this stay they will make a strong impression upon the entire world, leaving a tremendous influence for the immediate grave actions of men and history. The higher accomplishment of all this will be to bring in a new ecumenism which will be more powerful than even the old ecumenism which plagued earlier Fundamentalists.

There are two important truths which must motivate us at this ominous time in history. The first involves being humble; the second involves being bold. If a work is God's work and we have been misled by some person or persons, we must be *humble* enough to give way to the Holy Spirit and the Word of God so that we will not grieve, quench, or blaspheme God. If a work in our time is not

God's work and we are right and Biblical, we must be *bold* enough to stand up for the Holy Spirit and God, so that we will not grieve, quench, or blaspheme God. The danger is equal in either direction; the Holy Spirit will not approve anything that God's Word has condemned (I John 5:7; I Corinthians 2:10-13; II Peter 1:21). Paul said to the Corinthians:

> Wherefore I give you to understand, that no man speaking by the Spirit of God calleth Jesus accursed: and that no man can say that Jesus is the Lord, but by the Holy Ghost (I Corinthians 12:3).

In other words, we cannot pronounce error in the Name of the Lord Jesus with the sanction of the Holy Spirit, and we cannot pronounce truth in the Name of the Lord Jesus without the power of the Holy Spirit.

All the sounds of the time are siren sounds, and we must be able to discern their significances. The search for truth in this matter lies in the crucible of a trilogy. First, we must possess an inner life of devotion to the Lord Jesus Christ, and this comes from only the singular relationship of the New Birth. Second, we must possess an outer life of evangelism, service, spirituality, and fruit in the power of the Risen Lord and the Holy Spirit. And third, we must maintain a consistent life of Biblical integrity and intellectual honesty in the truth of the Word of God. This trilogy must be persuaded by the singular reality that the one thing that is greater than witnessing, soulwinning, supernatural signs, or personal piety or success is the personal exaltation of the Lord Jesus Christ through a daily faithfulness to His Word. Jesus said: "If ye love me, keep my commandments" (John 14:15). This singular reality must be cherished above theological systems, denominations, movements, personalities, and ecumenism.

There are three major areas in which we will pursue our investigation of the sounds, the signs, and the systems of thought as projected by Neo-Pentecostalism and Roman Catholic Charismatics. These words of Peter have become our guide:

For we have not followed cunningly devised fables, when
we made known unto you the power and coming of our
Lord Jesus Christ, but were eyewitnesses of his majesty.
For he received from God the Father honour and glory,
when there came such a voice to him from the excellent
glory, This is my beloved Son, in whom I am well pleased.
And this voice which came from heaven we heard, when
we were with him in the holy mount. We have also a more
sure word of prophecy; whereunto ye do well that ye take
heed, as unto a light that shineth in a dark place, until the
day dawn, and the day star arise in your hearts: Knowing
this first, that no prophecy of the scripture is of any
private interpretation. For the prophecy came not in old
time by the will of man: but holy men of God spake as they
were moved by the Holy Ghost (II Peter 1:16-21).

Peter presents three impressive witnesses in this
passage: (1) the fables, cunningly devised, which men
have followed and interpreted from history; (2) the
substantiating evidence that men have used from their
subjective *experience*; and (3) the exalted and more sure
word of all authorities—the very *Word* of God Itself. Peter
rejected the testimony of the fables from history. He
substantiated and validated his own testimony of the
Lord Jesus, by virtue of being an honorable eyewitness.
But he exalted the authority of the "more sure" Word of
God above all that history had noted and man had
experienced.

With these thoughts in mind, I have divided this book
into three parts:

    I. The Fallacy of Interpretive History
    II. The Weakness of Human Experience
    III. The Sufficiency of Divine Revelation.

PART ONE

THE FALLACY OF INTERPRETIVE HISTORY

1

The Fallacy of
Interpretive History

The ocean of contemporary religious thought in the late seventies is dominated by the eastern shoreline of European theologians of the intellectual and sophisticated *Heilsgeschichte* movements, and the western shoreline of the less pretentious American historians of the Classical Pentecostal, the Neo-Pentecostal, and the Roman Catholic Charismatic movements. The important word to be remembered in this observation is the word *history*; although it may not be obvious at first sight, there is a certain affinity between the two theological accounts.

Heilsgeschichte Versus Neo-Pentecostalism

When you read the profile of Neo-Christianity, you find it to be the composite of the influence of the intellectual *Heilsgeschichte*, and the very practical and pragmatic interpretations of the history presently being espoused in Pentecostalism. In all of this we see the Hegelian existentialism and synthesis culminating into an ecumenicity which allows the various forms of Neo-Christianity—and therefore of Neo-Orthodoxy, Neo-Evangelicalism, Neo-Morality, and Neo-Pentecostalism—to live compatibly within a fallacious interpretation of history as set forth and propounded by this neo-ecumenism. But the modern Pentecostal has his own unique way of interpreting history, just as does the *Heilsgeschichte* group.

Without getting too far into the analysis of Neo-Orthodoxy, we should at least illustrate with a meaningful description by the Neo-Evangelical, Carl F. H. Henry. The word *Heilsgeschichte*, simply rendered, means, "history of salvation." It is further defined as "that theological view of history as culminating in the formation and development of the people of God. European theologians widely hold this concept."[2]

Mr. Henry states:

> Then too, the Heilsgeschichte school itself includes an exegete as conservative as Oscar Cullman, whose theologically positive views embarrass some salvation-history scholars. In fact, just this extensive theological diversity within the modern *Heilsgeschichte* movement is one feature that differentiates it from the conservative camp. The salvation-history scholars are actually less unified in perspective than their mutual interest in historical revelation might indicate. They represent a wide variety of viewpoints and interests, although at this present time in the theological debate they manifest a common concern. Eduard Schweizer of Zurich is really a post-Bultmannian, Ulrich Wilckens of Berlin is numbered in the Pannenberg school, and Eduard Lohse of Berlin reflects much of the position of Jeremias, his former teacher.[3]

These words lead us to investigate three terms together. They are *Geschichtliche* ("that which happens and continues to happen"), *Heilsgeschichte* ("history of salvation"), and *Formgeschichte* ("the role of distinguishing Palestinian from Hellenic layers in the New Testament"). The European schools of theology have come in this century with a pretentious dialogue which has influenced many, as the Barth-Bultmann, Pannenberg, and Jeremias followers have pursued the matter. Probably, at this date, the Pannenberg school has gained the ascendancy.

Except for a very small colony of "genuine" Bultmannians, most of Bultmann's former students and disciples now modify or reject his emphasis that "the *preached* Jesus" is the ground of community between God and men. Fuchs and Ebeling seek to correlate the philosophical side of Bultmann's position with some of Luther's motifs as a corrective. Their conviction that the basis of community between God and men is the *historical* Jesus means, further, that the historical Jesus is the One who must be preached. "The historical Jesus—not the preached Jesus—is the one theme of the New Testament," insists Fuchs. Bultmann's failure to say this, he adds, is "the cause of the trouble among his disciples, and is a serious error."[4]

Do not misinterpret this disunity between the European theologians as catastrophic to their influence in the World Ecumenical Community and relationships, theologically, within their own ranks. We are merely viewing an argument *within* the existentialism of Neo-Orthodoxy in these differences concerning the "preached Jesus" and the "historical Jesus." But it does bear out that Barth's principal thesis that "God is God" is rendered inoperative. The refutation would be that God is not absolute in the metaphysical sense, but only in the "geschichtliche" sense of always occurring. "Heilsgeschichte" emphasizes that history is a record, while "geschichtliche" emphasizes history as an act. It concludes history as a record, past and history as an experience, present.

In a recent interview on *CATALYST* Tape Talk, Pannenberg presented the last word for the Neo-Orthodoxy voice in this discussion. The question was this: "Do you feel that there is a distinction between *Geschichte* and *Heilsgeschichte*? The answer stated:

Well, I always have disallowed this separation. A representative for the separation, of course, Oscar Cullmann in Protestant theology, as is, for instance, Karl Rahner in Roman Catholic theology. I have always opposed this separation because I think there is only one reality, and this one reality is understood in the biblical tradition as dominated by the God of Israel and of the

Christian faith. And this one reality under God is conceived as history in Jewish and Christian tradition.[5]

When we realize how the attitude toward history has changed from the days of Edward Gibbon and his account of *The Decline and Fall of the Roman Empire*, to the very modern and pretentious work of *A Study of History* by Arnold J. Toynbee, we can see that one of the problems directly influencing modern Christian thought is that of the various presuppositions that a modern historian adopts in his interpretation of that history. It is not merely a matter of studying facts; it also involves the presupposition and interpretation that dominate the facts and produce the conclusion of the modern historian.

On the more practical side, as well as on the American side of this ocean of modern thought, lies the neo-interpretation of history by the Classical Pentecostal, as well as the Neo-Pentecostal and Charismatic.

In my own observation of the typical Christian minister in the neo-camps, I have seen a moving away from the Biblical base in church administration and preaching to a base more acceptable to the world—education, music, psychology, speech, and history. Do not misunderstand: the arts, history, science, and proficiencies squarely based upon Biblical authority are most helpful to the ministry of the Lord Jesus Christ—especially in these days of cultural abuse. But unless all of our springs are flowing from the Biblical foundation and fountain, our human priorities will become the presupposition of our conclusions.

Let me illustrate. When I was a young pastor in Virginia, I observed another young man who was pastoring a church while attending a nearby college. His ministry was not squarely set upon a Biblical base. His messages were of a devotional nature. Instead of giving Bible expositions, he spiritualized his messages. He had a high regard for history and finally achieved a Ph.D. in that field. During those days he not only did not manifest much spiritual discernment of conditions existing in his denomination and state conference; he also did not manifest deep spiritual piety during prayer meeting or the preaching of the Word of God. I suppose that these things were especially marked in my mind because his father and my father were bishops in the same denomination and because my own soul, mind, and pastorate were consumed with the search of God and His Scriptures as I began to appraise the deterioration of that denomination in its orthodoxy and orthopraxy.

Years passed, and this young man suddenly loomed upon the modern Pentecostal horizon, having acquired a profusion of new spiritual manifestations, impressions, and demonstrations similar to the other Charismatic movements. I marvelled that his Charismatic experiences received from Notre Dame seemed to outweigh any former experience that he was reputed to possess through the New Birth. Becoming the vocal authority for Neo-Pentecostalism, he proceeded to cohere the older concepts from the Old-Line and Traditional denominations of Pentecostalism into the ultra-modern and even revolutionary ideas of Neo-Pentecostalism and the Roman Catholic Charismatics. This he has pursued even more zealously than he did his former positions in the church prior to his Notre Dame experience.

This led me to search out a reason for this man's change from an average pastor of unemotional ministries, without a particular emphasis upon the Bible, to a notable historian in the modern Pentecostal movement, as well as in his newly acquired emotional outbursts in his Charismatics.

After reading at least four of his books and a number of his periodicals, I felt that I had the answer for which I had been searching—the explanation of how he had managed such a change in his manner and message. Through the spirit which he had embraced from the Charismatics of Notre Dame, he proceeded to read into history a presupposition that all former Deeper Life movements of church history were being guided directly by a sovereign God to the present, great outpouring in the modern Pentecostal movements. It is my opinion that he adopted the wrong presupposition and therefore was brought to the wrong conclusion about this modern movement in history. I am firmly convinced that he had left the totalitarian authority of Scripture *prior* to his experience at Notre Dame, and that he took refuge in a fallacious interpretation which was built upon his own notable proficiency which he had found in his studies of history. This is not to say that the facts which he found in the historical studies were false or inferior; rather it was the way in which he arranged those facts that shaped in his mind illusions of grandeur concerning the Pentecostal heritage into which he was born. He wanted to believe, and he submitted to a certain spirit of things that gave him his presupposition; and he embraced an idea or theory outside the revealed Word of God.

This was not my first encounter with this particular temptation in life. In my earlier education I felt a dynamic pull to philosophy, music, and the power of public speaking. No minister is without temptation in the arena of history, philosophy, art, and science. Education is useful to the Lord only when it is captive to His Word. Every man has his natural, inspirational bias, and not one of us who reads the Bible and is genuinely born again is ignorant of the various devices of the Devil in this regard.

We are presently witnessing a dialectical treatment of history by many in the Neo-Christianity of the times. Roman Catholics reappraise their traditions and mutate into new positions through Vatican II; yet they continue, as in their former days, to deny the principles of the New Birth and justification by faith as taught from the Word of God by Martin Luther. There has been a shift in their emphasis, but not a change in their belief.

Sacred and secular historians are following all kinds of presuppositions to achieve certain results of modern propaganda in religion, science, and politics. Undoubtedly, there is an honorable correction to many events of history which should be made when other facts are found, and we should always observe the truth of things, no matter what it upsets in history. But history and the sovereign purposes of God are unchangeable at this end of the tube of time; and only the inerrant, infallible Word of God, as the base of our authority, could know everything and include everything that was needed to foretell and bring to pass that which God intended. This must be our presupposition in both heart and mind if we would dare to interpret the facts and readings of history. Otherwise, because we proceeded from the wrong starting point and motive, our conclusions will be greatly crippled or made erroneous.

The Present Ecumenical Pentecostal Movement

Later in our presentation we shall deal with a brief history of Pentecostalism prior to our modern time. Suffice it to say at this point that from the beginning of the twentieth century, there has been a wide diversity of groups among the Pentecostals. They include: (1) The Old-Line Pentecostal, (2) the Traditional Pentecostal, (3) the Classical Pentecostal, (4) the Neo-Pentecostal, and (5) the Charismatic Pentecostal.

At this point it would be hard to identify these five groups in a detailed description of their various distinctions, for we might view them in several ways.

The *Old-Line* and *Traditional Pentecostals* represent the first and second generation of Pentecostals associated with the origin of the twentieth century movement. Their particular distinctives center on the doctrine of sanctification and church government. In the theology of sanctification there was considerable debate and defense concerning the distinctive of sanctification as a second, definite work of grace, and sanctification as a process. In the former, the *crisis experience* was desired to be preserved; in the latter, the *process of holiness* was desired to be preserved. There was really no resolve found between the Pentecostals at this point in their history; and therefore, undoubtedly, the Old-Line emphasized the experience to the neglect of the process, and the Traditional emphasized the process to the neglect of the experience. There was therefore a tendency among the first-generation Pentecostals to either gravitate their position, theologically, toward sinless perfection or toward the more traditional view of experiential holiness being completed in death and Heaven. In addition, there was the distinctive of church government to be more episcopal in one group and more congregational in the other. We can observe, therefore, that the people themselves came from either the Wesley influence or the Baptist influence, respectively.

Because there was a reaction against the growing concern toward sinless perfection, or a hope for the consolidation of the two groups, the second-generation church leaders began to soften their emphasis upon the crisis and/or process in their teaching of sanctification, hoping that it would unite the various positions and effect a more acceptable Pentecostalism.

It is my firm conviction that the first-generation Pentecostal, although from a somewhat illiterate background and of limited understanding with regard to many things, was started upon a Biblical base where Biblical authority was besought by its bishops and demanded by its preachers. In those days there was a spirit in the air that effected in Pentecostalism's founding fathers many spiritual and Biblical insights that never again would manifest itself among the Pentecostals. I agree with Dr. Frank Garlock that those early Pentecostals brought back to Protestantism the warm and wonderful emphasis of the Second Coming of Christ.[6] The record should be kept straight; these humble, illiterate, early people had fled the formalism and liberalism of the Methodist and Baptist and Presbyterian churches which had been torn by nineteenth century Modernism and Liberalism. It would be hard to estimate the power of their prayer meetings and pious sermons and simple insights gained in their struggle away from formalism, poverty, and ignorance. Although their songs were without art, they were bright. Their sermons, though simple, were pure and Biblical. I believe that many of the spiritual and Godly and Biblical thoughts of those early Pentecostals finally found their way into the precincts of the evangelical and Fundamental camps during the time of the preaching of Moody, Morgan, Meyer, Finney, and Gordon.

It is becoming my position to set forth an untold account of the late Dr. N. J. Holmes, founder and first president of Holmes Theological Seminary, Greenville, South Carolina. After he had been in the practice of law for fourteen years, Dr. Holmes honored an earlier call to the ministry which the Lord had given him in his youth. From Dr. Holmes' own words we can discern what was at stake in his search for a constant walk with the Lord in the Presbyterian church:

> In the course of our evangelistic work in the Presbytery, going from place to place we found a great lack of spiritual life and power. It had been a great struggle for me to enter the ministry. I had resisted the call from the time I was sixteen until I became forty; but when I did yield I determined to do all I could. I went ahead preaching the gospel, as I had received it. I preached the law, its demands and our failures, sin, and repentance, regeneration and justification, and Christ as I apprehended Him, and prayer and the Bible. Churches were organized, sinners were converted and started on the Christian life, believers realized that they were not doing much for God or living as they ought to. They would try to consecrate and reconsecrate, and do better and live better, but they found a hard struggle, and we did too, but we did not know what else to do or say. Somewhere in our rounds we met up with a little book of Mr. Moody's, "The Secret of Power." We read it, and it made us very hungry for the work of the Holy Spirit in our lives. Some one told my wife about the Northfield Bible Conference at Mr. Moody's home, where he held this conference in July, every year for Bible study, and mainly on the work of the Holy Spirit. We became very anxious to attend it that we might learn about the Holy Spirit.[7]

This quotation portrays a man who was hungering for the Spirit-filled life which every true Christian has always desired; yet it equally describes a certain remnant of the first-generation Pentecostal as they sought God from the authority of the Biblical base.

After this incident, Dr. Holmes encountered some preachers who were preaching sanctification—that it might be received experientially in this life. He persists:

> Yet I became more and more anxious to know more about the Holy Spirit and His work. I wanted to know about that power or enduement for service that Mr. Moody spoke of in that little book, "The Secret of Power," and get something of the experience that he had received. I could feel the lack of that power in my own life, see it in my own work and in the lives and work of my brethren in the ministry and in the whole church, but had not learned the remedy, and, in fact, had not learned that there was a remedy.[8]

In the summer of 1891 Dr. and Mrs. Holmes went to Northfield, Massachusetts, and attended two conferences—the students' Conference, and the General Conference for Christian workers. Dr. Holmes had a private talk with Dr. Moody, from which we glean a gem concerning his increased hunger for the Spirit-filled life. Dr. Moody said, in part:

> God must have an humble man to fill with the Holy Spirit. That you might as well put a lunatic with a lighted match in his hand in a powder magazine as to fill a conceited, ambitious man with the Holy Spirit. He would explode the whole thing.[9]

Dr. Holmes closes his journal with the fact that after they had discussed the Holy Spirit, Dr. Moody prayed with him, and that later in the Conference Mr. F. B. Meyer of London, Dr. A. J. Gordon of Boston, and other teachers fed their hearts on this subject from the Word of God.[10]

The main burden of presenting this event in the life of N. J. Holmes is to point out that in those early years the first-generation Pentecostals—some of them, at least— were claiming the Biblical base and honorable piety.

A second-generation leader, Dr. H. P. Robinson of the Pentecostal Holiness Church, revealed that the

Pentecostal movement was making a change in another direction during his day. Three messages which he delivered at two General Conferences of his denomination indicated that his denomination was beginning to feel that change in the second-generation progress. The messages were these: "Evaluating the Mission of the Church" (General Conference Sermon, 1957); "Our Heritage and the Changing Emphasis" (General Conference, 1957); and, "Forward Through Purity" (General Conference Sermon, August, 1965, just four months before he died). From even a casual reading of these sermons one can easily discern that Dr. Robinson was concerned over the change that was beginning to manifest itself in the denominations of Pentecostalism, especially in his own denomination.[11]

Many times Dr. Robinson discussed with me, personally, the condition of his denomination; and being one of the General Assistants to the Bishop of the Pentecostal Holiness Church, he also ministered in, and knew the condition of, several other Pentecostal denominations.

In our conversations, Dr. Robinson would speak of "the old days" and the legacy which had been given to him. He loved the Word of God and inspired young ministers to dig into the Scripture and preach under the anointing of the Holy Spirit. In the following excerpt from one of the previously mentioned sermons he says of those men of the first-generation Pentecostal period:

> They were men of iron will and boundless energy, full of the Holy Ghost and faith, rugged individualists. They feared no one but God and hated nothing but sin. They were for the most part poor and illiterate; but they made up for any lack here with zeal, courage, and compassion.[12]

Dr. Robinson was at the point of the closing of the second generation of early Pentecostals, and he saw the continuing change that was being made on the threshold of the third-generation leaders. He gives a most moving presentation of that change.

> We are now in the third generation of our church. Few of

the "church fathers" remain among us. When they passed, we lost something of the pioneer spirit and spirit of sacrifice.

The first generation of our church was characterized by positive, powerful preaching on Holiness and Pentecost with a terrible attack on sin.

We are living in a day of change. The changes within and without the church in the past ten years are staggering. Change is necessary to progress. All change is not necessary and not good—change may be destructive if it is made just for the sake of change.

It is pretty easy to criticize the old-timers for their narrowness. They might have been narrow, but they were tall, and their shadow is falling over us in this generation. You laugh about their convictions on the Sabbath, divorce, hog meat, jewelry, and dress; but you'd better look a little closer. When I think of who they were, where they came from, what they had to work with, what they did, and the opposition they had, I want to go to their graves, pull off my hat, and bless their memory.

If we hope to have a church tomorrow, and for the next generation, we had better cling to some of the theology, principles, and convictions of our "church fathers."

They left us a heritage. Like Naboth we'd better tell Ahab we won't sell—we won't trade. We'll die first. We owe those men and women something. I thank God that I lived far enough back that I saw some of those men; I heard them preach; I saw some of them die.[13]

Dr. Robinson saw the "faith healers" coming; and realizing that they were a departure from his heritage in Christ and the Word of God, he denounced them:

It is quite different now. Everybody believes in miracles. Everybody has the miracle concept. Everybody from the Catholics to the come-outers practice faith healing. When somebody is healed now, the photographer is there to get his pictures and case history for TV, radio, newspapers and other publications. In a matter of hours—the world knows it, for the world is miracle-minded. That is the thought pattern. It isn't hard to get folks to believe something fantastic when they want to believe something fantastic, and they are conditioned into that concept of life.

This situation has given rise to a great surge of "faith healers." The healing evangelists are sweeping our nation and the world. They tell us that the world is experiencing a great revival. Each is constantly outstripping the other with a "more miraculous" manifestation of supernatural phenomenon.

This sort of situation would have been impossible fifty years ago among Pentecostal people. The healing evangelists are a product of our times. They are a natural outgrowth of our times. The soil is ripe for this kind of harvest.[14]

Dr. Robinson pleaded for a return to the Biblical base of his heritage:

What our church needs most is to hear somebody lift his voice above the din and roar of confusion and cry till it reverberates around the world, that it is still as it has always been—holiness or hell! That's the kind of gospel that this church was born in and if we are going to be the custodians of truth, let's preach the truth of holiness.

There are some who emphasize justification by faith; some whose major doctrine is sanctification. Others think the Baptism of the Holy Ghost, Divine Healing or water baptism are the things that should be prominent in their church teaching. But that is not our position ... We stand in the middle of the road and declare to all generations the whole gospel for the whole man, for the whole world. [15]

However, the change was not to be stalled, and there commenced among the Pentecostal leaderships of the second generation a *neutrality* to the change away from the Biblical base of judging their orthodoxy and orthopraxy.

A quotation from Dr. Vinson Synan, in his historical interpretation of the Pentecostal Holiness Church at that time, should sufficiently confirm the point. Dr. Synan's father was a second-generation bishop of the Pentecostal Holiness Church—Bishop J. A. Synan. Dr. Vinson Synan's quotation concerns the conflict that took place in the General Conference at Memphis, Tennessee, in 1953,

when Oral Roberts was a guest speaker at one of the
evening services. Roberts was an ordained minister in the
Pentecostal Holiness Church, and he had already
launched his somewhat independent, new Pentecostal
crusades that were based upon certain "audible voices"
he claimed from the Lord. The General Conference was a
heated controversy, indeed. Dr. Synan said:

> Robert's message to the conference was so well received
> that it was apparent that his support would be strong in
> the business sessions of the conference. In fact his
> strongest supporter, General Secretary Oscar Moore, a
> fellow Oklahoman, was elected General Superintendent in
> the place of T. A. Melton, who was relegated to the posi-
> tion of Assistant General Superintendent. Bishop Synan,
> who had not become publicly involved in the issue, was
> re-elected Senior Bishop and Chairman of the Gen-
> eral Board. Though the Bishop maintained his neutral-
> ity as presiding officer, he had harbored many reserva-
> tions about the claims and methods of Roberts. [16]

My father, Bishop Hubert T. Spence, was also a
second-generation Pentecostal, and he stood against
Roberts' ministry. Later my father was identified by Dr.
Vinson Synan as the last opponent in the church:

> The 1969 General Conference brought to an end not only a
> decade, but an era for the church. With the departure of
> Oral Roberts from the church in 1968, and the death of his
> greatest opponent in the church, H. T. Spence in July,
> 1969, the era of tension and bitterness that constituted the
> greatest threat to unity in the history of the church came to
> an end. [17]

Bishop Melton also stood against Roberts and lost his
position because of it.

There were leaders, such as Dr. R. O. Corvin and his
brother, Dr. W. R. Corvin, who were far from the Biblical
base in advocating positive existentialism in their
Pentecostalism. Dr. R. O. Corvin was one of the leading
spokesmen for the Pentecostal Holiness Church in the
second-generation leaderships. He was founder and first
president of Southwestern College, Oklahoma City,

Oklahoma; was one of the General Board Member officials of his denomination; and later was officially involved in the chartering and organization of Oral Roberts University and Graduate School. Dr. W. R. Corvin became president of the denominational school in Oklahoma City, and openly avowed confidence for "the Barthian emphasis on the Word of God and the Divine revelation," as well as other teachings of Karl Barth and Paul Tillich.[18] To my knowledge the teachings of these men were never questioned by denominational action on the part of their superiors. Later we shall see the overwhelming influence that existentialism and Paul Tillich had upon Oral Roberts' going into the Methodist Church.

Thus we can see that the change from a Biblical base of the first-generation Pentecostal into an acceptance of a new-revelationist, such as Oral Roberts, paved the way for a departure from earlier Pentecostalism which had emerged from a weariness of formalism, Modernism, and the lack of honorable emphasis upon a Spirit-filled life.

That which was happening in one denomination of Pentecostalism was happening generally in all of them as each entered, from its own distinctives, into the third generation. Their ecclesiastical policies, polity, and programs were undergoing great change, and they shared affinities with Scriptural and moral modifications which ultimately, because of their move to neutrality, would change their Biblical base.

The Classical Pentecostal

The third generation would finally identify the Classical Pentecostal.

Once again we set forth the diversity in Pentecostalism. It should be remembered, however, that the first and second generations of Pentecostals have passed away, and the present leadership of the Pentecostal denominations is in the hands of third-generation men. In other words, the present ecclesiastical leaders of Pentecostal denominations are men who, in the main, have been wholly produced by the Pentecostal denominations themselves. But included with that statement must be the acknowledgment that these leaders were produced by the new changes that came into those Pentecostal denominations as well:

1. The Old-Line Pentecostal and the Traditional Pentecostal commenced on a Biblical base in the first generation.

2. The Old-Line Pentecostal and the Traditional Pentecostal moved to the position of neutrality away from Biblical base in the second generation.

3. The Classical Pentecostal moved into a direct compromise, going further than earlier neutralities, in the third generation.

4. The Neo-Pentecostal commenced during the time of the third generation of the early Pentecostals, having already left the Protestant Biblical base under the old ecumenism of Modernism.

5. The Roman Catholic Charismatic commenced in the old apostasy of Romanism; but more recently it has manifested itself during the time of the third generation of early Pentecostals, and leads the new ecumenism.

The Classical Pentecostal found the presupposition that would make the transition from the Biblical base and the second-generation neutrality through a compromise in the denominations of Pentecostalism. In the light of the legacy of their first generation, this is doubly sad.

We may make this final presentation of the groups presently involved in the new ecumenism of modern Pentecostalism:

1. The Holiness-Pentecostal bodies, now guided by the Classical Pentecostal ecclesiastical and denominational leaders of certain Pentecostal denominations.

2. The Baptistic-Pentecostal bodies, now guided by the Classical Pentecostal ecclesiastical and denominational leaders of other Pentecostal denominations.

3. The Unitarian-Pentecostal bodies, now having been accepted into the World Pentecostal Fellowships

and Charismatic Conferences by the Classical Pentecostal ecclesiastical and denominational leaders of all Pentecostal denominations.

4. The Roman Catholic Pentecostal Communities now having been sanctioned by the Classical Pentecostal ecclesiastical and denominational leaders of all Pentecostal denominations.

One wonders if there could have been an effectual growth of the new ecumenism had there not been the compromise away from the Biblical base by the Classical Pentecostals.

These men compromised the Biblical base established by their founding fathers of the first generation of Pentecostalism.

They further compromised the Biblical base by not correcting the neutrality of the second generation of Pentecostalism.

They also compromised by accepting into their fellowships and conferences an anti-trinitarian group of the "Jesus Only" denomination. This was a direct rejection of one of the major fundamental doctrines of the Holy Scriptures and reveals from another side a departure from the Biblical base.[19]

They compromised still further by accepting the credibility of Roman Catholicism as a real Bible-believing people, when in reality, it has been the oldest apostasy in history. The Classical Pentecostal actually believes that this modern so-called outpouring of the Holy Spirit could do for the Roman Catholic Church what the reformers, the Holy Scriptures, and repentance should have done years ago. To assume that a Spirit, apart from a Biblical base, could bring an ecumenism that would exalt the Lord Jesus, is to believe that, in reality, the Holy Spirit works a different work than He did in giving us the Scriptures and that He works against Himself.

A simple path has been cut through the forest of Pentecostalism in the twentieth century—first, rejection of a Biblical base; second, a move to neutrality; third, the compromise; and fourth, the apostasy.

We must fully acknowledge that since early Pentecostalism there has been a remnant of people which has dared to be different. These people have struggled, debated, defended, suffered, and often been excommunicated because they endeavored to stand true to the Biblical base of the founding principles. Today they are either in the remote and unthreatening outposts of "Switchland Creek" in their denominations, or they have separated themselves from the neutrality and compromises of the Pentecostal denominations in which they labor. No one should underestimate how many have been moved or separated. I know of churches and ministers in the North and West, and a few in the South, who have separated in several major Pentecostal denominations. A line of demarcation has been drawn between the earlier Pentecostals who chose the Biblical base, and the modern third-generation denominational Pentecostals and the apostasy of the Unitarian-Pentecostal, the Neo-Pentecostal, and the Roman Catholic Charismatic.

The Historical Presupposition of the Classical Pentecostal

The Society for Pentecostal Studies has become the voice and clearing house for the Classical Pentecostal in his search for an explanation of the modern Pentecostal phenomenon that reverberates around the world and across all denominations, including the Roman Catholic Church.

A variety of voices in this Society has assisted in bringing about a revival of interest in Pentecostalism as well as in setting forth a notable compilation of Pentecostal histories. Dr. Vinson Synan, of the Pentecostal Holiness Church, has rendered outstanding service in his search for the historical pieces for both Pentecostalism and his own denomination, although I do not agree with his presupposition and interpretation. It is Dr. Synan's conviction that Pentecostalism developed within the Holiness-Pentecostal tradition. Synan admits, however, that "his delineation of the development of the Holiness movement is based largely on secondary sources prepared by representatives of Methodism and the classical Holiness tradition who have not given particular attention to the features that have more directly led into Pentecostalism."[20]

From another point of view, Donald W. Dayton, a member of the Wesleyan Church, made a written contribution to the third annual meeting of the assembled members and guests of the Society for Pentecostal Studies at Lee College, Cleveland, Tennessee, late in 1973. The burden of his work opened the line of thought that the history of Pentecostalism could be traced to certain influences of the Keswick movement and Moody.[21]

To say the least, speculation is large with regard to the origins and sources of influence that led up to the Pentecostal movements of twentieth century Pentecostalism.

But there is something else that must be understood from the histories as presented to us by the Classical Pentecostals: the early Methodists and Baptists never intended that they be considered as heading into the present Pentecostal movements. In fact, many of the Methodists and Baptists regarded all Pentecostals as heretics. Their doctrinal positions were quite clear; their quest for God and spiritual things were in an entirely different direction.

Let us note Dayton's remarks:

In spite of extensive recent scholarship devoted to the history of pentecostalism, the origins and background of the movement are still obscure. Earlier history has been combed for occurrences of glossolalia, but there has been little attempt to delineate carefully the development of the complex of theological and religious ideas that culminated in pentecostalism.[22]

Dayton further states that an assumption may be taken for granted from earlier writings of Pentecostalism to identify itself with Methodism and the Wesleys and yet be incorrect.

Some students of pentecostalism have assumed that this doctrine (the Baptism of the Holy Ghost) derives ultimately from early Methodism and the Wesleys. Hollenweger comments, for example, that "John Wesley ... had already made a distinction between the sanctified, or those who had been baptized in the Spirit, and ordinary Christians." But such a statement is at best oversimplified and at worst completely misleading. Wesley taught a doctrine of Christian perfection and not a Baptism of the Holy Spirit. Indeed, if we may trust the recent study of Herbert McGonigle, Wesley seems not even to have put major emphasis on the place of the Holy Spirit in the work of sanctification. His development of the doctrine in the *Plain Account of Christian Perfection* is almost entirely Christocentric in character. Wesley does use the expression "Baptism of the Holy Spirit" a very few times, but always, McGonigle concludes, in reference to conversion or "justifying grace."[23]

Although Dayton is merely clearing up that Wesley, in spirit and theology, should not be understood as a direct believer of the modern Pentecostal movement, and Synan is merely referring to the technical data of his sources in an honorable search, both men, as is typical of the Classical Pentecostal's presupposition, proceed to use their position in modern history to read back into the historical evidences a consistent and continuing work of God and the Holy Spirit in bringing about the present twentieth century movement of Pentecostalism.

We are alarmed at this presupposition. It is presumption! We could not believe that a sovereign God was moving through movements in previous Protestant history, based on Biblical fundamentals, into a present movement involved in an apostasy. You can do many things with sand, but you cannot build a foundation on it. The Methodist and Baptistic doctrines preclude building on their foundations a superstructure built on its own foundations that would be diverse to the foundational principles themselves. The sovereign work of the Holy Spirit in a succeeding age or generation would never build upon that which He had rejected in a previous generation, nor would He bring in error to a generation and upon a work through which previously He had revealed truth.

At this point, we should illustrate the manner in which the Classical Pentecostal historian, in a practical way, uses his presupposition. Dr. Synan, in his *Charismatic Bridges*, is typical. Actually, he makes a synthesis between his own studies in history and his human experience with the Charismatics. Dr. Synan went to speak at the Sixth International Conference on the Charismatic Renewal in the Catholic Church, which convened on the campus of Notre Dame, in June 1972, and he came to the following, glowing conclusion:

> Before the conference, I became thoroughly convinced that God could do anything he wished to do without consulting me or any one else. My research into the history of pentecostalism had convinced me that there was no reason why the Holy Spirit could not be poured out upon any Christian who was open to and prepared for the pentecostal experience. Reading David Wells' *Revolution in Rome* and Kilian McDonnell's *Catholic Pentecostalism—Problems in Evaluation* proved to me that the Catholic Church was in a state of theological ferment unprecedented since before the Protestant Reformation. Widespread reading of the Bible, now encouraged among Catholics rather than prohibited, was bound to have a profound effect on the church, for "the unfolding of thy words gives light. . ." (Psalm 119:130).
>
> Since Vatican II, I was told, the Roman Catholic Church had abandoned its "ghetto mentality" and "fortress theology" which had insisted on a monolithic uniformity in the face of the challenge of the Reformers. Competing schools of theology could contend with each other within the Church as had been the case before Luther. Now a pentecostal spirituality was possible in Catholicism without the theological problems that would have attended such a movement before the 1950's. With the English mass, the guitar mass, and the cursillo movement of the 1950's, the stage had been set for the mighty government of the Holy Spirit in the Roman Church. The Lord was now "putting it all together" in the charismatic movement.[24]

But the writer does not follow *just* this historical appraisal of things which his mind has already accepted. This interpretation of history, which he had personally embraced, motivated by his personal involvement and the modern interpretation set forth by Roman Catholic writers, caused him to believe that the present Pentecostal movements were "set for a mighty government of the Holy Spirit in the Roman Church." Notice his human involvement which received confirmation through his own human experience:

> Despite all this theoretical knowledge of what could happen, I was hardly prepared for what I saw and experienced at Notre Dame upon attending my first Catholic Charismatic prayer meeting. After my arrival on campus, I was told that a "little" preliminary prayer meeting was in progress in the basketball coliseum. I hurried to the building and was flabbergasted to see over 10,000 already gathered for the informal meeting. Testimonies were given about the wonderful works of the Lord in many places. The atmosphere was warm and inviting. Soon the huge throng was asked to praise the Lord in the Spirit. Suddenly all hands were raised and the most beautiful harmony filled the air. It seemed that everyone there was praying and singing in other tongues and praising God. All around me were priests, nuns, and apparent college students with seraphic expressions on their faces. I had frankly been skeptical as to how "pentecostal" these Catholics would be, but my skepticism turned to wonder and praise as the gifts of the Spirit began to flow.

> The tongues, prophecies, scripture, homilies, and choruses came forth with such power and conviction that I was quite literally overwhelmed. They were singing "our" songs and exercising "our" gifts. It was more than I could take. A kind of cultural and theological shock sent me running to a room where for about fifteen minutes I was unable to do anything more than weep. This was quite surprising to me since I am not overly emotional and had a reputation for being quite critical of "over-done" spiritual manifestations.[25]

At this point we need to consider another reaction expressed by Synan in his own denominational publication, *The Advocate*. It concerned the same service at Notre Dame:

> It would be unrealistic to say that there are not problems between the Catholic Pentecostals and those of the traditional Pentecostal movements. It is a fact that many Catholic charismatics continue their devotion to Mary and the rosary. Others still drink and smoke. This constitutes a serious barrier to fellowship and understanding with us in the older Pentecostal tradition. However, I understand from talking to dozens of participants that the Holy Spirit is convicting of sin and delivering many of them from these habits and customs.[26]

Looking back upon these extended quotations from one who identifies himself as a Classical Pentecostal, we are beset with a flood of questions: How could Dr. Synan, before he attended the Notre Dame Conference, have believed from reading literature by Roman Catholics that they were trustworthy? Is this not a shift from the Biblical base of authority in his life? Is it not true that the Roman Catholic priests have been reading the Bible for centuries without finding saving grace through Christ? (Merely reading the Bible carries no magic if the heart is not right with God.) Should we simply and completely trust Vatican II and a shift of method in their manner of presentation, and expect them to come to the truth by Spirit rather than through the infallible Word of God? Does a certain liberty in dialogue within the Roman Catholic Church in schools of theology indicate repentance from error and a return to the Biblical base of the Word of God in a context of historical apostasy? What could the English mass and the guitar mass have to do with a return to the true and living God? Is the cursillo movement of the 1950's the same as the Protestant Reformation? Was the Lord "putting it all together" regardless of whether or not the pattern of Scripture was followed? Is it possible that this "putting together" was simply another, but new, ecumenicity? If Dr. Synan was following a wrong conclusion from the Roman Catholic writers, as well as a wrong presupposition from his own studies of history, could this not lead him to embrace the tremendous emotional experience that he found at Notre Dame? If the first is wrong, could it not be that he simply validated that error through another error? If a person embraces an intellectual error, could there not be the possibility of an emotional confirmation of the same? Could it be that his "cultural and theological shock" was a sort of last outpost of his former background of the early days of Pentecostalism when there was a Biblical base? Was his emotional reaction which he experienced at Notre Dame simply the final break with all ties to the former truth of the Biblical base? Does this not mean that he, as a third-generation grandchild, has now rejected the first-generation Biblical base and is substantially announcing that the first-generation was in error? Is it not important to deal with the problems which came to his mind with regard to "devotion to Mary," "the rosary," and "drink," and the "smoke," and the belief that people may be filled with the Holy Spirit prior to conviction for sin and the New Birth by the Holy Spirit?

It is possible to presuppose a particular interpretation to history, presuppose that Roman Catholic writers express Biblical truth, have it confirmed by an experience through emotion, and finally come to ERROR! The Christian must build his faith upon a Bible base; then, and only then, may we be sure that the agreement of the Holy Spirit through the mind, heart, emotion, and conscience is trustworthy.

But we have labored with questions. There remains a sequel to these quotations which must bring us to a series of principles to be laid down in this matter of the presupposition of anyone's interpretation of history. Let us read the typical conclusion of the Neo-Pentecostal to his own presuppositions, as Dr. Synan continues to speak of the Notre Dame experience:

> The Lord did a mighty work in my heart that week that has continued to this day. . . .

I made a new covenant with the Lord that summer to do all within my power to pray for and contribute to this movement, since I felt clearly that it was a genuine move of the Holy Spirit to renew the church in our time. I began to see the worldwide Roman Catholic Church as one of the greatest fields for revival in the world. What a marvelous victory would come for the Kingdom of Christ and for mankind in general, if this 600,000,000-member church could experience a new pentecost.

Since the Lord has allowed me to see all the foregoing evidences of the mighty outpouring of the Holy Spirit in our day, I have felt compelled to bear witness to those things to anyone who will listen ... In short, I have endeavored to build bridges of love and understanding between the classical pentecostals, the neo-pentecostals, and the charismatic Catholics. I realize fully the doctrinal and historical problems that still divide Christians who come from different backgrounds and traditions. Yet I have faith in the Holy Spirit that He will continue to break down those barriers in His own time and way.

All that I have seen has convinced me that the Lord has called us to a new type of unity—an ecumenicity of the Spirit. Without claiming to be part of any ecumenical movement, the charismatics have become the greatest *de facto* example of interchurch prayer and worship in recent times. It seems that the old ecumenism which has repeatedly run aground on the rocks of doctrinal and structural differences has already failed to achieve the high hopes of its originators and promoters. These have failed because the priorities were wrong. Spiritual unity must always precede structural unity.[27]

These last paragraphs are very sad. To me they sound like the death of the Biblical base of early Pentecostalism, and are, in fact, a contradiction and denial of the truth propounded by a number of early Pentecostals. How do you change the oldest apostate church in history from within, where there is no Biblical base? When the Lord really shows *His* servants the "evidences," it will be found in the Word of God, and the results will be Scriptural, indeed. To build bridges from a neutral or compromising position away from the Biblical base, to an apostate church, is to remove all distinctions which formerly identified the Christian faith with the Biblical base. I do not really know what Dr. Synan means by "the doctrinal and historical problems," in the context of his own presupposition; but it should be shouted from the housetop that no amount of pragmatic success of an old or new ecumenicity is worth the price that is paid when one departs from the Biblical base of the infallible Word of God. The doctrine of Romanism was never based upon the Word of God. And it is true that Neo-Pentecostalism does not have to pay homage to the old ecumenism; it is gobbling up the "old" as a deceptive device to make people believe that it is not an ecumenical movement of the old error. However, the new ecumenism will be a more deceptive shift. This time it will not make the Biblical base the catalyst of faith, any more than did the old ecumenism; rather, the ingredient will be *spirit*.

As this shift of the old to the new ecumenism comes about, we note something of a Swan Song in the implication of Synan as he looks back with some trepidation of spirit in his appraisal of Martin Luther:

> Yet one wonders what might have been had Luther and the Roman Catholic Church been willing to seriously attempt renewal.[28]

It would have been wonderful if the Roman Catholic Church had been willing to repent and return to the Biblical base; but be assured of this—LUTHER WAS FIXED. Luther's conscience was captive to the Word of God. The answer to Synan's "wonder" with regard to what might have been had Luther been willing to seriously attempt "renewal" in the sense that Dr. Synan meant is this: THERE WOULD HAVE BEEN NO PROTESTANT REFORMATION AT ALL—THE ENTIRE CHURCH WOULD HAVE REMAINED IN THE APOSTASY!

A Personal Conclusion

In giving these extended quotations from Dr. Vinson Synan, I have not meant to parade or refute him above another. It is apparent, however, that he has become the spokesman for many of the older and more traditional Pentecostals and for the third-generation leaderships of Pentecostal denominations. At the same time he speaks, personally, as a Classical Pentecostal. Knowing Dr. Synan and his dear father, Bishop J. A. Synan, both of the Pentecostal Holiness Church, I must with careful announcement make it clear that the present position of Dr. Synan was not the position of his own denomination and its leaders in earlier days. Synan has betrayed a trust. The early men commenced on the infallible authority of the Bible base, and Bishop J. H. King, G. F. Taylor, N. J. Holmes—all of the first-generation ministers and teachers—ministered from the Biblical base.[29]

Bishop King was well known as the authoritarian of Biblical authority, and he was never known to measure by anything other than his understanding of the Bible. Bishop T. A. Melton, the bishop under whom I was ordained, loved the Bible above all else. In the second-generation leadership, I shall always remember Dr. H. P. Robinson as God's messenger who wrote and preached from the Biblical base. To Dr. Robinson, there was no doubt with regard to the victory of Protestant Reformation and Martin Luther.

I have spent hours of private conversation with a number of the men I have mentioned, and the Word of God was the basis for the inspiration which I received. I am utterly amazed, therefore, that Dr. Synan, with his notable and proficient historical pen, has given such little attention to the great controversies, defenses, board meetings, General Conferences, and host of other events which endeavored to stay off the present expansion into Neo-Pentecostalism. No doubt many of the other Pentecostal denominations have followed the same pattern. It is my opinion that Synan has followed the usual ecclesiastical logistic of ignoring those who were fired, pushed out of churches, voted off boards, or made to suffer some other action perpetrated against those who refused to follow the teachings, sponsorships, crusades, and popularity of the new breed of independent Pentecostal personalities that emerged during the second-generation leaderships. In the light of former commitments to Christ and His Word, it is astounding to hear the third-generation leaderships speak so glowingly of the Charismatic movement. Although Dr. Synan ably reveals the ecclesiastical hierarchy and their underhanded way of dealing with the Biblical men in their denomination,[30] he does not seem to see that his own system is doing the same thing to its ministers.

Years have passed, and this volume has been written from the standpoint of the Pentecostal spectrum. There is a story worth telling—and one not to be forgotten—with regard to the heritage and legacy of the past.

In the early days when there suddenly loomed upon the horizon such personalities as McKay, Branham, A. A. Allen, and Oral Roberts, a courageous group stood true to the Word of God, though at high personal cost. This, too, has part in Pentecostal history. In all historical Pentecostal denominations of the early days there was a remnant who laid their ministries on the line for the Word of God. Having ministered in seven of the older and larger Pentecostal denominations, I have been able to witness a remnant through those days. There has been a half century between the early Pentecostals and the present Neo-Pentecostal movements; and that half century has been marked by Pentecostal positions further apart than the average person of our time can realize. It is unfortunate that many ministers and churches, having no place to be taught from the Bible base, had to go to an independent position that led them out into legalism. But because of the departure of their denominations, hundreds of Pentecostal churches have sprung up across the United States in quest of a Biblical base and a separated, holy life in these times when Biblical separation is so right and necessary.

As I have already stated (Preface), it is because I could no longer remain in the Pentecostal denomination that

Foundations Bible College, of which I am founder and president, came into existence. The third-generation leaderships having compromised their legacy from their forefathers, and my being a third-generation Pentecostal, I felt that I must sever all relations with that compromise. I must add that in all the years of my pastoring Pentecostal churches in Pennsylvania, Virginia, Washington, D.C., and North Carolina, I took a firm stand. I had entered the ministry in 1950, and for twenty-four years had been a member of two Pentecostal denominations. I served as a member of the staff and faculty of Holmes Theological Seminary, Greenville, South Carolina, which is the oldest, continuing Pentecostal Bible school in the world. After nine years I was dismissed because of my strong Biblical position. I accepted an invitation to be founder and president of Heritage Bible College of the Pentecostal Free Will Baptist Church; but after three years, having been disillusioned by the lack of Biblical authority among the leadership, I resigned. Three years had been ample time for me to realize that Neo-Pentecostalism had made deep inroads into all of the third-generation leaderships, and that eventually it would completely absorb them.

Dangers Involved in Interpretive History

It is not that we believe a historian should preclude his own presupposition, but that there must be a check and a criterion to be sure that the presupposition is on the Biblical base of God's infallible Word. There are dangers associated with historical interpretation, and we should constantly remind ourselves of these dangers and bring them to the only revelation man has that is directly from the Lord to men. The dangers involve several points:

1. Forgetting that the data from which history is drawn often comes from secondary sources of the past as well as an inaccurate bias of the present.

2. Leaving out pertinent detail that reveals another side of historical interpretation, including minority-forces that truly influenced the mainstream of the

majority-forces.

3. Adopting a presupposition of history that includes one's own subjective involvement in the material that the historian gives as facts.

4. Assuming a confidence in other historians who interpret with the same presupposition, or mistakes, that the historian himself adopts. This is a reasoning process according to itself.

5. Thinking that an erroneous presupposition of a different kind than a former erroneous presupposition is really different from error of a new ecumenism.

6. Believing that a *true* presupposition of history founded on an old *false* presupposition of history can be brought to a *true* synthesis in its conclusion.

7. Believing that a *false* presupposition of history founded upon an old *true* presupposition of history can maintain *true* integrity in its conclusion.

Or, more pointedly, in the subject at hand, we must acknowledge certain facts in the conclusion which the Neo-Pentecostal might draw from his false presupposition involved in his interpretation of history:

1. We do not have enough Biblical evidence in the base of Roman Catholicism in the twentieth century to indicate that it is truly experiencing return, renewal, and reform in the Biblical sense.

2. We have not heard from Vatican II of a genuine return to the Biblical base of authority that is necessary for us to respect their so-called return, renewal, and reform. Indeed, they persist in their own dogmas, their papacy, and their apostasy.

3. We do not see in the conclusions the modern Pentecostal has drawn from his own interpretation of history the totalitarian authority of the Biblical base that is needed for an objective and true interpretation of that history.

4. We believe that among modern Pentecostals are certain teachings which are in opposition to the Biblical teachings founded upon the Biblical base of authority. Some of these teachings embrace the

following beliefs:

a. Roman Catholics may be filled with the Spirit prior
to being convicted by the Holy Spirit of their sins
and entering into the New Birth (justification by
faith).
b. A Spirit-filled life allows the practice of error and
sin in that life, without a Biblical separation.
c. The Holy Spirit is able or willing to correct with a
spiritual unity that which was refused to be
corrected with a Biblical unity.
d. The new ecumenism is not linked with the old
ecumenism. Whereas old Modernism was a
departure from the Word of God through a *doubt* of
the supernatural, the modern, new Pentecostal
teachings espouse a departure from the Word of
God through a *false teaching* of the supernatural.
e. The work of the Protestant Reformation was not
conclusively a work of the Holy Spirit, in its
own right, awaiting the final capstone in the
present work of the Charismatics.
f. The work of the modern Pentecostal movement
supercedes the Protestant Reformation, although
we know from objective history that the Protestant Reformation, although not without limitations, is the greatest demonstration in church
history of what the Gospel could do in all of the
compartments of life—science, art, and religion.
g. All praises, songs, ceremonies, Bible readings, and
other effects as demonstrated in services at Notre
Dame are rooted in Biblical causes. In other words,
these effects can be substituted and counterfeited.
They have been in history without being proof that
the Holy Spirit is in it.
h. We are living in the days of a Holy Ghost
Awakening, rather than the final Apostasy. The
Bible teaches the latter, and we are witnessing it.
Yet there is a true outpouring of the Holy Spirit in
these days illuminating God's saints to see this
Apostasy and proclaim God's Word.

i. The denominational programs and progresses have been following the path of orthodoxy and orthopraxy and their decisions, through their respective ecclesiastical machinery, have been a direct work of the Holy Spirit, leading to the Charismatic renewal.

j. The Deeper Life Movements of past history have been a part of the modern Pentecostal movement in spite of the presence of erroneous teachings as set forth in Romanism and the unitarian concept in the error of anti-trinitarianism of the "Jesus Only" Pentecostals.

k. The modern movements of the National Association of Evangelicals, as well as the World Pentecostal Fellowships and other affiliate organizations, are a result of the on-moving work of the Holy Spirit in our time—in spite of the fact that there have been links through these groups with personalities and movements in membership with the World Council of Churches, including Chilean Pentecostals and personalities such as David J. Du Plessis, who not only joined the World Council, but who also has accepted the dogma of papal infallibility.

l. There is no other possible presupposition that could be accepted as a basis of interpreting history apart from the Classical Pentecostal and the Charismatic one, though they are not founded upon the Biblical base of authority.

Whenever we move away from the Biblical base of authority, we are left open to formulate our own directions in the interpretations of history and in our own human experience. But interpretations of history have fallacies, and human experience has weaknesses.

Possible Views of History

It should be remembered that the conclusions which we draw from history and human experience depend upon the presupposition with which we commence.

It might be profitable to observe at least three possible views, using charts (p. 46) to illustrate them. We shall designate these charts A, B, and C, with the following explanation (God is represented by the dotted line, invisible; man the solid line, visible):

Chart A represents a view of history based upon the presupposition that all the actions of men are synonymous with the actions of God. It is a somewhat panthe-historical view that God is in history and history is synonymous with God.

Chart B represents a view of history based upon the presupposition that man and his experiences are the main thrust of action, and that therefore, man is in the driver's seat of the actions manifested. It is a kind of deist-historical or anthropo-historical view that man is the significant channel and chain from which consummation is brought about.

Chart C represents a view of history based upon the presupposition that God and His sovereign will are the main thrust of action, and therefore, God is in the driver's seat of the actions manifested. This is a theist-historical approach that indicates God Himself, both transcendent and immanent, brings about His consummation of things, as man performs his own will distinct from God's will, but not divorced from God's will.

Chart C, perhaps, could be positioned into two panels that would indicate the invisible or providential actions of God's working behind the visible scenes, and the visible and miraculous actions of God's working openly, at times, in the visible scenes of history and human experience.

Undoubtedly, it would be important to know the world-view a person is taking when he approaches both history and human experience. That view would determine the presupposition that would be read into the facts of history and human experience and ultimately would determine the conclusion reached by those facts and experiences.

Although we are definitely grappling with an old problem and a tremendous line of thought, each of us, as a

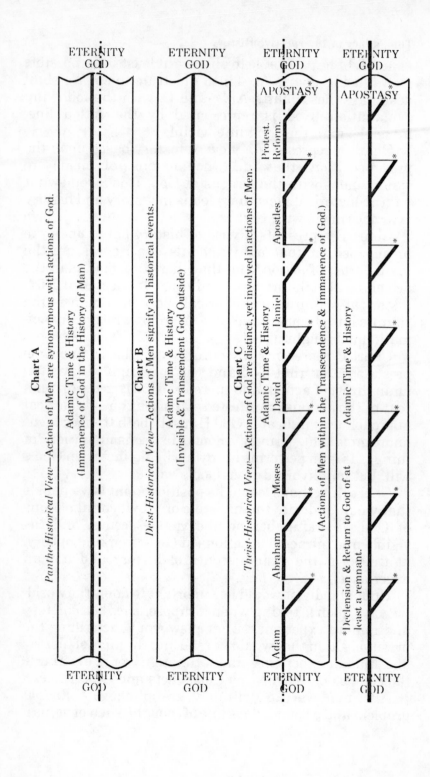

Chart A

Panthe-Historical View—Actions of Men are synonymous with actions of God.

Adamic Time & History
(Immanence of God in the History of Man)

Chart B

Deist-Historical View—Actions of Men signify all historical events.

Adamic Time & History
(Invisible & Transcendent God Outside)

Chart C

Theist-Historical View—Actions of God are distinct, yet involved in actions of Men.

Adamic Time & History

(Actions of Men within the Transcendence & Immanence of God.)

Adamic Time & History

ETERNITY GOD

ETERNITY GOD

ETERNITY GOD

ETERNITY GOD

APOSTASY

APOSTASY

Protest. Reform.

Apostles

Daniel

David

Moses

Abraham

Adam

*Declension & Return to God of at least a remnant.

ETERNITY GOD

ETERNITY GOD

ETERNITY GOD

ETERNITY GOD

Christian, must choose the view that exemplifies the Biblical base and yardstick of authority which God intended through His inspired and inerrant Word.

If we accept the totalitarian authority of Scripture, Chart C seems to be the best choice. (Since man is born a sinner, we assume that Satan, demons, and men are working cooperatively in all their actions; the Christian would be following the will of God.)

It should be carefully understood that at different times in history, as well as in different events in human experience, God may choose to manifest Himself in different ways. Allow us to illustrate this in the metaphor of Solomon. "His left hand is under my head, and his right hand doth embrace me" (Song of Solomon 2:6; 8:3).

God may choose to manifest Himself in history in the figure of the "left hand"—unseen and invisible, when man does not, on the average, recognize it. Elisha's servant (II Kings 6:13-17), as well as the prophet Habakkuk (1:1-4), and many others, did not see the hidden hand of God, behind the head, away from the front of the eyes, working His plan and will. However, there are other times when the "right hand" of God works in an obvious fashion, before the eyes, in front of the face, performing the supernatural and the miracle right there in history and human experience. But keep in mind that if we had eyes in the back of our heads, so to speak, we could see both the right- and left-hand manifestations through Biblical insight and spiritual discernment. We would see that God is there working all the time. The problem seems to become more difficult when we recognize that God often works His hand in a glove, hiding it even more. But later, in His will, according to His Word, He removes His hand from the glove and there appears—in time, space, history, world—the very manifestation of "the finger of God."

Needless to say, the problem of man is not the matter of rejection of the unseen, providential, left hand of God, or the seen, miraculous, right hand of God. The problem is to discern when the action is from the true, supernatural

God of the Holy Bible, or the false, supernatural (unnatural) hand of the Devil, demons, error, counterfeits, or
actions of mere men.

Two things are very evident in the Scriptures: One,
God and Satan are both super-to-the-natural of natural
man; and two, God and Satan are capable of producing
signs, wonders, miracles, and works which are
supernatural (cf. Joshua 10; Matthew 8:14-18; 7:21-23;
Revelation 13:13-15; 16:13-14). Of course, God is superior
in all these things. Man must be able to distinguish
between the power behind both the natural order of
things in history and human experience, and the
supernatural order of things in history and human
experience. The only way that a man can know this
distinction is through the infallible Word of God—the
Bible!

This explains how we can understand that Pharaoh
and his magicians were able to do only a limited number
of miracles through their Satanic enchantments, and
Moses, a servant of the true God and through the power of
God, could proceed to a greater manifestation of
miraculous power in the salvation and exodus of Israel.
Gideon would test his "fleece" (Judges 6) twice, simply to
be sure the matter was from the Lord. Elijah would test
his "altar" (I Kings 18) by pouring on twelve barrels of
water, in a time of drought when water was precious, to
prove that the fire was real and not "rigged." Across the
centuries, the beloved John would set forth this principle
in the Word of God: "Beloved, believe not every spirit, but
try the spirits whether they are of God: because many
false prophets are gone out into the world" (I John 4:1).
We can still hear the Biblical echo of the Virgin Mary
when she heard about the greatest miracle ever known
before concerning the Incarnation of the Son of God in the
flesh: "Be it unto me according to thy word" (Luke 1:38b).
For a final criterion we turn again to John: "And this is
the confidence that we have in him, that, if we ask any
thing according to his will, he heareth us: And if we know
that he hear us, whatsoever we ask, we know that we have

the petitions that we desired of him" (I John 5:14-15).

We must test history and human experience by the authority of the Word of God; we do not bend the Bible down to history's happenings and human experience. Every man must bring his presuppositions and experiences up to the Word of God, or be rid of them and find the presupposition and experience and life of God's Word.

There are times when the actions of God and man proceed through history in a more harmonious fashion than at other times. I believe that the Protestant Reformation was one of those times.

There are also times when man's actions depart from God and become a complete detour, a tangent, an apostasy; but God continues in the direct, straight line of His sovereign will.

But there is never an action that can be perpetrated or devised by man totally outside the sovereignty of God; for God, inherently, through His providential order of things, triumphs over the wickedness and weaknesses of man, no matter what man's will might be. This observation is true no matter what position one may hold toward predestination. This does not primarily concern the problem of sovereignty or free will in the point that we are making about history; and the point is not primarily concerned here in the matter of salvation. Rather, it is a matter of God's involvement in human history.

It should be thoroughly understood that whenever God, whether by His Word or Holy Spirit, sends or endorses an awakening, a renewal, or a reform through a spiritual movement on earth, it will be authoritatively pronounced through the doctrine, preaching, and teaching of His Holy Word.

If an earthly movement cannot receive the endorsement of the Word of God, it is false; and those who have found the Word of God in that generation must condemn it with all their heart and mind. Though it is an awesome duty, it is a necessary one.

2

The Doctrine of the Holy Spirit in Church History

At this point in history—beyond the legacy of creeds and councils from Nicea, Constantinople, Ephesus, Chalcedon, and others—the Christian must announce his own witness in keeping with the spirit of born-again Christians of all ages.

The first four church Councils—Nicea (325), Constantinople (381), Ephesus (431), and Chalcedon (451)—were by far the most important and far-reaching councils because they settled the orthodox faith on the Trinity of the Godhead and the Incarnation of the Lord Jesus Christ as the Son of God. The second Council of Constantinople (553), which condemned the Three (Nestorian) Chapters, was a mere supplement to the previous councils of Ephesus and Chalcedon. The third Council of Constantinople (680) condemned Monothelitism; and the second Council of Nicea (787) settled other things.[31]

As we look back across the centuries of church history, we realize that there has been a sovereign God working behind the screening and facade of man's trek into present apostasy. In the early years creeds and councils worked slowly, carefully, and completely to a formal and final resolve of the full deity of each member in the Godhead. We can hardly overestimate the value of this initial activity. Although the doctrine of justification by faith was not prominent in those early years, we can see that the foundation of the Trinity was most necessary for the work of the Lord later on in history.

It is not the purpose of this book to unravel the myriad problems involved in the early creeds; rather, it is to announce the fact of the final step in the full recognition of the deity of the Son and the relationship of the Holy Spirit in the Godhead.

The Creeds and Councils made it clear that orthodox theology believes and proclaims and defends the Trinity of the Godhead as revealed in Scriptures. At this point in the study of Neo-Pentecostalism, there must be an acknowledgment that something has basically happened to the present concept of pneumatology (the doctrine of the Holy Spirit) as taught by this movement. The years of departure from God's Word reveal a departure from the Trinitarian theology as well. This has been observed before in the "Jesus Only" Pentecostals.

Added to the Nicene Creed at the Third Council of Toledo in Spain (589) was the Latin word *filioque* ("and the Son"). This is often spoken of as the last nail for the Nicene Creed that thoroughly repudiated Arianism (the idea that Christ was distinct from God). From this presentation of the *filioque,* it became an acknowledged fact that the Holy Spirit proceeded not only from the Father, as Nicea said, but also from the Son.[32]

This makes it crystal clear that both the Holy Spirit and Jesus Christ are as much God as is the Father. Also, it sets forth the important fact that the teaching of Christology must be the presupposition and foundation for all teachings of the Holy Spirit that might follow. Theology, Christology, Pneumatology—this is the order in God's revelation to man.

There are numerous New Testament passages that declare an interchangeable terminology between Jesus the Son and the Holy Spirit. Although they are distinct in their personalities of the Godhead, there is equality between the two; and the work of Christ is necessary before the provisions and benefits of the Holy Spirit are realized. In a very practical way we are reminded of the many acknowledgments in church history that have distinguished the work of Christ *for* us, and the work of the Holy Spirit *in* us. These provisions proceed from the Father and the Son. Both Christ and the Holy Spirit share mutually the title "Spirit" (Romans 8:9-11); and Jesus Christ is called "truth" (John 14:6), and the Holy Spirit is called "the Spirit of truth" (John 16:13).[33]

Many Christians would agree that there is a difference between being *born* of the Spirit and being *filled* with the Holy Spirit; but none would agree that the New Birth is *servant* of or *subsequent* to any teaching of the baptism or infilling of the Holy Spirit. Standing on the authority of the Biblical base, we would never accept the idea that the infilling of the Holy Spirit could be a *substitute* for the New Birth. The essential and fundamental truth of the salvation of man lies singularly in a belief in the priority and presupposition of the New Birth above all other spiritual experiences. The glorious infillings of the Holy Spirit are not something beyond the New Birth, but something out of and for only born-again believers (John 14:16-17). The entire Divine Depositum, which includes all of the benefits of the atoning sacrifice of the Lord Jesus Christ put to the account of the believer, commences at the New Birth and becomes God's test for the reality of all these succeeding experiences in the life of the Christian.

It is not my purpose to decry a true, Biblical teaching and distinctive concerning the deeper life of a Christian; nor would I deny the place and reality of the gifts of the Holy Spirit in the Body of Christ, set there by the sovereignty of God. It is my desire to trumpet an alarm against so-called super-spiritualities being something higher than that which God announces through His Word as the highest—"Ye must be born again" (John 3:7). It is becoming to us, to the legacy to which we were born, and to the heritage to which we owe a great debt, to sound the trumpet and call back to the Bible of our fathers in church history those who earnestly desire a deeper, daily, and experiential life in Christ. We must quit the claims built upon the existential and superficial and flee to the Rock of Ages and the Word of God.

We cannot accept unbiblical claims of extant dreams, visions, and audible voices, for they are outside the pale of the infallible Word of God. We believe in Holy Spirit impressions and demonstrations of genuine praise; but every manifestation must be tested in the light of infallible Truth. This is the critical point: Holy Ghost manifestations *must* proceed from the Word of God and the Son. This must be considered as the direct order of procession, without the human subjectivism of false suppositions and human experience.

The Christian Church, throughout the world at this point, is passing through a crucial hour. It is being plagued with "miraculous oil," "blessing pacts," "miraculous-horn-of-plenty," "red strings," "holy wallets," "seed-faith," "prayer cloths," and a multitude of other idols and images. Far too often these are set forth by the "rigged" claims, phony deals, weird utterances, "Hollywood-alka-seltzer" enthusiasms of a brand of "Pentecostal professionals" who claim powers in their hands, punctuated by the world's sound of the "rock beat," and those who are suffering from Pentecostal fevers rather than the true, Biblical Pentecostal fires. These professionals are turning people from the pure, simple, separated Gospel of the Lord Jesus Christ to unbiblical trends and tangents that are bringing reproach to the Scriptural men of evangelism, the honorable methods of soulwinning, and other Biblical truth that builds the saint up in the most holy faith. The modern Neo-Pentecostal obscures the profound, simple Gospel with a super-profundity that lies beyond the human heart and mind and calls the individual to something mystical which he thinks will make him spiritual. The fundamentals are being lost in the shift of emphasis to "spirit" when they should be "Back to the Cross and the Word of God."

The Trinity Versus a Schizophrenic Godhead

Having dealt with the Creeds and Councils of church history, we move to another observation which other writers have ably presented in their refutation of Neo-Pentecostalism.

There is little, if anything, that can be written to improve the wording of the human presentation of the Biblical doctrine of the Trinity. The early Fathers did their job well, and Christians owe a great debt of gratitude to them for their persistence in firming up a foundation that settled the historic belief of the Biblical Godhead. Probably no one answered more questions, extended more illustrations, cleared more definitions, and yet was unable to fully explain the Trinity than Augustine. We doubt that anyone will ever raise a serious question that Augustine did not discuss in his declaration of belief in the Trinity.

The extended doctrine of the Holy Spirit at the third Council of Toledo (589) contributed the final expression needed to fill out the fabric of man's response in a balanced understanding of the Godhead Trinity. This doctrine (*filioque*) definitely stabilized our understanding of the relationship of the Holy Spirit with the Father and Son, as well as completed a historical dogmatic in final expression.

But throughout these same years, as the confirmation has increased in strength, there has been a definite moving of error. Parallel to the confirmation there has been a growing departure—first a trend, then a tangent, and presently the erroneous concepts propounded by Neo-Christianity. The Fundamentalist is able to see this more clearly because his dedication has been to the centrality of essential truth as revealed in Scripture.

During the days of the prophet Samuel there was a rejection of the theocracy. This period in Israel's history was marked, particularly, with a rejection of God Himself. It was that grand period when God the Father was so very prominent in the promise of His coming Son, the Messiah, as well as the "glory of the Lord" accompanying certain actions through Israel as the Holy Spirit. It was a time when the Father's administration was particularly obvious and the preliminary preparation and longing for Messiah and the Holy Spirit prevailed (Isaiah 61:1-4). But we see Israel condemned by God for their demand for a king. In reality, they had rejected God, not merely the prophet, Samuel.

> And the Lord said unto Samuel, Hearken unto the voice of the people in all that they say unto thee: for they have not rejected thee, but they have rejected me, that I should not reign over them (I Samuel 8:7).

When the Messiah, the Lord Jesus Christ, came into the world, there was a similar rejection of the Son of God. The nations of the earth, as initiated by Israel and individual Jewish leaders who had rejected God under the Old Covenant, rejected the Son of God as well (John 19:7, 16; Acts 4:26-28). "Then answered all the people, and said, His blood be on us, and on our children" (Matthew 27:25). Of course, this became the most peculiar sin in the history of the world (John 16:9). The crucifixion, historically, witnesses that rejection; and the rejection of Jesus Christ is, of course, the true index to the rejection of the Trinity, completely. We can see this with considerable importance in the entire New Testament. The Holy Spirit would convict the world of the sin of not believing on Jesus Christ (John 16:8-9).

> Who is a liar but he that denieth that Jesus is the Christ? He is antichrist, that denieth the Father and the Son. Whosoever denieth the Son, the same hath not the Father: [but] he that acknowledgeth the Son hath the Father also (I John 2:22, 23).

> Wherefore I give you to understand, that no man speaking by the Spirit of God calleth Jesus accursed: and that no man can say that Jesus is Lord, but by the Holy Ghost (I Corinthians 12:3).

At the stoning of Stephen the rejection proceeded to the last Member of the Trinity—the Holy Spirit. Stephen set the record straight in the final pronouncement of the

Jewish rejection of God. He had already adequately
spoken of the Father (Acts 7) and of Jesus, His Son (Acts
6:14; 7:52, 53). In fact, we should carefully note that once
again Jesus Christ becomes the catalyst for their
rejection of the Holy Spirit as well. Having rejected the
work of Christ *for* them, there could be no work of the Holy
Spirit *in* them.

> Ye stiffnecked and uncircumcised in heart and ears, ye do
> always resist the Holy Ghost: as your fathers did, so do ye
> (Acts 7:51).

Israel had turned their backs on the Trinity of God,
with the final demonstration being set forth in the
crucifixion of Jesus Christ, the centrality of all their
rejection. But also, they had rejected the Pentecostal
advent of the Holy Spirit in the Upper Room.

During the Gentile period now, we are witnessing a
parallel rejection through the history of the church.

We can see why it was so very important to give creed
and council to the truth of the Trinity—the distinction
and equality of the Son and the Holy Spirit proceeding
from the Father and the Son. In looking back, we observe
that history has been something like a giant catechism
class, always starting with the question: "Who is God?" It
has been a necessary exercise in the history of the church
to return to that question. And it is equally true that the
way the church and the world regard the Trinity is an
index to the truth or error of an age.

Although across the intervening years we have
viewed several historical situations of overemphasis
upon "Spirit," none of it has compared with the present
error in Neo-Pentecostalism. (Some Pentecostals in our
time no longer believe that these past movements were in
error, but rather a part of that which God intended for our
time.)

There was a group called the Montanists. Montanus
was a pagan priest who was converted to Christianity in
150 A.D. He was a Phrygian and a heretic who with his
"prophetesses entered into ecstatic states and spoke
unintelligibly." It was said of one of the Montanist

prophetesses that she "in an ecstasy of the spirit ... conversed with angels, and, sometimes with the Lord Himself." [34]

Celsus reported that among the Gnostics there was some form of ecstatic utterances around 180 A.D.[35]

Justin Martyr (100-165 A.D.) mentions "spiritual gifts." However, he mentions a limited number: understanding, counsel, healing, foreknowledge, strength, teaching, and fear of God.[36] We do not know whether this new listing included all gifts mentioned in the New Testament.

Irenaeus (c. 140-203 A.D.) wrote that he had "heard" that many "through the Spirit of God do speak in all kinds of languages."[37] There are two observations that should be made in this account. Irenaeus had only "heard" of this, and we do not fully know what is meant by "kinds of languages."

During the 1600's there appeared the Cevenol Prophets with prophetical tongues in a Christian community.

Following the revocation of the Edict of Nantes, which took place after the Reformation, there were persecuted Protestants in southern France who claimed the gifts of prophecy and tongues.[38]

During the 1700's there were the Jansenists, a group of Roman Catholics who held night meetings at the tomb of their former leader (1731). Here were reported ecstatic phenomena including tongues.[39]

In 1776 the Shaker community was founded near Troy, New York, by "mother" Ann Lee. Followers believed that she was the "female principle in Christ," "that the second coming of Christ was fulfilled in her," and that sexual intercourse was the cause of corruption in humans. Therefore, to "mortify" the flesh they danced together naked while speaking in tongues.[40]

In the 1800's tongue-speaking appeared again in a group under Edward Irving, who was of Scotch Presbyterian background. He founded the Irvingites in London, and later they became known as the Catholic Apostolic Church. Irving taught that all the apostolic

gifts should be in evidence in his day. Mary Campbell, a
young female member, was the first to receive the gift of
tongues (1830). Soon others began to demonstrate
"spiritual gifts" of tongues, prophecy, healing, and new
revelations. Mary Campbell later confessed that it was
her own voice, not God's, and that she had lied. Robert
Baxter, who had claimed the gift of prophecy, renounced
the whole movement, including his gifts, as the work of
demons. Immorality was reported among the Irvingites,
although we do not know that it is true.[41]

In the 1800's the Mormons commenced their movement. They have always held to tongue-speaking as a
phenomenon; and when the Salt Lake City Temple was
dedicated, hundreds of elders are said to have spoken in
tongues. It is perpetuated and revered that Brigham
Young prayed in the "pure Adamic language."[42]

In 1902 the A. J. Tomlinson group claims the estab-
lishment of a denomination. Actually, Tomlinson was
dismissed from the original Church of God, a Pentecostal
denomination dating back to the oldest Pentecostal
organization. But in all fairness the A. J. Tomlinson
group should not be identified with the first-generation
Pentecostals as we think of them. "Tongues and other
ecstatic phenomena were not uncommon" among the
Tomlinson group.[43]

This, by no means, completes the historical outline of a
certain "spiritual" phenomenon, but it bears evidence of
many "excesses" appearing adjacent to the Christian
community of church history.

There appeared in the first part of this twentieth
century a wide profusion of Pentecostal denominations
from Baptistic, Methodist, and Unitarian backgrounds.
We have already presented this particular segment of
history, and we expressed the belief that some of them
commenced on a Biblical base.

For fifty years the Pentecostal Holiness Church had
nothing to say in their Discipline concerning the
distinctives and manifestations of "the gifts" in their
churches. It was, in those early days, the most unim-

portant of their emphases, although at times, in some
places, there were excesses. And as we have said before—
even within the first-generation of the Pentecostal
denominations, a struggle took place, especially among a
certain remnant.

A strong layman, like A. E. Robinson, was a great man
for Bible reading; and in his writings, he warned against
the excesses. But Bishop J. H. King, of the Pentecostal
Holiness Church, of the first-generation leadership,
probably said more against the excesses than any leader
in the history of the denomination. Bishop King had a
great distaste, and often expressed it, concerning the
Stamps-Baxter music in those early days. There were a
few times when he refused to preach in a service—and at
least one time, left the pulpit and went to his room—
because of not only the lengthy musical renditions, but
also the type of music presented. My father told me of a
time when Bishop King stopped the preliminary part of
the service because it had been filled with "praises" and
Stamps-Baxter "songs," and told them he had received a
message from the Lord and wanted to preach. He rebuked
them for the "disorder"; then he expounded on "The
Grace of God." It was noted by my father that people did
not shout as much for the sermon as they had for the
songs.

Some of the people in those early days were genuine
Christians who had left cold, "Liberal" denominations
which had become dead in formalism and their departure
from the evangelistic and evangelical principles of the
Word of God. Gifts and tongues were not the major issue
at all; Biblical separation and purity were the greatest
hopes of their hearts. There was a Bible base in those
days; there was a Biblical authority among some of the
ministers. The Second Coming of Christ and the living
hope of Christ's return was a major thrust of truth, but
echoes were rumbling against men like Bishop King and
the discipline of A. E. Robinson. The second-generation
leaderships gave manifestation of a shift to neutrality,
away from the Biblical base in the Pentecostal denom-

inations. The excesses were tolerated without correction, and the new-breed of extravagant Pentecostal personalities were allowed to speak of new-revelationism completely away from and in contradiction of the Biblical base.

Another Perspective in History Leading to Modern Pentecostalism

The previous observations of schizophrenia in the teachings of the Neo-Pentecostal brings us to another important event further back in history. In viewing modern Pentecostalism, we should acquaint ourselves with, and remind ourselves of, this other perspective. It has not received due attention by many writers of our time; yet it gives understanding in this growing problem of religious schizophrenia.

The Trinity has been under attack in other ways by those not directly related to the Pentecostal spectrum, but it is part of the climate and atmosphere at this time in the religious mood of things.

The Universalist Churches of the United States, starting in New England, have modified the orthodox Christian system as expressed in the historic creeds; they endeavor to retain a reverence for Christ without acknowledging His deity, and a belief in the immortality of the soul with suitable awards after death for conduct in this world. The New England Convention of Universalist Churches, at a meeting in Winchester, New Hampshire, in 1803, adopted a Profession of Belief in three articles. In 1899 the General Convention, meeting in Boston, added to the Winchester Profession clauses, giving "The Conditions of Fellowship." At a meeting of the Convention in Winchester, 1903, which celebrated the adoption of the Profession, its three articles were spoken of "as the first explicit statement in the creed of what is known as liberal Christianity."[44]

The Statement of Article II was liberal enough to attract some Trinitarians and Modernists to a unity in the matter. But under "The Conditions of Fellowship" there was a phrase that became the great emphasis of the

Universalists: "We believe in the Universal Fatherhood of God."[45]

The Unitarians, although a free association of societies laying stress upon practical aims and requiring no subscription to a doctrinal formula, published a formula by James Freeman Clarke and published by the Unitarian Sunday School Union. This formula affirms: "We believe in the fatherhood of God, the brotherhood of man, the leadership of Jesus, salvation by character, the progress of mankind upward and onward forever."[46]

The Unitarians founded their movement in 1825 as the American Unitarian Association. Their object was "to diffuse the knowledge and promote the interest of pure Christianity." The older Unitarians, represented by W. E. Channing, rejected binding creedal formulas, the doctrines of the Trinity and total depravity, and what was called the bleak Calvinism of New England; yet they held to a sort of exaltation of Christ.[47]

It is obvious that these liberal movements of Universalists and Unitarians aborted the hypostatic union of the Lord Jesus Christ and the great paradox and truth of the Biblical Trinity. They were a God-the-Father-only movement which rejected the inerrant and infallible Word of God, which declares the equality of Jesus Christ as God, and the emphatic cry of the Creeds in the proceeding equality of the Holy Spirit.

From this unitarian heresy has flourished also certain efforts and movements in our century that have set forth an overemphasis upon a "Jesus-only" concept in Pentecostalism. In reality, this group came from a doctrinal division in the Assemblies of God between 1914-1916. Often referred to as the "unitarian-pentecostals" or "the United Pentecostals," they "do not believe that the Godhead consists of a Trinity composed of Father, Son, and Holy Ghost":

> This group teaches that there is only one person who can be called God, and that is Jesus Christ. According to this view, the Biblical references to the "Father" and the "Holy

Spirit" are merely "titles" referring to Jesus, who alone is
God.

These churches believe, furthermore, that Christian
baptism must be administered "in the name of Jesus only"
in order to be valid, and that this sacrament is not
complete until the initiate has been baptized with the Holy
Spirit with the evidence of speaking with other
tongues—in the baptismal pool.

Known by the trinitarian pentecostals as the "Jesus only"
movement, the unitarian pentecostals prefer to be known
as the "Jesus name" or "oneness" movement. [48]

However, in 1916, after the separation of the "Jesus
Only" Pentecostals from the Assemblies of God Church,
there has been a return to the mutual fellowship of all of
these Pentecostals in the Charismatic movement and
Notre Dame and Kansas City fellowships. Just as the
original Unitarian movement was a part of the old
ecumenism of Liberalism, so this fellowship of the "Jesus
Only" Pentecostals reveals that the new ecumenism is a
part of the old ecumenism as well.

In Unitarianism Jesus is presented as the ultra-
human, without being deity, and considerable attention
is drawn to the Sermon on the Mount and the ethical
teaching connected with human morality and conduct.
Total depravity is denied; yet Christ is viewed only as the
paragon of all humanity. He is the great Person and
Peerless Example, but their teaching of the Lord Jesus is
heretical because they have an unbiblical base in the
doctrine of the Trinity. The "Jesus Only" Pentecostals
share the same heresy in another way.

In the neo-orthodoxy of Karl Barth we can see a
circumventing of the Trinity in still another way. Karl
Barth espoused a christocentric philosophical theology
instead of a true God-centered, trinitarian one. In his
earlier writings Barth is accused of not believing in the
Holy Spirit in the Biblical sense at all. In his later
writings he endeavors to straighten out his teachings on
this matter, but it is doubtful that he did. Whether or not
he succeeds in his expression of it, we cannot conclude

that he actually saw the Father and the Holy Spirit in the true, historical sense of Christianity as taught upon the Bible base. Barth's teachings, along with those of many other neo-orthodox theologians, have greatly influenced modern Christian thought in the years between the old Liberalism, which he denied, and the Neo-Christianity, including Neo-Pentecostalism, which he helped to build.

But the Fatherhood of God movements and the teachings concerning the Peerless Humanity of Christ, both erroneously believed and proclaimed, have now given way from an old ecumenism into a new ecumenism. Both were a departure from the Biblical base, and each is but the extension of the other. These movements made their contribution by adding certain erroneous ingredients, and then were swept along to a greater influence in our time, thus bringing in a new mutation with old species error. The new ecumenicity includes error from the past brought up into Neo-Orthodoxy, Neo-Evangelicalism, Neo-Morality, and Neo-Pentecostalism.

History has already suffered a "God-the-Father Only" and "Jesus Only" error. Now in Neo-Pentecostalism we are suffering a "Holy Ghost Only" error. Not only is there an overemphasis upon the Holy Spirit, but also modern Pentecostalism has embraced anti-trinitarian doctrine as well as Romanism.

In these latter days, because of the extreme excesses and lack of Biblical authority and Biblical separation, we can see these movements going on into total schism from the Trinity-View, headed toward a spiritualism and even occultism. It is not necessary to deny the doctrine of the Trinity, theologically, although that is equally involved. A movement may achieve the same thing by an unbalanced teaching of the Holy Spirit. The existential principle that is working in Neo-Pentecostalism and being applied in a Pentecostal context, is resulting in a dangerous direction toward demonism. In some of the preaching of the Neo-Pentecostals is even appearing an alarm that the demonic and occult powers are already working deep among them. David Wilkerson, in his sermon "The Charismatic Itch," sets forth the sound of this prevalent danger of demon power among his Pentecostal followers.[49] It is unfortunate that Wilkerson does not realize that he has done as much as any other man to produce the very thing he condemns.

Many Neo-Pentecostals are calling their services "Holy Ghost Services," which could be said in a rightful sense if they were on the Biblical base. But the services persist and boast that they are being maintained by "Holy Ghost Only Powers." Bishop T. A. Melton mentioned to this author that for several weeks a certain Pentecostal pastor in Richmond, Virginia, had been unable to preach in the services. Bishop Melton expressed alarm about this condition and the pastor involved. One church boasted of nineteen Sundays without the preaching of the Word of God. It is feared, because of some complaints which I have heard by preachers involved in this, that the pastors had not been able to prepare a sermon for the week and decided that it would be an appropriate time for a "Holy Ghost Service" so that no preaching would be needed. I believe in Biblical *praise*; but I fear that in the future, *praise* will replace preaching among the Charismatics. This praise will be predominantly songs and the glossolalia. Because of their commitment to the glossolalia, emotion in music, and the acceptability of "rock gospel," this facility of praise will be the mark of spirituality among them. That is, involvement in erroneous praise will be the mark of spirituality.

It hardly needs to be emphasized that in our day there could not possibly be a church that was so Biblical and spiritual that the people could actually go for nineteen Sundays without the Word of God. I do not believe that there is such a church in the world. I would be among the first to appreciate times when a true manifestation of the Holy Spirit appears in a service; but the importance of this statement turns upon the fact that whenever I have witnessed a manifestation, it was when and as the Word of God was going forth.

What Does This Mean?

Down through history there has been a growing error in the camp of professing Christianity. On the one hand, there has been an unbiblical emphasis upon "Spirit" *within* the Trinitarian camp by some; and on the other hand, there has been an unbiblical emphasis upon "Spirit" *away from* the Trinitarian camp and doctrine by others. It matters not to the Enemy whether hot excesses plague the church, or cold rationalism; it matters not whether "Spiritualism" or "formalism" captures the people. From either direction the entire aggregation of error proceeds from an overemphasis that brings about schizophrenia in the Godhead teachings of the Bible.

The fact that the old ecumenism is a contrast in spirit to the new ecumenism will make it much more deceptive to the people. What is happening in the twentieth century, the age of aggressive apostasy, is the result of a long neglect by many in the Christian camps of the world. The Modernist has been among us; and rationalism and humanism have been exalted there. Neo-Christianity has gone in another direction: super-spiritualities and Charismatics and tongue-speaking have been exalted above the Holy Spirit and the Scriptures. For the ultimate purpose of Satan, it seems necessary that false religion be a coming-together of these extremes so that it will carry with it the deception that is needed to take the masses. So, the "Liberals," the Roman Catholics, the denominations, the sects, the cults, the Jesus People, and many others are being swept away from the blessedness of Biblical authority and the fundamental principles of saving grace; and the new emphasis will be in the name of "praise," "rejoicing," and "song," with the hiatus reaching the claim of the "glossolalia." It will be deceptive, because no one, generally speaking, would want to attack praise or legislate praise that is Biblically sound.

In looking back over the history of the early Pentecostals, we can see the less important place of the glossolalia being simply that of Holy Spirit unctionized "praise," and for many years the gifts were not even mentioned in some of the denominational presentations of faith and practice. They took the position that the gifts remained in the Body of Christ throughout church history; but I always heard them speak of it as a Biblical distinctive apart from personal salvation of the individual, and never more than an "initial" evidence of a manifested Holy Spirit.

The modern "tongue-speakers" are deeply involved in a judgmental appraisal of tongues. They take upon themselves the selection of certain linguistical syllables to be uttered before the individual can experience the glossolalia. Some of these judges distinguish between a mental glossolalia and a stuttering tongue, which are only preliminary to the more genuine and superior glossolalia. This is ridiculous. The "pipe," "harp," and "trumpet" of their delusion have a very narrow range; and since there were no tape-recorders in the time of the Book of Acts, who in this day is capable of informing a person when he has acquired and set forth, under the unction of the Holy Spirit a Biblical phonetic of audible, spiritual reality? This would be simply a subjective judgment by an individual, which is a part of the heart of the heresy: man measures his own meaning in the endeavor to verify another in his own glossolalia. Many judges, so-called, have taken it upon themselves to inform another person receiving such a manifestation of the Holy Spirit exactly *when* he had achieved the glossolalia. A minister in Maryland, at an altar of prayer, told a young convert the exact syllables to say; and when the bishop of that denomination and his council of men were informed, the matter was ignored.

In the Kansas City Charismatic gathering, July 20-24, 1977, Rev. Rick Bradford, in his workshop on "How to Receive the Baptism of the Holy Spirit," "directed the petitioners to 'take a step of faith and start praising (God) in a language you never learned . . . just start with sounds, any sounds.' A sort of low chant emerged from the front rows. For a minute or two a soft sibilant chanting sound grew, punctuated by an occasional 'Thank you, Jesus.' " Soon the sound quieted somewhat and Bradford suggested that the group "begin to sing in the Spirit," "as the entire convention did periodically during the evening mass meetings at the stadium. This time a singing sound arose on a single musical note or a harmonic of it, like a faulty pipe organ. Soon this died away, too." After someone else started a familiar Charismatic hymn, it seemed to trigger the speaking in tongues. "Sometimes the Holy Spirit comes so quietly and beautifully you're not sure you've gotten it," Bradford said. "Some of you have not received all you will experience. My wife received the baptism of the Spirit about 10:20 one morning, with only a few quiet prayers; but about 2:30 the next morning she awakened with a flood of new words.... Asked if she had received the Spirit baptism, Cindye Davidson of Fairbanks, Alaska, who was still wiping her eyes as she left the room, replied with a faint air of bewilderment, 'I must have.' "50

In observations of these matters, it is not dependent upon whether the gifts are present in the Body of Christ today. The whole turn of this matter is the clear Biblical evidence that reveals the delusion and error involved in the present Charismatic movements. In either case, we are not talking about Biblical absolutes and fundamentals. We have read of certain martyrs of the Christian faith whose tongues were cut out of their heads because of their persistent, audible testimony for Christ. However, we certainly *could* not rightfully argue against the reality of their personal salvation through faith in the Lord Jesus Christ, and we *should* not deny the reality of the indwelling of the Holy Spirit in their lives.

Charismatics, like the Corinthians, have made too much of the glossolalia. In the future, no doubt, we shall see an increase in this delusion. It is obvious, in the Corinthian catastrophe, that when people gravitate toward the overemphasis of the glossolalia, the gift of prophecy, which is so vitally linked with the Holy Scriptures, is despised and made inferior. This is just another way of saying that the Biblical base is no longer the authority of that people.

More and more we find people embracing this false "praise" as the touchstone of fellowship and faith. They go to all-night Gospel Sings and Rock Gospel concerts; but they cannot endure, to say nothing of enjoy, a Bible preacher who preaches beyond 12:00 noon on Sundays. It is inconsistent to all that we know in the spirituality of the Christian life. There is a root and fruit in this matter, and it is my own personal opinion that it is rooted in the flesh and sexuality, and the fruit of it will lead to an unseparated life and the occult. This is strong language, but I say it after some years of thought and prayer. God has never asked us to show our love to Him by headlong zeal, emotional songs, and ecstatic praises; He wants us to show our love to Him BY SIMPLE OBEDIENCE TO HIS WORD. Jesus said:

> If ye love me, keep my commandments. And I will pray the Father, and he shall give you another Comforter, that he may abide with you for ever; Even the Spirit of truth; whom the world cannot receive, because it seeth him not, neither knoweth him: but ye know him; for he dwelleth with you, and shall be in you (John 14:15-17).

There are many more effective ways of exalting the Lord Jesus Christ in our lives than by saying words of praise. I believe in praise, but obedience has priority. You cannot substitute praises and songs for living a life that exalts Jesus Christ. Often the Charismatic will actually suggest that praise should be the utterance of the mouth rather than the judgment through Scripture preached to the condemnation of sin and the sinner. Their commitment to the glossolalia hinders their seeing the need—yea, the urgent need—of the gift of prophesying. The gift of prophesying sets forth edification, exhortation, and comfort, in the light of revelation, knowledge, and doctrine (I Corinthians 14:3, 6). They cannot "take" that work of the Holy Spirit through the Word of God as set forth in the immediate anointing of the Holy Spirit in the preached Word.

More and more we are hearing, and are going to hear, of "Sharing" groups, "Praise the Lord" clubs, "700 clubs," "Full Gospel Business Men's Fellowships," and other satellite efforts springing up to emphasize praise and song instead of the Word of God among the Charismatics. I do not mean that the Bible will not be used in their meetings; I mean that there will be the use of the Bible for this presupposition of the glossolalia and Charismatics away from the Biblical base. More and more the genuine Christian is going to be misunderstood in his stand and defense of the preaching of the Word; for, "who would be against 'Gospel Song' and 'praise'?" they will ask.

Nevertheless, the Word of the Lord must be our guide and defense, and there is a great harvest out there who will desire the truth. I know of no passage more appropriate in this point than the words of Ezekiel, when he said:

> And they come unto thee as the people cometh, and they sit before thee as my people, and they hear thy words, but they will not do them: for with their mouth they shew much love, but their heart goeth after their covetousness.
>
> And, lo, thou art unto them as a very lovely song of one that hath a pleasant voice, and can play well on an instrument: for they hear thy words, but they do them not.
>
> And when this cometh to pass, (lo, it will come,) then shall they know that a prophet hath been among them (Ezekiel 33:31-33).

This was the response of the people after Ezekiel entered the second half of his ministry. A messenger had come announcing that Jerusalem had fallen; and when the captives at Chebar heard it, they had hoped that the prophet would preach something comforting, with messages like lovely songs, pleasant voices, and musical instruments. But Ezekiel proceeded with greater messages of judgment to come. The people of the world are tired and in trouble. They long for comforting songs and praises, but the Word of God announces greater judgment to come. That Word, however, will meet the need of every heart in the glorious hope of the Gospel.

3

Historical Implications of Neo-Pentecostalism

Neo-Pentecostalism is a "new" (Greek, *neos*) teaching of "the baptism in the Spirit," the "Charismatic gifts," and the "glossolalia" (tongue-speaking).

It is not possible to pinpoint the exact date of the beginning of Neo-Pentecostalism, although the decades of the sixties will be remembered historically as the time of its birth.

We might establish the birth of Neo-Pentecostalism by three personality incidents. The first incident involved a California businessman by the name of Demos Shakarian. Through his leadership there emerged the Full Gospel Business Men's Fellowship. After several failures in business ventures, Shakarian consulted with Oral Roberts about founding a businessman's association. His efforts met with little success until in 1953 he "implored heaven for a sign from God concerning the future. He and his wife had a vision given to them in tongues in which throughout the world millions of men, who had seemed dead, 'threw up their hands and started magnifying God.'"[51] I might add that since this date quite a number of Pentecostals have testified to similar visions.

From the date of his "visions," Shakarian found the direction and momentum to build FGBMFI. Primarily interdenominational among the Pentecostals, it brought

together from various business activities men who
wanted the fellowship of sharing the "full gospel" in
settings such as prayer breakfasts, small Bible cell study
groups, and weekend retreats. It should be remembered
that *materialistic prosperity* was the quest and thrust in
the final evaluation of the practical side of Neo-
Pentecostalism.

Another force bringing Neo-Pentecostalism into
existence from the 1950's was the ministry of Oral
Roberts. The son of a first-generation Pentecostal
Holiness preacher, Roberts was brought up in the
Pentecostal Holiness Church and became a minister in
that denomination. In 1968, however, he defected to the
Methodist Church.

In the 1950's Roberts stirred intense interest in his
Healing Wings Revival Ministry, which was a well-
organized effort to reach believers through small rallies
in suburban centers. Roberts also made effective use of
radio, television, and his magazine—*Abundant Life*.[52]

As a result of Roberts' ministry, no visible inroads
were made during the 1950's within main-line American
Protestantism; yet in all Pentecostal denominations
there was a growing change which was greatly
influenced by Roberts. Other denominations listened to
his message with a growing interest.

The third personality incident leading to Neo-
Pentecostalism occurred in 1960 in an Episcopalian
parish in Van Nuys, California. Many Neo-Pentecostals
cite this incident as the birth of their movement. It should
be remembered, however, that there could not have been
that effective birth without a *neutrality* in the second-
generation Pentecostal leaders and the full compromise
of the independent personalities of the Pentecostal
denominations. According to reports, the rector of this
Episcopalian parish—Dennis J. Bennett—had received
the gift of tongues and for several months had quietly
ministered the second blessing to members of his parish.
About seventy members came to experience "the baptism
in the Holy Spirit." It is reported that "inevitably rumors

and gossip about these meetings spread through the congregation" and that Bennett brought the issue into the open in April by reading a letter to his congregation explaining what he understood by the transforming power of the Holy Spirit Baptism and what he hoped it could do for his parish."[53]

There it is: Pentecostalism had broken across denominational boundaries. A definite movement had been born because of the wedded-union of the Pentecostal denominational move from the Biblical base (leaders and individual Pentecostal personalities formerly associated with those denominations), and the move of certain other denominations from a liberal and unbiblical base involved in the apostasy.

Throughout the 1960's this movement appeared to be strongest among Episcopalians, Lutherans, and Baptists, and to a lesser degree among Methodists, Congregationalists, and Presbyterians.[54]

Finally, in the early 1970's, the Neo-Pentecostal impact came upon the Roman Catholics.

The number of church people involved in Neo-Pentecostals in those days is unknown. One minister estimated that "eleven percent of the members of the major denominations have opted for a tongues experience."[55] Others labeled it "the third force in Christendom." And by 1970 it was generally conceded that "the pentecostal churches are almost certainly the fastest-growing Christian communities in the world."[56]

The following historical sketch reveals the extent of the phenomenon of those days through 1977:

In 1966, two laymen and other members of the faculty of Duquesne University, Pittsburgh, Pennsylvania, shared a spiritual experience similar to that which Bennett had previously experienced.

In August, 1966, two young men in attendance at the National Cursillo Convention (a Catholic renewal movement born in Europe in the late 1940's and stressing the need for a personal experience) introduced in this circle a book which had intrigued

them: David Wilkerson's *The Cross and the Switch-
blade*. This, too, resulted into certain Neo-Pentecostal
characteristics.

In January 1967, contacts were made with Protestant Charismatics in the Pittsburgh area, and by
February several Duquesne faculty members had
received the Neo-Pentecostal's experience.

In January 1967, news of the Pittsburgh area happenings reached the University of Notre Dame. This
endeavor was encouraged and assisted by members of
the Full Gospel Business Men's Fellowship, and the
Neo-Pentecostal group increased.

In February 1967, "the Duquesne Weekend" had
become a familiar phrase marking this experience.

After Easter 1967, the "First Annual National
Catholic Pentecostal Conference" was held on the
Notre Dame campus. About 100 students, priests, and
faculty members, chiefly from Notre Dame and
Michigan State, were in attendance.

In 1967, according to Edward Plowman, "historian
of the movement," the Jesus People movement, like
the Catholic Pentecostal movement, got its start.
Some of the hippies of Haight-Ashbury, San Francisco, "discovered Jesus" that year. Mr. Plowman
speaks of these as basically Pentecostal.

In 1967 the "experience" touched Missouri Synod
circles. It is also known, however, that the American
Lutheran Church saw most of the early Neo-
Pentecostal action in the earlier 1960's. Several of the
ministers of the Missouri Synod were "defrocked"
because of public statements on the issue.

In 1969 the first special conference for leaders of the
Neo-Pentecostal movement drew about 50 in the
month of January. The second and third drew 300 to
500. Regional conferences were also instituted. Over
1,000 found their way to the Third Regional Conference, held in New Jersey.

In 1969 a "Communication Center" was established at Notre Dame, specifically to serve the Cath-

olic Charismatic renewal. The Center publishes a
Directory of Catholic Charismatic Groups.

In 1969 the American Catholic bishops decided to
allow the Charismatic renewal within the Catholic
Church to have free course. In the opinion of Bishop
Joseph C. McKinney, Auxiliary Bishop of Grand
Rapids, he believes that 90% of the bishops see the
movement as a good thing.

In the spring of 1972 there was established the
nation's first nonterritorial Catholic Pentecostal
parish, the Community of the Holy Spirit, in St.
Charles, Illinois.

In June 1972, almost 12,000 Roman Catholics
gathered at Notre Dame University in Indiana for the
Sixth Conference, with seven bishops and 400 priests
attending it. This is familiarly known as "Pneuma
72."

In June 1972, Protestants in attendance at the
Sixth International Conference at Notre Dame were
forbidden to receive Communion.

In 1972 the Lutheran Church of America
established a special commission to study the matter
of Neo-Pentecostalism within their own group.

In 1972 more than 10,000 attended the First
International Lutheran Conference on the Holy Spirit
held in Minneapolis, Minnesota. This August meeting
reveals the penetration of the Neo-Pentecostalism
message into Lutheran circles.

In January 1972, A National Presbyterian
Conference on the Holy Spirit was held in St. Louis,
Missouri, which drew 150 ministers. A "Charismatic
Communion of Presbyterian Ministers" has attracted
350 members; and it is estimated that between ten and
fifteen thousand members of the United Presbyterian
Church and the Presbyterian Church in the United
States have received the "Pentecostal baptism" to this
date. All of this has come about since the 1970 General
Assembly of the United Presbyterian Church in the
U.S.A. issued its report on "The Work of the Holy

Spirit," which was the result of two years of study. It has been hailed as one of the best official statements on the Charismatic renewal and has brought about considerable growth in the movement.

June, 1972, undoubtedly, marks the most significant development for Neo-Pentecostalism on the *international* scene. It was established by the Vatican (Secretariat for Promoting Christian Unity) to extend a five-year dialogue on the theology and experiential elements of "Pentecostalism," with representatives from all Pentecostal movements. In the first session, it was co-chairmaned by David Du Plessis, who has been instrumental in opening the doors for the experience in ecumenical circles, along with Father Kilian McDonnell, Executive Director of the Institute for Ecumenical and Cultural Research, Collegeville, Minnesota. The next session of the dialogue was held June 1973, in Italy.[57]

July 20-24, 1977, the Charismatics massed 45,000 in the night services held in the Kansas City football stadium. "For four days and nights they heard their leaders proclaim their movement to be unstoppable, a new 'great awakening,' the greatest gathering of Christians in 800 years." Let us note a number of observations of this most recent meeting.

1. Rev. Vinson Synan, general secretary of the Pentecostal Holiness Church, said, "This conference has demonstrated to the nation and the world that this is an increasingly powerful movement, growing tremendously in breadth and strength. ... We see many things together in many ways, and now we're moving together in a cohesive direction for the future."

2. When reporters asked many of the visitors why they had come hundreds and thousands of miles, the answer came back almost universally: "To praise God!"

3. A Nazarene pastor ousted for his involvement in the movement, the Rev. Warren Black of Kansas

City, said he knew of about 60 other Nazarene ministers who in recent years "have been put out because they received the gift of the Holy Spirit."

4. It was reported in this meeting that there are 10 million Charismatics in the United States, one-half of whom have emerged in the last 15 years, and about 50 million world-wide.

5. Persons attending and participating included: Kevin Ranaghan of Notre Dame; Pentecostal Ecumenist David Du Plessis; Ruth Carter Stapleton; Catherine Marshall; and Southern Baptist minister, Charles Simpson.

6. Conference Chairman, Catholic theologian Kevin M. Ranaghan of Notre Dame, said, "Something happened here to establish a new level of Christian unity in the United States."

7. The conference, the first national ecumenical gathering of Charismatics, included Roman Catholics, Lutherans, Episcopalians, Methodists, Presbyterians, Baptists, and Pentecostals.

8. President Carter sent a message to the conference on Saturday asking for prayers that "I may make the right decisions toward bringing about world peace and better understanding between the different nations and those of different beliefs ... Please pray for human freedom and that liberty may be enhanced by the teachings of Christ. Please remember I need you and your support of prayer in the days to come."

9. With Charismatic caucuses already existing in most denominations, new ones took shape here among members of the United Church of Christ, and several churches of Wesleyan tradition, including the Free Methodist, the Christian Missionary Alliance, and the Nazarenes.

10. The "Shepherd" ministry of ministers were present, individually, which is a relatively new group of the Charismatic community, involving such men as Derek Prince, Hagen, Copeland, ... "This is a rather highly structured charismatic community, the

Church of the Good Shepherd, where about 80
dedicated members nurture and strengthen each
other's spiritual growth under the direction of the
'Shepherd' who exercises authority over every aspect
of his parishioners' lives." This particular group once
again reveals another characteristic of the Roman
Catholic Church, reminding us of the Confessional
Booth, and the error of destroying the Biblical privacy
of thought, mind, conscience, temptation, and sin.
Joseph Garcia of Fort Lauderdale, Florida, a former
lifelong Roman Catholic, after suffering failure in his
marriage and his business, came to and consulted
with the "Shepherd" of this particular Charismatic
community, and was present in this meeting with his
life-changing experience, which he testifies as the
original counseling session received one night from
the "Shepherd."

November 28—December 2, 1977, marks the days of
the claim Larry Flynt made of being "born again."
His own testimony sets forth an array of names
involved in both Neo-Evangelical and Neo-Pentecostal circles. Of course, we will always remember
Flynt as founder and editor of *Hustler* and *Chic*
magazines, both filled with pornographic material.
His conversion occurred in a jet headed for the West
Coast and in the presence of Ruth Carter Stapleton.
He claims to have had a vision in which appeared "a
man laughing heartily and calling himself Paul" who
"stood with Jesus Christ." A number of observations
should be made from the events and testimony of this
notorious individual.

1. The personalities linked into his testimony at
this time were Ruth Carter Stapleton, Chuck Colson,
Bob Harrington, Lenny Bruce, former senator Harold
Hughes, Bert Lance, and Johny Cash.
2. He is a Charismatic; he spoke in tongues at the
time of his "conversion" and "vision." In the "vision"
he speaks of animals eating at his neck—"like ba-

boons and monkeys, gnawing at me." He was informed in the "vision" (by Paul) "there had been a distortion of His Word, which confirmed my thing on religion: there are a lot of religions, but only one God." In the vision, also, he "witnessed the saving of Lenny Bruce from hell."

3. His language remains foul, even after his experience of having been "born again"; and "curbing an enormous sexual appetite," Flynt admits, "is one of the tougher commandments by which he must now abide."

4. Flynt plans to turn his corporation "into a non-profit company to publish an illustrated Bible, and to produce a spiritual and religious 'Roots.'" "His task as he sees it: to address those beliefs in his magazines while still pleasing both his new Christian friends and his several million readers."

Another View of the Former and Latter Rain

In these first three chapters we have been observing the Neo-Pentecostal's attitude toward history. We have called attention to the voices of the Creeds and Councils of church history, and the presupposition that modern Pentecostals take in reading back into history a message that they have preconceived with their own human experience, having left the authority of the Biblical base. They do not seem to realize that there could possibly be a presupposition different from theirs in the interpretation of history.

For the sake of distinction, I offer another possible view of one of their favorite passages of Scripture. It concerns the Biblical presentations of the former and latter rains, and is one of the emphases of the Classical Pentecostal's thrust in the hope of convincing others that the Holy Spirit is moving in the world in the present Charismatic renewal. This group believes that we are living in the great Awakening that God has always desired to bring to the world.

We need to give, at length, these passages of Scripture

from the prophet Joel and the apostle Peter:

> And it shall come to pass afterward, that I will pour out my
> spirit upon all flesh; and your sons and your daughters
> shall prophesy, your old men shall dream dreams, your
> young men shall see visions: And also upon the servants
> and upon the handmaids in those days will I pour out my
> spirit. And I will shew wonders in the heavens and in the
> earth, blood, and fire, and pillars of smoke. The sun shall
> be turned into darkness, and the moon into blood, before
> the great and the terrible day of the Lord come. And it
> shall come to pass, that whosoever shall call upon the
> name of the Lord shall be delivered: for in mount Zion and
> in Jerusalem shall be deliverance, as the Lord hath said,
> and in the remnant whom the Lord shall call (Joel 2:28-32).

> But Peter, standing up with the eleven, lifted up his voice,
> and said unto them, Ye men of Judaea, and all ye that
> dwell at Jerusalem, be this known unto you, and hearken
> to my words: For these are not drunken, as ye suppose,
> seeing it is but the third hour of the day. But this is that
> which was spoken by the prophet Joel; And it shall come to
> pass in the last days, saith God, I will pour out of my Spirit
> upon all flesh: and your sons and your daughters shall
> prophesy, and your young men shall see visions, and your
> old men shall dream dreams: And on my servants and on
> my handmaidens I will pour out in those days of my Spirit;
> and they shall prophesy: And I will shew wonders in
> heaven above, and signs in the earth beneath; blood, and
> fire, and vapour of smoke: The sun shall be turned into
> darkness, and the moon into blood, before that great and
> notable day of the Lord come: And it shall come to pass,
> that whosoever shall call on the name of the Lord shall be
> saved (Acts 2:14-21).

From these outstanding passages of Scripture comes
one of the most important prophecies to the modern Neo-
Pentecostal. In fact, I wonder if more emphasis is placed
upon these somewhat limited passages than the Lord
ever intended in the light of so many other passages of
Scripture dealing with the salvation of man by the grace
of God. It is typical of sects and cults and heresies to
magnify in a passage from the Bible much that is not
cardinal to the fundamentals of the Christian Faith. In

other words, there are many great doctrines of the Cross and the Bible that occupy much more consideration than those that I have quoted above.

My greater purpose for bringing this matter to the reader's attention at this time is to show another possible interpretation of these passages—even in the light of the modern Pentecostal interpretation.

The usual position of the modern Pentecostal is that the events of the Day of Pentecost were a *partial* fulfillment of Joel's prophecy, but that the complete fulfillment would be a *latter* rain outpouring of the Holy Spirit in the last days before the Rapture and Second Coming of Jesus. To the modern Pentecostal, the present demonstration of the Pentecostal and Charismatic outpourings are a direct fulfillment of that latter rain. In fact, many of them will actually go so far as to say that they believe that in only such a present profusion of the Charismatic outpourings could the words of Peter possibly be true: God would "pour out" His Spirit "upon all flesh."

Quickly, we must deny such an absolute meaning to "all" (Greek; *pasan*). Nowhere in the Bible does the word mean absolutely "all" in an all-inclusive sense. The context must decide; the context qualifies. If we would take this to its conclusion, it would mean that everyone in the world would be filled with the Holy Spirit.

Even in our beloved King James Version we would not interpret the following verse to be absolutely "all" things, including things physical, psychical, and so on:

> Therefore, if any man be in Christ, he is a new creature: old things are passed away; behold, all things are become new (II Corinthians 5:17).

When a person is born again, we would not conclude that absolutely all things in that person would become new—hair, teeth, skin, brains, et cetera.

The words for "all" (Greek: *pas, panta, hapas, holos, pantos, hosa,* etc.), including synonyms and cognates, would always be understood in each context to pertain to that which is suggested in the context, and not everything suggested in the universe.

The Rains

We understand from the language of Scripture that the "former rain" is the rain of autumn, which follows the drought of summer and prepares the ground for plowing and the sowing of seed; the "latter rain" is the rain of their spring, which concludes the rainy season and is necessary before the sickle and the harvest ingathering. There were two purposes in the mind of God for sending these two rains. The sending of the former was to prepare the sown seed for the birth of the crop, and the sending of the latter was for the harvest of the crop. Often the withholding of these rains was the sign of an act of judgment.

But rainfall is also used in Scripture as a figure of spiritual refreshment (cf. Hosea 6:3), where God is expected to visit His people "as the rain, as the latter rain that waters the earth." It might be understood that while the first and second comings of Christ are peak-moments of divine blessing, the people of God may at all times pray for a revival of His work "in the midst of the years" (Habakkuk 3:2), as well.

Even Job implies an understanding of the former and latter rains (29:23), and there are possibly eight other references to this matter (Deuteronomy 11:14; 32:2; Proverbs 16:15; Jeremiah 3:3; Hosea 6:3; Joel 2:23; Zechariah 10:1; James 5:7).

The passage in Deuteronomy, chapter eleven, presents a more complete report of exactly what the former and latter rains meant in the sense of physical blessing. Moses is speaking of their entrance into the Land of Canaan and the natural provision that God was going to give them through the rains:

> For the land, whither thou goest in to possess it, is not as the land of Egypt, from whence ye came out, where thou sowedst thy seed, and wateredst it with thy foot, as a garden of herbs: But the land, whither ye go to possess it, is a land of hills and valleys, and drinketh water of the rain

of heaven: A land which the Lord thy God careth for: the eyes of the Lord thy God are always upon it, from the beginning of the year even unto the end of the year. And it shall come to pass, if ye shall hearken diligently unto my commandments, which I command you this day, to love the Lord your God, and to serve him with all your heart and with all your soul, That I will give you the rain of your land in his due season, the first rain and the latter rain, that thou mayest gather in thy corn, and thy wine, and thine oil (Deuteronomy 11:10-14).

It is obvious that this was a blessed provision which God gave to Israel as they entered the land. When they were under Egyptian bondage, they had to artificially irrigate the land with their "foot" (the water tread-mill), which lifted the water from the river level to the various levels of their farm areas. In Canaan God was going to send special rains from Heaven which would indicate His care and concern in their labors of the land. The provision of this chapter in Deuteronomy was a physical provision for a physical land, but it hints toward future spiritual blessings.

As the years went by, God's covenant included those spiritual blessings identified by these physical benefits. Solomon, in his prayer of dedication in the Temple, would commence to set forth certain spiritual overtones that would deepen in the years ahead:

When heaven is shut up, and there is no rain, because they have sinned against thee; if they pray toward this place, and confess thy name, and turn from their sin, when thou afflictest them: Then hear thou in heaven, and forgive the sin of thy servants, and of thy people Israel, that thou teach them the good way wherein they should walk, and give rain upon thy land, which thou hast given to thy people for an inheritance. If there be in the land famine, if there be pestilence, blasting, mildew, locust, or if there be caterpiller; if their enemy besiege them in the land of their cities ... (I Kings 8:35-37a; cf. II Chronicles 7:12-14).

The prophet Joel describes a time when the four stages of the locust had devoured the blessings of the land. Israel

had sinned, and the land was suffering under the
judgment of God, as Solomon had prayed. Joel's
prophetic eye sees down through the years the saving of
the Gentiles and the restoration of Israel, and he
prophesies that God will come and refresh the land as the
people turn to God:

> Be glad then, ye children of Zion, and rejoice in the Lord
> your God: for he hath given you the former rain
> moderately, and he will cause to come down for you the
> rain, the former rain, and the latter rain in the first month
> (Joel 2:23).

From this blessing, the land would once again bud and
bring forth the corn, wine, and oil. The devastating locust
would depart, and the rains which had been stayed
because of Israel's backslidings would return.

So, we can see a very definite relationship in this
matter of Israel and the rains.

Joel speaks of the "afterward" which Peter calls "the
last days," and which really commenced at the First
Coming of Christ to earth. We can see in this both the
harmony of the Word of God and the immediate
inspiration and illumination of the Holy Spirit to Peter on
the Day of Pentecost.

The modern Pentecostal takes the spiritual significance of these rains (the former and the latter) to
simply mean that the *former* outpouring of the Holy
Spirit came on the Day of Pentecost and continued
through the first century as seen in the Book of Acts. They
believe that the world is presently passing through the
fulfillment of the *latter* rain—that the present manifestation of Neo-Pentecostalism and the Roman Catholic
Charismatics is genuinely sent by a sovereign act of the
Holy Spirit, reaching across denominational boundaries
to all flesh. They explain that between these two spiritual
rainy seasons lies the middle church history with its
dearth of spiritual blessings.

Finally, the modern Pentecostal believes that First-
Century Christianity received the spiritual former rain in
the outpouring of the Holy Spirit in the Book of Acts; and

that now, in Twentieth-Century Neo-Christianity, the last rain, which is the latter rain, is being poured out by the Holy Spirit. To them, the Dark Ages and the Medieval Periods are passed, and the Charismatic powers are working through the modern Pentecostal movements. This they interpret as the *new* ecumenical movement.

Another Presupposition

In order that we might show the possibility of another presupposition of this matter, we offer this thought: Is it possible that the basic principles mentioned above could be right but that the conclusion is wrong? Many of the Protestant theological systems flowing out of the Reformation accept certain implications of the above-rendered presentation. By this we mean that we can find some of the ingredients mentioned in the various Biblical interpretations of historical Christianity. Such error always has in it some truth. It might well be that some would object to the latter rain's having such pre-dominance among the Gentiles, and would suggest that the message in Joel, and confirmed by Peter, should be ultimately understood as Jewish—the return of the Jews to God, probably in the Tribulation Period.

In view of the fact that both Joel and Peter conclude the prophecy with the final phenomena of judgment from God during the coming Tribulation Period, the Pre-Millennialist can see that he has come to *something* of that time, generally speaking, to say the least, in the fulfillment of prophecy. We particularly draw attention to the matter of the manifestations in the heavens and on the earth:

> And I will shew wonders in heaven above, and signs in the earth beneath; blood, and fire, and vapour of smoke: The sun shall be turned into darkness, and the moon into blood, before that great and notable day of the Lord come ... (Acts 2:19-20).

Let us take a backward glimpse, at this point, of the Biblical rains and a certain implication.

In Genesis we saw, at Creation, that which a former

rain was initiated to be in the Garden of Eden:

> But there went up a mist from the earth, and watered the
> whole face of the ground (Genesis 2:6).

After 1656 years, God sent a latter rain, typically, in an
entirely different manner and of great consequence—the
Flood! The former "mist" was a blessed, refreshment rain
at the beginning of creation. The latter was a powerful,
destructive rain in the "flood of waters" (Hebrew:
mabbul, flood, deluge; not a "mist," *ed*, vapour). The
former was the beginning of an age; the latter was the
closing of an age.

This is significant. During the history of Israel, when
they were obediently following God, He sent the former
rains for the planting of their seed in the land, according
to the preceding pattern which was really another origin
and birth-life through seed. Also according to Biblical
pattern, He sent a latter rain for the ingathering—the
sickle and the judgment of the harvest.

The Day of Pentecost, according to the same pattern,
was a time of recreating, regenerating, redeeming,
planting, sowing, and initiating the work of Christ in the
Gospel to the whole world. The Holy Spirit was poured out
for the specific work of commencing, extending the work
of the Gospel.

In this twentieth century, as in the days of Noah which
Jesus said would return, we are living in a time of the
outpouring of the Holy Spirit to prepare for the Biblical
separation, restraint, and pronouncements against the
apostasy, in the light of the coming of Christ and
Antichrist. This is not a time of renewal or national
revival. It is not a time of awakening and true, Biblical
ecumenism. The judgment of God is ahead, and also the
end of this age. This is a glorious time of Holy Spirit
insight and spiritual discernment, but only if the
Christian is anchored into the Biblical base and
following daily the teachings of Scripture.

Instead of the latter rain's indicating an outpouring of
the seed-planting and birth of the church as set forth in
the Book of Acts, it should be understood that we are

approaching the end of the age typically presented in James, chapter five. Instead of these days being days of the acceptance of Neo-Christianity, they are exactly the opposite: the Holy Spirit is sending a revival of light to the true saints of God in order that they might recognize the rejection of the Biblical base by the people involved in Neo-Christianity. The Holy Spirit, through the Word of God, is revealing not an awakening, but the apostasy. Though Neo-Pentecostalism is a part of that apostasy, they insist that it is an awakening.

This is not the New Testament seed-planting of the commencement of the Christian Faith in history; it is the New Testament pronouncement of the culminating of the Christian Church in history. The Holy Spirit is revealing to the people of God the *error* of the neo-ecumenism, not the outpouring of the Holy Spirit upon and through the neo-ecumenism. Instead of its being the presupposition that Neo-Pentecostalism is the fulfillment of the prophecy of Joel and Peter, it is the Biblical presupposition that God is separating from these heresies a people for the return of His Son. The Holy Spirit is anointing "young men" with clear vision to "see" Christ-centered, Biblical principles of the Gospel as a true vision of exalting Jesus through His Word in these last days. The Holy Spirit is using "old men" (in their past ministries in a time when there was a firm stand, without compromise, in the exalting of Jesus Christ and His Word) to inspire all who believe the Gospel. A host of "old men" have dreamed their dreams. Some are deceased, having left behind a record of unwavering faithfulness to the Word of God, but others are still active in the battle. The Reformers envisioned what the Gospel could do, and they have left upon us a lasting impression. Others, at a time not so far distant from the present battle, warned us in our first-generation initiation of this century, during the time of Modernism, of crucial days ahead.

It is great to be a Christian in any age; it is especially great to see these matters and be the Christians we should be in this time. It is not simply a matter of whether or not we are experiencing an outpouring of the Holy Spirit now; it is more a matter of recognizing, through the Word of God and the Holy Spirit, the purpose of this outpouring to us. Not all outpourings are for the same purpose in the mind of God—some are for blessing; others are for preparation. I am constantly amazed at the number of friends I have found, personally, across the denominational lines and theological systems, who see only what is happening at this time in history. But thank God there is a true remnant of saints being brought together for the battle and for the restraint that is needed in our time against sin and error.

There is a great difference in believing that we are witnessing an awakening rather than an apostasy. If it is the former, the neo-ecumenical world is right; if it is the latter, the ones that the neo-ecumenical world rejects are right. No matter what the current opinion might be, only those who are founded on the Biblical base are right. The Biblical base extends its own presupposition; and that is what we must follow. The pattern is consistent: the former and latter rain has a significance at Creation; the former and latter rain has a significance in Israel's bringing the Messiah; and the former and latter rain has a final significance in the End-Time when Christ will return in judgment and then peace. We should not forget the "harvest" in the seven parables of the Lord Jesus concerning the End (Matthew 13).

The presupposition takes the same facts, but draws a different conclusion according to its own identity. An example may be shown through the selection of four letters in the alphabet and several conclusions of different words drawn. Consider the letters T, S, R, and A. Four words may be spelled: RATS (an ugly pest); TARS (an utilitarian product); ARTS (a beautiful talent); and STAR (a brilliant light). From RATS to STAR is a wide distance in meaning, but it is most important to know which is which.

Some people consider the Neo-ecumenism of the present Neo-Christianity and conclude that the Holy

Spirit is bringing a world-wide awakening! Others conclude that the Holy Spirit is revealing the final apostasy! Needless to say, one of the basic problems of the time is the lack of spiritual discernment through the Word of God. Spiritual discernment is also the work of the Holy Spirit, and it is desperately needed in our time.

For young men and old men to have fulfillment of their visions and dreams in evangelism and character, always exalting Jesus Christ, there must be nothing less than the outpouring of the Holy Spirit upon all of us. There are four groups of ages from childhood to old age: the potential vision of the infant, the preparing vision of our young people, the prime vision of leadership, and the past vision of old age for our inspiration and encouragement. From the child in the Christian home all the way through the aged minister of the Lord Jesus Christ, this generation must possess the concerted vision of all of us, and of our entire families, if as Christians we meet the challenge of soulwinning, separation, anointed preaching, and the exaltation of Jesus Christ from the Biblical base.

Another View of the Book of Acts

As we have already observed, the Book of Acts is most important to the Neo-Pentecostals. Sometimes it seems to be to them the most exclusive part of the Bible.

But with the background of our previous presentation of the former and latter rain, we must now advance to another view of Acts which is not usually considered in the Charismatic view.

By the end of the first century the wonderful manifestation of the Holy Spirit in planting the seed of the Gospel began to take on another manifestation in the world and the church. The later epistles of Paul, Peter, James, John, and Jude reveal a definite deterioration in the churches. The Book of Acts records the wonder of the early days of the first century and the spiritual success that accompanied the time of planting of the Gospel in the Roman Empire. The Epistles reveal the onset of a falling

away in the visible church communities, which is in
harmony with the "tares," "tree," "leaven," and "bad"
fish in the parables of the Lord (Matthew 13).

Instead of the modern Pentecostal's unusual emphasis
upon the wonder of the beginnings of Pentecost, as
prominently presented in Acts, we need to note what was
taking place by the end of the century. When Paul, in his
earnest desires to go to Rome, first viewed the capital city,
he thought of it as his greatest crusade; when he finally
arrived there, however, it became his most sufferable
crucible. We wonder if that is true in our day. We hear
much boasting of great crusades, great successes, and
fantastic happenings and awakenings. But is it as
wonderful as men think? Has the crusade not become the
crucible by which God tests the preacher and the
Christian?

James introduces the subject of the "last days" and
speaks of the cry of the poor to the Lord. Then he
admonishes and encourages believers with these words:

> Be patient therefore, brethren, unto the coming of the
> Lord. Behold, the husbandman waiteth for the precious
> fruit of the earth, and hath long patience for it, until he
> receive the early and latter rain (James 5:7)

James is describing the last days (cf. v. 3) as a time of
falling away. The latter rain refers to the apostasy and
the sickle (Mark 4:29; Revelation 14:14-20) which soon
will be demonstrated in the earth. It is not a time of "the
commencement" of Acts; it is the time of "the harvest" of
James. James is not speaking out of gloom; he is offering
inspiration and encouragement. It is the time of the
greatest hope in history! There is the "good ground," the
"wheat," the "herbs," and the "good" fish, promising
fulfilled hope in Christ (Matthew 13).

The eschatology of the Neo-Pentecostal is optimistic
about the *salvage* of an age. The Bible does not teach that
we can save the world; it teaches that the world lieth in
wickedness, under the Wicked One (I John 5:19). The
Charismatic's "Awakening" is not possible, for it will
take nothing less than the personal coming of Christ to

regenerate the earth. Man, the institutional church, Charismatic personalities, other instruments—none of these can effect this change. We long for it, but we cannot usher it into existence.

There is a vast difference in the Biblical revival and reformation, and the Charismatic awakening. The Bible does not promise the awakening that the Charismatic claims. It is too humanistic and worldly; it seeks aggrandizement of the creature. Paul agrees with James that first there must be a "falling away" (II Thessalonians 2). All Scripture is given by inspiration of God (II Timothy 3:16), and the seven parables of the Lord (Matthew 13) mark congruity between the Gospels and the Epistles.

John, in the Book of Revelation (2:7ff), reveals the Holy Spirit speaking to declining churches. The Seven Churches are being admonished continually. They are falling away. The Christ Who had commenced to walk in the midst of the churches (the candlesticks 1:13), finally is put outside the door of the Laodicean Church (3:14-19). There He stands, earnestly entreating the *individual* of the Church (3:20-22). The apostasy is present there; the institutional church is lukewarm, and the Spirit counsels people about the need of tried gold, the separation of the white raiment, and the increased need of eyesalve so that the person might see. Yes, once again, young men must see (cf. Acts 2:17) the great message of the Bible against the backdrop of the apostasy.

Another View of the Corinthian Catastrophe

Our previous presentations of the rains and the Book of Acts leads us now to a consideration of another possible view of the Corinthian catastrophe.

As we stated in the Introduction, Paul makes his position clear in his plea to the Corinthians:

1. The more excellent "way" (Greek: *hodos*, road, way) of I Corinthians 12:31 is the *Agape* of God shed abroad in the believer's heart by the Holy Spirit (Romans 5:5), which leads to Biblical separation, holiness, and Godly

character (I Corinthians 13).

2. There is a definite order in the gifts: "first apostles [proton], secondarily prophets [deuteron], thirdly teachers [triton], and after that miracles [epeita], then gifts of healings, helps, governments, diversities of tongues" (I Corinthians 12:28).

3. The gift of prophecy is definitely greater than the gift of tongues (I Corinthians 14).

4. The gift of tongues is presented in two different ways: Paul versus Corinth. Paul's understanding of the gifts led him to *know* that the gift of prophecy was the greatest of the gifts; the Corinthian's understanding of the gifts led them to *think* that the gift of tongues was the greatest of the gifts. Paul desired to present the gifts as the Lord had revealed them to him; he did not want to see the continuation of the gifts in the manner of the Corinthians. Paul could not deny the gifts, for they were from the Lord for the Body of Christ. Yet he dared not condone the excesses, for they were from the flesh and error. Paul approves the gifts under the sovereignty of God, but he condemns the erroneous gifts being perpetrated under the volition and excesses of men.

Let us observe in I Corinthians 14 the contrast between Paul's view and that of the Corinthians. It should be noted that in the King James Version the word "unknown," used in connection with "tongue," is italicized, indicating that it was not in the Greek Text. The word is used at least six times in the context (I Corinthians 14:2, 4, 13, 14, 19, 27).

The views of both Paul and the Corinthians came out of the truth of the gifts given by the Holy Spirit; but one was honorably held, and the other abused. In the outworking manifestation of the gifts, Paul's view included a definition of the gifts that the Corinthians, in general, did not know. Without doubt there was a remnant of people at Corinth who comprehended Paul's words, and the Apostle's understanding and explanation of the gifts of the Holy Spirit was a blessed assistance to the Body of Christ. But the Corinthians' understanding of the gifts brought harm to the church. Paul's view was

Paul

1. "I would that ye all spake with tongues, but rather that ye prophesied" (v. 5a).

2. "For he that speaketh in an *unknown* tongue speaketh not unto men, but unto God" (v. 2).

3. "Howbeit [tongues] in the spirit he speaketh mysteries (v. 2b).

4. "He that speaketh in an *unknown* tongue edifieth himself" (v. 4).

5. To Paul, the gift of tongues involved the manifestation of thanksgiving and praise (vv. 16-17; cf. vv. 2-4).

6. Evidently, Paul had to inform the Corinthians that he spoke in tongues more than all of them, which could have indicated that the Holy Spirit manifested this gift through Paul more privately, or away from the presence of the Corinthians, at other churches (cf. vv. 18, 28; "speak to himself"). There was something about this gift with Paul that the Corinthians did not understand or did not believe that he experienced.

The Corinthians

1. In the manifestation of tongues in the church, there must be the interpretation of tongues (v. 13).

2. The gift of tongues is not for the unlearned one (one who is receptive to the Gospel, learning the rudiments of the Gospel; v. 16).

3. The gift of tongues is not for unbelievers who might be in the church service (one who is not presently receptive to the Gospel; v. 23).

4. The gift of tongues, as practiced by the Corinthians, was, in reality, a judgment against themselves (vv. 21-22), as Isaiah refers to the foreign king who came in judgment against Israel. To one who did not know it, the jabbering of Corinth was no more than the jabbering of a foreign language.

5. The Corinthian catastrophe was a manifestation of a false gift of tongues that brought misunderstanding; outsiders attending service and hearing it would have thought them mad (v. 23).

6. The Corinthian Catastrophe involved the erroneous practice of tongues, which demanded Paul to establish corrections, controls, and restraints, as follows:
   a. Paul demands that the gift be subject, "by course" (vv. 27, 39), which indicated that several were practicing the gift of tongues, so-called, simultaneously—interrupting each other. This practice, of course, led to confusion.

b. Paul demands that the gift be subject to a definite interpretation by at least one, preferably two, and more conclusively by three other persons (vv. 27, 28); or, it may be that we are to understand that Paul is declaring that no more than three persons should speak in tongues in any public service of worship.

c. Paul also demands that the Biblical principle of the authority of man over woman be established in the public worship services. Apparently, the Corinthians had other problems than the erroneous use of tongues; the women at Corinth must cease speaking in tongues, entirely, as well as speaking out in the public service in other matters (cf. vv. 34, 35).

7. To Paul, the church should "covet to prophesy," which denotes preaching (not the delivery, simply, of a carefully prepared sermon), with the immediate unction and anointing of the Holy Spirit, unto edification, comfort, in the vernacular of the congregation before the minister (vv. 3, 5b, 19, 39; "five words with understanding").

7. Undoubtedly, the gift of tongues was demonstrated at Corinth as a volitional act of the human will rather than of the will of the Holy Spirit Who gives utterance (Acts 2:4; I Corinthians 14:19, 26). It is obvious that the Corinthians, prior to Paul's warning, did not realize that the gift of prophecy was greater than the gift of tongues. This reveals that they were not understanding the gift from the Biblical base.

8. Forbid not to speak with tongues (v. 39b). This simply means that we are not to deny the gifts because of the abuse of them.

8. Apparently, indecency and disorder accompanied the erroneous manifestation of the Corinthian use of tongues, revealing the flesh and the error of the catastrophe.

held in Biblical truth on the Biblical base; the Corinthians' view was held in carnal and divisive error.

The Corinthian catastrophe was rooted in error, self-will, pride, and false doctrine; and it is our belief that the local catastrophe of the first century has blossomed into the international Charismatic catastrophe of the twentieth century. In other words, at work in Corinth were two entirely different sets of definitions, beliefs, purposes, and conclusions, and the same condition exists today in Neo-Pentecostalism. Corinth *supposed* a great unity but yielded great division. Neo-Pentecostalism presupposes a great ecumenism, but it is bringing error and apostasy. Over and over again we must repeat that the Holy Spirit will not put His approval on that which the Word of God condemns. The Holy Spirit is not directing or approving the new-revelationism which has been at work since their first supernatural "audible voice," the absence of the Biblical base, separation, and holiness, or the positive Unitarian and Roman Catholic error. The Lord did not reveal that to us by an impression, or subjective experience; He revealed it to us through His infallible Word—the Bible!

Although there may be a difference of opinion among certain Fundamentalists concerning the actuality of all of the gifts of the Holy Spirit being presently manifested in the Body of Christ, there still remains the prerogative of the Holy Spirit to discontinue the exercise of these gifts as He sovereignly wills it. He must draw His own line of demarcation between truth and error in the various movements of church history. There is an agreement between the Word of God and the work of the Holy Spirit in making clear that which is false and that which is true in any age. As the Word of God reveals truth, so the Holy Spirit, in any age, will check, correct, control, and restrain by His own manifestation in accordance to the Word of God. In these last days, the Bible-believing, separated Christian will be led by, and therefore recognize, the sovereign line which God draws between delusion and truth, just as He did at Corinth.

PART TWO

THE WEAKNESS OF
HUMAN EXPERIENCE

4

The Weakness of Human Experience

Prior to the Protestant Reformation, the *hope* of personal salvation, as presented in the theologies of those years, was viewed mainly through a *process.*

After the Protestant Reformation, the *reality* of salvation was proclaimed through an experience—the New Birth, more familiarly known as justification by faith.

Of course, experientially, aside from the sovereign Divine Depositum, we can see now that the outworking of this glorious salvation for the individual is presented in the Word of God as both an experience and a process:

> Believe on the Lord Jesus Christ, and thou shalt be saved ... (Acts 16:31b).

> ... work out your own salvation with fear and trembling (Philippians 2:12b).

> But he that shall endure unto the end, the same shall be saved (Matthew 24:13).

> To him that overcometh ... (Revelation 3:21a).

We can see an experience of saving grace working in our lives through a process actually bringing us to the end of that salvation. The presupposition to this presentation must be that we are believing these truths of the Biblical base that Christ died for our sins according to the Scriptures (I Corinthians 15:3), and the Divine Depositum from Calvary has been given to us through the New Birth. We can see no other way to view this and at the same time be Scripturally sound.

In the days prior to the Protestant Reformation, the presupposition of Romanism was not upon a Biblical base; therefore the process would not have worked. Nothing works, from the Biblical base, in the life of a person, if it does not flow out of the Biblical experience of the New Birth. All of Romanism's history is filled with the long tedium and hope through good works, sacraments, priest, pope, and even purgatory.

The Reformation broke that chain, proclaiming straight from the Scriptures that justification is by faith through the grace of the Lord Jesus ALONE! There was to be a crisis experience of the New Birth, and many began to enter into this great evangelistic truth that Christ instantaneously sets the sinner-slaves free!

Although this truth was greatly needed at the time of the slavery of Romanism, in these extended days of Protestantism and the growing apostasy there has been an ever-increasing tendency to overemphasize the *experience* to the neglect of the *process*. As a result, we have been accused—and rightfully so in some circles of evangelism—of proclaiming "cheap grace." Romanism did not teach the New Birth or a right process; but on this side of that religious slavery the Reformers and many of their succeeding students have thoroughly weighed and proclaimed the Biblical fundamentals of the Gospel of the Lord Jesus Christ. We have a rich heritage, and access to a great treasury, which is a part of the dreams of our "old men." It is important that we not betray these Biblical "dreams" as we see our own "visions" as set forth in the proclamations of our "young men."

There is not only the evangelistic call to the most necessary *experience* of the New Birth; there is the call of Scripture to the *process* of a deeper walk with the Lord Jesus in the power of the Holy Spirit. It is not Charismatics that we are talking about; it is Godly character proceeding out of the New Birth.

We might think of this matter in several ways and still maintain our Biblical base. The fundamentals of the Faith have been worked out in doctrinal principles in church history; but it may well be that the Biblical distinctives of the Christian life need greater consideration in our day. We venture a simple presentation at this point to set forth the experience of the New Birth and the process which, experientially, is the outworking of grace into the entire Christian life: (1) The life-giving experience of salvation, when man passes from death to life in the New Birth. (2) The sin-removing stage of salvation, when the believer passes from a life dominated by sin into a life in Christ Jesus and a walk in the Spirit, unto victory over the power of sin. (3) The fruit-producing stage of salvation, when man is anointed with the unction of the Holy Spirit, and the outer witness in the fruit of evangelism.

We might think of this process as related to the provisions of the Atonement as set forth in the New Birth, Sanctification, and the Infilling of the Holy Spirit. The wonder of it all is a direct result of the Divine Depositum given to us in the New Birth, and the outworking of it into our lives, experientially, in the crisis-process through our lives *all* our lives. Undoubtedly, these things could be said another way and still remain on the Biblical base, but the fruit would be comparable. Often, I have found that these precious benefits are a matter of true, spiritual semantics, as long as they remain on the Biblical base.

As we have already explained, there has been a tendency since the Protestant Reformation to overemphasize the *experience* of salvation to the neglect of the *process* of salvation. The result is an orthodoxy without separated, effective orthopraxy among a truly evangelical people, and the rise of super-spiritualities of the Charismatics.

We live in a day when often the professing Christian makes a cheap "decision," a shallow "commitment," an easy "renewal," or a short "vision," for human "reform." The mass meeting and the media of statistics have both blessed and cursed us in a century when there is a tendency to measure achievement in the vein of three easy lessons, dehydrated foods, and automatic assembly lines. The methodology of Neo-Evangelicalism has crystalized this weakness and conformity; and compromise has erupted in the methods of evangelism.

We must return to the Biblical reality that builds the Christian life the long, hard way—with days of prayer, Bible reading, and Bible living on the Biblical base. There is no substitute for this. Too many people rely on an *experience* received from a mass meeting, and neglect the faithful walk in the Spirit in the ordinary and common duties, disciplines, and delights of every day. Many people return to their homes after the luxury and pomp and super-claims of methodology and the Charismatic fevers, and do not seem to know what to do there. This is exemplified in the near-extinction of the housewife and the upsurge of the career woman. They return to the ordinary place in life, as the shepherds "returned" to their ordinary sheep-work; but they do not possess the "shepherd-life," which glorifies and praises God and makes "known abroad the saying which was told them concerning this child" Jesus (cf. Luke 2:20 & 17). Too many are interested in the *great* blessing, the *great* religious excitement, the *great* signs, the *great* happenings, the *great* personalities, the *great* crowd, and the *great* experience. It is unnatural and unbiblical to live in the "great" realm as the world and the Charismatics think of it today. It is a land of fantasy and fable. The ever-increasing emphasis of existentialism has greatly assisted this impetus because it carries with it such language as the "thing," the "trip," the "crisis," and the "happening."

Christianity, on the Biblical base, carries with it the message of the Christian experience and the crisis; but as we will see a little later, the great truths of the Bible rest on and often survive by being part of other truth in a paradox. The ordinary part of a Christian life is as important as the extraordinary part; this we saw in our discussion of the left and right hands of God. When there is no miracle, there is always God's providence. Both are equally wonderful, for both come from above. And the paradox of the experience and the process, the super-natural and the natural, the *manifestation* of the Holy Spirit and the *abiding* of the Holy Spirit, is equally a part of the Christian life. When the Christian isolates Christian experience from the process and the normal, daily life, he tends to magnify a single moment, a single impression, a single manifestation, and a single feeling to a sacrifice of the whole life. To exalt the Lord Jesus through the whole life is the purpose of the Christian life.

We continue to notice a strong implication coming through modern Pentecostals that spiritual things, *per se,* religiously rendered, are more important than secular things, humanly rendered. Dr. Bob Jones, Sr., in his unusual ministry, often emphasized that there was no "difference between the secular and the sacred in a Christian's life." His presupposition, of course, was based upon the pronouncement that first the person must be born again and in the will of God. This is a most important principle in the Christian life.

Oh, how we need great spirituality in the ordinary acts of the Christian life. The moment of the glossolalia and the moment of the gifts, as the Charismatics claim them, are erroneous moments. Even the true, Biblical gifts in the New Testament are no greater than the moments of simple witness, honest labor, joyous family, and honor-able play. Oral Roberts has made famous the saying, "Expect a miracle every minute." That capitalizes on the moment only. On the Biblical base, we can say that we have lived a miracle throughout life, and the presence of God's goodness and mercy can prove it.

Human Experience is Momentary; Human Experience is Weak

Besides the limitation of human experience as being the emphasis of a moment, we should remember that human experience has certain weaknesses. Without destroying, on the Biblical base, the great fundamental experiences of the Word of God, we must keep in mind that we cannot build the Christian life on what we feel, or think, or have experienced. The Lord often takes our feelings away so that we will not rely on feeling.

As our presuppositions must be firmly founded on the Word of God in our interpretations of history, so must we bring every experience to the Word of God. It is possible to think too much of a Notre Dame experience. We can turn our historical trends into experiential tangents and ultimately lead ourselves into error and the apostasy.

It should not be necessary for us to go into a great extension of this point, for the Word of God is clear. Isaac, in his encounter with his sons, Jacob and Esau, is a great reminder of the fallacy of sense-perceived feelings.

Even in the field of philosophy there are multitudinous concepts which prove the weaknesses and fallacies of human experience and sense perception. Once again, we recognize the involvement of pragmatism, empiricism, secularism, behaviorism, and psychology in the spreading, erroneous philosophy of modern existentialism. Hegel and Kierkegaard have done much damage, which has become a working virus in Neo-Christianity.

In the days of Martin Luther there was an exegetical and theological shift from the exposition of philosophers to the Scriptures, and this is what made the Protestant Reformation effective. It touched all parts of life without being a part of worldly philosophy. And the modern Pentecostal movement shares affinities with the existentialists of the time.

In the days of John Wesley there was an exegetical and theological shift and emphasis from the Biblical fundamentals to the Biblical distinctives of the Christian life. The truths in the Biblical distinctives of the Christian life brought the emphases of sanctification, separation, perfect love, holiness, sin, temptation, et cetera, to an unprecedented point in history.

As long as the Reformers followed the inerrant and

authoritative Word of God in their pursuit of the
fundamentals of the Christian Faith and the distinctives
of the Christian life, there was a complementing effect
upon the Christian world, even though all of them did not
see the Biblical distinctives of the Christian life in exactly the same way and to the same degree. All teachings
presupposed the authority and infallibility of the
Scriptures, at least for awhile, and therefore were rooted
in the sufficiency of Scripture. The argument was not
whether the authority of Scripture was the Source of
truth, but whether the Scriptures said what these
reformers believed the Bible said. It was not *if* the
Scriptures said it; it was a matter of *what* the Scriptures
said.

In our own time, the premise deals with what the Holy
Spirit might reveal to a person, personally, and what the
Bible might reveal to the world, totally. A schizophrenia
has been drawn by modern Pentecostals between the
Holy Spirit Who inspired the Scriptures, and the Holy
Spirit Who is purported to have brought forward the
modern Charismatic movement.

History Past, Experience Present

It should be obvious by now that the fallacies of
history, as presented earlier, are compounded by the
weaknesses of human experience which we have just
presented. Only the Word of God can be fully trusted.

History is but the record of human experience
multiplied through many events and many years. As we
suggested previously, God has been doing His work, man
has been doing his work, and Satan has been doing his
work. The presuppositions produce the various views of
history—whether God, according to His will and purpose,
or Satan and the sinner according to their wills. But all
are within the will of our God—to an end and a purpose
and permission of His choosing—without its being
construed that God condones it. God has not personally
sponsored every religious awakening in history. Many of
them were inspired by error and evil. Therefore, we

cannot afford a false presupposition in our interpretation of history past; nor can we afford to follow a weak, human experience in our interpretation and witness to history in the present century in which we live.

Without fear of contradiction, we can say that the *Biblical fundamentals* of the Christian Faith have been worked out into a practical and honorable presentation. These great fundamental principles of the Bible are well known by anyone who wants to know them, and they are still preached with the Holy Spirit's anointing and power in some pulpits and places. The World Congress of Fundamentalists, held in Edinburgh, Scotland, June, 1976, gave a clarion call to these Biblical principles:

Definition of Fundamentalism

A Fundamentalist is a born-again believer in the Lord Jesus Christ who

1. Maintains an immovable allegiance to the inerrant, infallible, and verbally inspired Bible;
2. Believes that whatever the Bible says is so;
3. Judges all things by the Bible and is judged only by the Bible;
4. Affirms the foundational truths of the historic Christian Faith:
   The doctrine of the Trinity
   The incarnation, virgin birth, substitutionary atonement, bodily resurrection, ascension into heaven and the Second Coming of the Lord Jesus Christ
   The new birth through regeneration of the Holy Spirit
   The resurrection of the saints to life eternal
   The resurrection of the ungodly to final judgment and eternal death
   The fellowship of the saints, who are the body of Christ;
5. Practices fidelity to that Faith and endeavors to preach it to every creature;
6. Exposes and separates from all ecclesiastical denial of that Faith, compromise with error, and apostasy from the Truth; and
7. Earnestly contends for the Faith once delivered.[58]

When we speak of these fundamentals—with clear announcement and without apology—we do not preclude the individual Christian and his Biblical distinctive of the Christian life, as long as it remains upon the Biblical base of the above-mentioned declaration of truth. I shall always be thankful for the accompanying postscript to the above document passed in Edinburgh, Scotland:

> Therefore, Fundamentalism is militant orthodoxy set on fire with soulwinning zeal. While Fundamentalists may differ on certain interpretations of Scripture, we join in unity of heart and common purpose for the defense of the Faith and the preaching of the Gospel, without compromise or division.

The *Biblical fundamentals* of the Christian Faith have been set forth in a practical understanding for all of us, yet the Biblical distinctives of the Christian life remain the responsibility of the individual Christian. It may be that we need deeper concern and proclamation of the distinctives in the time in which we live. In any case, only the Biblical distinctives built upon Biblical fundamentals received from the Biblical base have assisted us in our quest.

Neo-Pentecostals and Roman Catholic Charismatics are endeavoring to build Christian Experience upon the fragments of certain aspects of the fundamentals; yet they do not believe in the totality and sufficiency of the Bible. They speak of a deeper life, a deeper experience, the gifts of the Holy Spirit, the glossolalia, and a host of other super-spiritualities reputed to be a part of the legacy of history and human experience, from presuppositions not founded upon the Biblical base. It is beyond us to understand how a movement could participate in, and fellowship with, those who have been a part of the original apostasy, as well as those who deliberately teach anti-trinitarian principles, if they, in reality, were following the inerrancy and authority of Scripture. You cannot build a deeper, spiritual life upon error.

There is no solution to the position of the Classical Pentecostal who would bring about a synthesis between the earlier Pentecostals and the present ecumenicity. We can only record a summary of our previous words. They have brought in error (1) by reading into history past the presupposition that God has been moving toward this Charismatic Hour; (2) by reading and adding the modern Roman Catholic writers who propound the same presupposition; and (3) by accepting, in confirmation, the witness of human experience from Notre Dame meetings as the final acceptance of that which had already been presupposed.

Some years ago a young man with whom I grew up in Washington, D. C., and who led a jazz band of which I was a member, was converted to Christianity. A little later I, too, was born again. He and I entered the ministry about the same time, and he pastored a church near the nation's capitol. Oral Roberts came to Washington with one of his crusades. My young ministerial friend, seeking to justify his acceptance of this crusade, told me the following story:

"Before Oral Roberts came to Washington, D. C., in that meeting, I prayed, asking God to prove Himself in the campaign, for I was going to attend it to find out if it were of the Lord. If the crusade were real and the Holy Spirit were present, I wanted God to speak in tongues through me. When the evening arrived for me to go to the service, I experienced the most profound and wonderful manifestation of the glossolalia I had experienced in my Christian life."

I asked, "When you prayed that prayer and attended that service, what did you do with the Biblical authority of your Christian life?" He has never answered that question.

There are two other incidents that aptly illustrate the point.

At a Sunday School Convention held at Oklahoma City by a Pentecostal denomination in the 1960's, two unusual services demonstrated several strange experiences. In one service a Neo-Pentecostal threw down his Bible with some verbal violence and shouted: "I used to study the theology and doctrine of that Book, but since I have received the Holy Ghost I have a new teacher." The audience went up with a shout and a manifestation of their glossolalia.

In another service of that convention a popular Neo-Pentecostal couple impressively presented to the denomination an automobile van for its work with young people and evangelism. There was no Scripture reading or other acknowledgment to the Lord. The evangelist's wife mounted the stage. As she paraded across the stage in her mini-dress and champagne-pink dyed hair to join her husband and present the keys of the van, a spontaneous praise commenced; and once again there went up a shout and a manifestation of the glossolalia. It was one of the first times I had ever seen so much flesh gratified in a so-called religious sensation. The audience responded emotionally either because they were embarrassed over her worldliness, or because they were gratified by her manner. Such incidents have led me to believe that sex is at the root of some Pentecostalism.

In both of these instances my heart was broken in prayer, as I reacted against the parade of flesh in a context of unseparated and unbiblical actions. I knew well these matters and realized that they grieved the Lord and the Holy Spirit.

Another ministerial friend told me later that when these things happened in the services, his emotions broke loose with uncontrollable manifestations. Returning to his room, he gained rational understanding that his reaction had been against the Lord; and he regretted his outburst.

The experiences of these two young ministers could be multiplied over and over again in modern, Neo-Pentecostal contexts. I have had many ministers and laymen to tell me privately of similar reactions; yet most of them would return to participate and fellowship with that which they had condemned. I am persuaded that there are millions in the world who are involved with emotions and commitments which earlier in their experience they would not have followed. Human experience is weak and must be tested in the light of Scripture.

Existentialism is the grand "trip" of the emotions of man. It is no wonder that we read of Oral Roberts, in his going to the Methodist Church, that Paul Tillich greatly influenced his move.[59] It should be remembered that Diane Kennedy Pike, the widow of Bishop James Pike, while waiting in a Jerusalem hotel for news of her husband from his wanderings near the Dead Sea, saw him leaving his body in a filmy cloudlike substance. In her spiritualistic vision "Mrs. Pike also had a glimpse of the bishop's welcome and warm embrace by his old friend and teacher, Paul Tillich, the renowned theologian who was called the 'father of the death-of-God school.'"[60]

Reference having been made of Roberts' demands, we give an account of certain Pentecostal personalities and situations built on experientialism.

Pentecostal Experientialists

One of the world's foremost Neo-Pentecostals, Oral Roberts, has boasted of a number of "audible voices" and new revelations from God. We quote extensively to illustrate a typical manner in which the sufficiency of Scripture is *not* sustained. The quotation will speak for itself, but several observations will be drawn:

(1) The Title: "A New Revelation from God...What God Has Shown Me is Shortly Coming to Pass."

(2) The Request: "Please open your mind and hear what God has shown me, for it will surely affect your life."

(3) The Revelation: ("...five things as God showed them to me.")

  "I. There is Going to Be a Visitation of Men by Angels As in Bible Times.

  II. There will be a New World-Wide Emphasis on Healing And Supernatural Deliverance
  in the established church.
  in the medical profession.
  among mankind generally.

  III. There will be Mass Healings Among Large

Audiences. (Point of Contact)

IV. There Is To Be A New Foreign Missionary Drive Through Mighty Signs and Wonders.

V. There is to be a Coming Together of God's Anointed for the Final Revival."

(4) The Authority of the New Revelation: "These five things are shortly coming to pass. God has spoken, and His Word is true. His Word will not return unto him void."[61]

Let us analyze some of the things mentioned here.

First, the title makes it clear that the claim is reputed to be a "new revelation from God...What God has" revealed to Mr. Roberts. It is an added revelation, to say nothing of the fact that the contents contain false utterance in the light of the Biblical fact of the apostasy of the last days. The thought of the gathering together of "God's Anointed for the Final Revival" is the same as the modern Ecumenical Movement—the new ecumenism.

Second, the claim of this revelation declares its authority to be co-equal with the Bible, in spite of the fact that Scripture is used to verify its appeal and content. "His Word will not return unto him void," said Roberts. By taking the liberty of using that verse—Isaiah 55:11—to substantiate his claim, Roberts projected himself and his so-called revelation to the level of Biblical authority. This is error. Isaiah's announcement referred to Scripture alone! Scripture is sufficient within itself and consummated within itself—"it shall not return unto me [God] void." Only the "holy men of old" possessed this degree of authority, and when the last one gave his utterance, the Bible became complete. There remains no man with that authority today.

Third, we should consider the implication of this quotation. Where is Roberts getting his information? I say that he is a false prophet who is receiving information from the "god of this age." That "god" is preparing the stage for the Antichrist, and the ingredients of Roberts' message are part of the propaganda which is necessary for the educating of the masses for the general acceptance of the "man of sin." New attitudes in the churches, new

attitudes toward the medical field and medicine, and
other implications are a part of the education that is
necessary to effect belief for the coming False One.

Another example is the following quotation from an
article on "Demons."

> I discern demons three ways. First, through God's
> presence that comes upon me, which I usually feel through
> my hand. Second, by the breath of the person, and third,
> by the person's eyes.
>
> The name of the chief demon is Beelzebub, which means
> god of the flesh, or god of corruption. Now, the very nature
> of a demon is unclean and when he possesses a human
> being, he gives off a stench to his breath which is unlike
> any other odor or stench you ever smelled. It is not just bad
> breath, it is more powerful than that. Then the eyes of a
> demon-possessed person take on a luster which is
> uncommonly bright and which reminds one of the eyes of
> a poisonous serpent. It is an unforgettable experience to
> see the leering eyes of a demon.
>
> The Lord told me I would know the number and name of
> demons and would have His power to cast them out. When
> I am anointed and His Spirit is powerfully moving
> through my spirit, I have this power and am able to cast
> out demons. When I am not anointed and when the Spirit
> of God is not upon me, I am an utter failure when I come to
> deal with such people. This is the chief reason I do not like
> to make private prayers and why I prefer to pray for people
> in our campaigns. In the campaigns, I preach and get
> myself in a harmony with God which I am not able to have
> at other times. This enables me to have this anointing
> upon me much more.[62]

This information about demons, although thoroughly
interesting, is outside Bible revelation. Yet Roberts says,
"The Lord told me." What does he mean by this phrase?
In his writings contemporary to the decade of this quoted
article, he called certain revelations "audible voices."
This is also seen in his earlier books and is an original
description by him. He has, at times, called attention to
his name that his parents gave him at birth as Oral, with
not only revealed significance to his actual birth, but also

to his name in connection with *oral* communication from
God.

Also, he speaks in the demon article about getting
himself "in harmony with God." On the face of it, this
statement seems very innocent. I have not been able to
decide whether it is a contradiction of what he said later
in his seminars at his University, or whether it is simply
an extension and explanation of the matter. In his
seminars in the summer of the sixties, in the early years of
his University, Roberts presented a message on "The
Reciprocity of the Holy Spirit." In this message he
referred to the statement of getting himself "in harmony
with God." He spoke about the Spirit-filled life and
volitional tongue-speaking and stated that when a person
is baptized with the Holy Spirit, he becomes synchronized
(reciprocity; "a mutual exchange of privileges") with the
Holy Spirit. This places the Spirit-filled believer in a
position, as Roberts would say it, to speak in tongues by
his own volition.

Two persons who were present on that occasion told
me that one of Roberts' assistants questioned him during
a time of public discussion. The man enquired, "Brother
Roberts, would this not mean that the Holy Spirit did not
know when to speak in tongues, and we had to tell Him?"
Mr. Roberts replied that he did not understand the
question.

At the close of the service Roberts called for a line to be
formed and the ministers to come before him expectant
that as he laid his hands upon each of them, they would
volitionally speak in tongues at their own will. This is
unscriptural. Scripture says that at Pentecost they
"began to speak with other tongues, as the Spirit gave
them utterance" (Acts 2:4; cf. 10:44, 46). It is clearly stated
that when Paul laid his hands upon the twelve Ephesians, the Holy Ghost came upon them of His own volition (Acts 19:6), and not that of the individual believer.
The gifts of the Holy Spirit are not in the physical bodies
of the believers, resident, monopolized by their own
franchise;   the   gifts   were   set   in   the   Mystical

Body of Christ and exercised by the sovereignty of God
Himself.

T. L. Osborn, in his book on *Healing*, actually goes so
far as to say that although the Bible speaks of six ways
that God heals in our modern time, God has revealed to
him, personally, a seventh way. God had given to him the
gift "of the creative power of the word of faith."[63] Mr.
Osborn goes on to explain that when he speaks, his own
words create faith in the heart of the hearer for him to
have faith for the miracle that he seeks. This, too, is
heresy; it is mere experiential subjectivity or positive
suggestion, psychologically, if anything. Positive thinking is very prominent among all Pentecostals. For any
man to claim the gift or power of creating words or faith
would substantially mean that he is claiming to be *Logos*
("the word," John 1:1, which is only the prerogative of
Christ) or that he was the Holy Spirit Who generates faith
in the human heart.

In each of these cases, we must assume that each
of these men is a true prophet without Biblical
credentials—or at least that is what they want and expect
us to assume. If we accept their messages as authoritative
from God, who is to say who else and what else should be
included to the true prophet and the truth? We are simply
declaring that we cannot accept the mere words of a man
as proof of that man's being a true prophet of the Lord.
His authority must come from Scripture. This is an old
necessity down through church history, and we must
contend for it in this twentieth century apostasy. Where
the Bible speaks, we will proclaim, defend, and believe it.
Where the Bible is silent, we will not proceed, on our own,
assuming that we have special light, and neither will we
endorse it in another. We cannot accept a man on the
basis of the silence of Scripture or on the personal word of
his own authority, separate from Scripture. We can
support only the man who, by the authority of Scripture,
supports the authority of Scripture.

In more recent days, Roberts is presenting "a new
delivery system from God," which is the gift of an

"Alabaster Box" of anointing oil. He says, "I have prayed over the oil and I know this will be a powerful New Point of Contact for your total healing needs."[64] This is indeed something new, because it is reputed to give "many divine healings" in advance of being sick.

Presently, Mr. Osborn is presenting a piece of burlap which the person is to return with an offering. When Osborn receives the burlap again, he will fast and pray for three days and three nights; then he will return the cloth for healing.[65] If it were not so serious, we would have to laugh in the face of this claim. Imagine God's being constrained to wait three days and three nights before prayer can be answered.

History is replete with the claims of human, subjective revelations. In our generation, we have heard of one pope who declared that Jesus appeared to him in his bedchamber when he was ill. We must reject the claims of new revelations, so-called, no matter how powerful or popular a man and his system might be.

5

The New Ecumenism

Up to this point, our considerations have taken us back in history; yet we have kept clearly before us the twentieth century Neo-Christianity. Neo-Pentecostalism is not an island; it is a part of the mainstream of the ecumenical movement. Personalities from all of the neo-world are fellowshipping with, or are optimistic about, the mushrooming "new ecumenism." Earlier we mentioned that the methodology of New-Evangelicalism is an accompanying force. For years, men from the Neo-Evangelical camps have been speakers and participants in the efforts of the Neo-Pentecostal. The Full Gospel Business Men's Fellowship has greatly assisted this integration of denominations and movements as has Billy Graham's participation in the dedication of Oral Roberts University.

Influence of Methodology

At some point in our reflections we need to consider the influence of *methodology*, as propounded by the Neo-Evangelicals, and their involvement in the claim of the Neo-Pentecostal with regard to the *power* of the Holy Spirit. Methodology and power are a strong combination. Their teachings mutually assist the success of their work.

Apostolic Succeedings

There are a number of elements involved in taking the Gospel "into all the world." There must be a message, a man, a mission, a method, and a means. It is obvious that the Gospel is to be carried by human instrumentality sent on a mission using some method or means. Not in the history of the world has man had access to wider opportunities in missions, methods, and means to advance the glorious message of our Lord Jesus. I would not deny the value of these instruments. It is encouraging to know that we do not have to spread the Gospel via the horse-and-buggy and other former creeping methods. The invention of the printing press, radio and television, transportation and other mechanical and technological avenues—all of these have opened far wider horizons for the keeping of the Great Commission.

In our time, however—particularly in the institutional church—there is a considerable difference of opinion regarding the management of the man, the mission, the method, and the means in relationship to the Gospel message itself. Who would have thought that an increase in the availability of methods and means would become a snare, effecting in world evangelization such diversity of opinion?

One of the main problems of modern Christendom is that of knowing how far a person, denomination, minister, or other organization should go with methodology. To what extent should we use the ever-increasing tools of psychology? To what degree should we "relate" to the sinner in leading him to Christ? What about the tricks of emotion, music, money-raising programs, contests, and awards in this great quest for the souls of men? Is the method—are all methods—the means of salvation, or does the Gospel alone have the power to bring the sinner to Christ?

Church history is filled with examples of tangents and failures that have issued from the abuse of methods and means. Although former church history lacked the modern tools of evangelism, new problems were present even then. Certain apostolic succeedings are clearly recorded in the minutes of the meetings in history, and we would do well to note them. We tend to think that today's problems are unrelated to the past; but as we have already observed, there is a common species of sin. We cannot afford to repeat the abuses of the methods and means of past history. A flood of "neo's" does not mean that we are totally different from the past. Total depravity of the individual is totally involved in our history. In our earnest desire for Christianity to "relate" to others, and fearing the label of being "hung up" on doctrine, separation, and discipline, we might assume that we need a new dimension beyond that of our forefathers. However, we must set forth the man, the means, the mission, and the methods in the genuine light of sanctified motives and of the supremacy of the message of Jesus Christ.

The Apostle Paul makes it clear that the message (the Gospel) should be the main item on the "agenda" of our committee reports and evangelistic statistics:

> For I am not ashamed of the gospel of Christ: for it is the power of God unto salvation to every one that believeth; to the Jew first, and also to the Greek. For therein is the righteousness of God revealed from faith to faith: as it is written, The just shall live by faith (Romans 1:16-17).

Two things are obvious in these verses: (1) The *Gospel* is the power of God unto salvation. Inherent in the Gospel is the power of God to do the job of saving souls from sin. (2) The Gospel is the revelation ("therein") of the righteousness of God and faith, rather than simply the mission, the method, the means, or the man.

In Neo-Evangelicalism and Neo-Pentecostalism there is a methodology that actually hinders the power of God in the power of the Gospel. But let us consider this further:

First, we encountered in church history the "Apostolic Succession" of *man*.

This arose from the clamor for human authority in the early days of church history. Apostolic Succession has been defined as "the doctrine that properly ordained bishops convey the grace of God through an unbroken chain of the laying on of hands going back to the first apostles of Christ. The Roman, Eastern, and Anglican churches hold that such unbroken physical succession is essential to a valid Christian ministry."[66]

Contrary to the more popular accounts of the history of popery—and there are several routes that may be presented to gain the truth of the matter—there is another way in which Romanism should be considered. It was not until the days of Pope Leo I (440-461 A.D.) that the first leader spoke of his demands in singular authority. There were, at that time, four bishops in Antioch, Alexandria, Constantinople, and Rome. The Roman bishop, Leo I, sought headship in this authority. Pope Gregory the Great (590 A.D.), in response to the cry or claim for a singular authority, took the attitude of humility, or servant. This, of course, was hypocritical of Pope Gregory, but it brought the sentiment of the people to a greater receptivity to the claim of pope. It was Pope Leo III (800 A.D.) who first achieved the full office of authority when he crowned Emperor Charles the Great, indicating the growing authority of popes over kings. This increased to an unprecedented power as exercised under Pope Gregory VII (1073 A.D.), also named Hildebrand, who used the great weapon of authority as an interdict against Henry IV. The king was required to stand barefooted in the snow for three days as an act of repentance, before Pope Hildebrand would accept his solicitous words toward restoration.

The point is well made that *man* must not be taken to be more important than the *message* of the Gospel. It is our hope that we have learned this lesson well; but it is possible that we are viewing a repeat in history, from a Protestant spectrum, through some of the Neo-Pentecostal personalities who have accepted the infallibility of the pope. But from Peter down to the present pope, it is clear that man, whether a pope or peasant, is nothing when it comes to the matter of the Gospel. History records the contradiction of popes, and yet people continue to believe in their "infallibility" and accept their voices as the mouthpiece of God ("ex cathedra"). Romanism must explain the fact that some of their popes, such as Pope Liberius, were Arians (an heretical group), and that some popes, such as Pope Honorius, were actually deposed for heresy. If the popes are infallible and actually speak as the mouthpiece of God, how could any of them possibly embrace a heresy or a lie?

There were sixteen Vulgate popes who claimed that the Latin Vulgate, written by Jerome, was infallible; yet Pope Clementine had to change many blatant mistakes found there. The condemnation of Galileo, seventeenth century, is another incident that continues to be a mystery. It is said that Galileo endured trial and imprisonment, and on his knees, with an oath, had to renounce the truths of his scientific creeds. How could Romanism take a man of conscience and make him perjure himself in order to be saved from the stake? This is not a matter of ignorance; it is a matter of coercion.

Is it not clear that the *man* of church history is susceptible to mistakes and sin? How can the Neo-Pentecostal, under any consideration, speak of a Spirit-filled relationship with a church that has not denounced this as heresy? To me it seemed important to give account of this matter in this book. Popery has not changed. In our own time, consider Ireland, Spain, and South America. The power of Romanism remains. The *moods* of Romanism change with any movement or opportunity, for casuistry—"the end justifies the means"—is their stratagem. But the message and error and apostasy are ever the same.

The exegesis of Matthew 16:18 continues to be pertinent to the Romanists' argument of Peter as the first pope. It was not the *man*, Peter, but his confession of the Christ that magnifies the message of the Gospel. "Peter" remains in the Greek Text as "piece of a rock" (masculine gender), rather than Peter as "this the rock" (feminine gender). Actually, Peter was to be "of a rock" (cf. John

1:42; 21:15-19; I Peter 2:1-8)—that is, part of a rock. The use of two different Greek words distinguishes between Peter and the Christ. We must keep the record straight: upon the Biblical base, only Jesus Christ, the Son of the Living God, could be The Rock. We must ever remember that man is man and God is God. All of us have our callings, gifts, positions, and privileges in Christ, but we are restricted to the place of man the creature. Roman Catholics still endeavor to get around this exegesis by quoting from the Latin Vulgate in which there is not the gender distinction as in the Greek. It is not "Apostolic Succession" but the apostolic *message* that the Word of God says is to be the succession down through the years.

We can observe in modern Pentecostalism, Pentecostal popes of a kind. They make their claims of new revelations, powers, and gifts. They teach an erroneous doctrine that divides the Body of Christ into different kinds of Christians—the Charismatics and the fundamental ones, etc. The Word of God does not allow such ideas.

The Means of Grace

Second, we observe that church history records the *means.* In some contexts it is defined as the "means of grace," and is expressed as "instrumentalities of salvation, as faith, prayer, Scripture, and sacraments."[67]

It is interesting that "Scripture" is included as *a* means rather than *the* means; but undoubtedly, the definition is referring to the mechanical, written means of Scripture.

There are true, Biblical means of grace. But these means have often been abused. Once again, Romanism developed an impressive list of "Seven Sacraments":

1. *Baptism.* To the Romanists this sacrament is representative of the death and resurrection of Christ. They teach bluntly that through the means of baptism the child dies to sin and is regenerated and made a member of the Church and the Body of Christ. Although they speak of a "Baptism of Desire" for men like the thief

on the cross, Baptism of water is considered essential to salvation. In our times some Protestant churches still insist that "Baptismal Regeneration" is efficacious.

2. *Confirmation.* This sacrament, to the Roman Catholic, signifies maturity. He believes that it imparts power to help him fulfill public duty and life. Romanists believe they receive the Holy Spirit in this sacrament, and considerable instruction is given to the person involved.

3. *Eucharist.* This is the sacrament of the Lord's Supper, or the sacrifice of the Mass. It claims transubstantiation in which it is believed that the elements are no longer wine and bread, that only the *appearance* remains the same as before the act of the Mass.

4. *Penance.* This sacrament is believed to reconcile the sinner to God as often as he sins after Baptism. Generally speaking, three things are involved in this means: contrition, confession (Confessional Booth), and satisfaction.

5. *Extreme Unction* (Anointing the Sick with oil). This is a sacrament which is supposed to impart grace from the Holy Spirit Whose anointing takes away sin. Both physical and spiritual benefits are believed to be involved, though the latter is more important.

6. *Holy Orders.* This is the sacrament of hierarchical power imparted by a competent minister by the imposition of hands, and leads to the Roman Catholic priesthood and other positions in the Church.

7. *Matrimony.* This sacrament confers grace to sanctify the unique union of husband and wife. Without this, it is believed that any other means of marriage would be a state of adultery.

It should be kept in mind that Romanism regards every sacrament as a direct means of grace. The Bible teaches certain ordinances, such as Water Baptism and the Lord's Supper, and in the government of the church these ordinances should be maintained regularly. However, in the history of the church there has been the mistake of overemphasizing the man and the means, to the neglect of the message of the Gospel.

Today we are seeing among Charismatics the practice of a great use and development of the "laying on of hands," and we predict that this particular act will increase for many future expressions and ceremonies. The abuse of James' admonition with regard to "praying for the sick" (ch. 5) will increase. Note the similarity between the sacrament of "Extreme Unction" and the Pentecostals' "praying for the sick."

It seems appropriate, at this point, to consider a certain meeting of the Charismatics at Kansas City, July 20-24, 1977. Significantly, the Roman Catholic Church was the prominent leader of the convention. A Catholic magazine advertised the meeting in these words:

> This celebration is one united conference, and at the same time many conferences. The National Conference on Charismatic Renewal in the Catholic Church, traditionally held at Notre Dame, will be held this year in Kansas City as a part of the 1977 Conference on Charismatic Renewal in the Christian Churches. Other denominational groups and fellowships will be doing the same thing—holding their national conferences as a part of this one, united conference. They include Lutherans, Episcopalians, Baptists, Messianic Jews, Pentecostals and people from non-denominational backgrounds.... The planning committee for the conference includes prominent leaders from many different traditions who share a desire to see unity in the Body of Christ.[68]

Among those addressing the convention were Kevin Ranaghan of Notre Dame, Pentecostal ecumenist David Du Plessis, Ruth Carter Stapleton, Catherine Marshall, and Southern Baptist minister Charles Simpson.

As we have mentioned before, Christians need to understand that often the new ecumenism is couched in the language of Scripture, but a far different meaning is attached to the words. When a Charismatic says that he has been "born again" or "saved," does he mean that he has become a Christian by personal repentance and faith in the Blood of Christ alone, as the Bible reveals?

Cardinal Leo Joseph Suenens, whom we have

mentioned before as involved in the Charismatic Renewal, has clearly explained what Catholic Charismatics mean by the "new birth" or "conversion":

Once we have clarified our terminology, we are ready to speak about what seems to me to be one of the most important contributions the charismatic renewal might make to the Church in the coming years: to give all Christians a renewed awareness of what their baptism implies.

In the beginning of the Church, baptism was conferred upon converted adults; later on, when baptism was conferred upon infants, an important change took place in the way people were initiated to Christianity by heredity, by family education, and by the support of Christian society, created a new type of Christian. For the most part, Christians were no longer converts who met Jesus as their Lord and Savior and who chose their fellowship in full freedom and consciousness.

Today we need Christians who are fully aware of the reality and the meaning of their baptism and who are fully open to Jesus, having met him personally in their lives. This suggests a new catechumenate for Christian adults who have been baptised and confirmed as children, but who now accept in a new, adult way the truth of what they already are sacramentally.

Baptism of children has to continue; this tradition is solidly founded and remains valid. But we need a place for a renewed commitment to the Lord.

This is what people in the charismatic renewal refer to as being "baptized in the Spirit": a renewed, personal Pentecost, in keeping with the sacraments of baptism and confirmation, but with a new awareness and acceptance. ("New Covenant," 2/77).[69]

No one could read this quotation and not realize that Cardinal Suenens was giving full announcement, in 1977, that the Roman Catholic Church continues to believe exactly what it has always believed and that Baptism and Confirmation, as well as all other Sacraments, remain exactly the same as before in the Roman Catholic Church. He is also announcing just as

clearly that the Roman Catholic Charismatics are
committed to the very same belief. The "New Birth" or
"Renewal," as they use the term, is on the same apostate base. In other words, the Charismatic "renewal"
is merely another approach to that which has always
been believed by the Roman Catholic Church
"sacramentally."

The only conclusion to draw is that "renewal" means
that the Roman Catholic becomes a *better* Roman
Catholic Christian, not a *converted* born-again Christian. The greater conclusion is also clear: the Roman
Catholic Charismatic movement is a giant step toward
greater ecumenicity and is a breakdown of the Biblical
separation, as revealed from the Biblical base, that is so
badly needed in this time of apostasy.

The parade of "stars" at the Kansas City convention of
July, 1977—whether by Pentecostal denominations or
non-denominational Pentecostals—are making their
contributions to this tremendous growth of the World
Ecumenical Movement (which is but an extension of the
old ecumenism). It is a coming together of Neo-
Christianity around an old heresy and an old apostasy.
AND ROMANISM IS THE LEADER!

It is becoming clearer why the Neo-Pentecostal and the
Roman Catholic Charismatic share a common ecumenicity. It is more than the common indulgence of the
glossolalia; there are also deep affinities for "great
signs," the supernatural, new revelations, impressions,
and a host of old things all the way back in history. It was
presented in the earlier days under the Roman papacy,
and now it is presented again, in a new guise, under the
Charismatic papacy. There were Roman Catholic Sacraments in the old Roman Catholic apostasy, and Cardinal
Suenens assures us that these Sacraments remain in the
new Charismatic apostasy. Not having been on the
Biblical base in their old apostasy, they are still setting
forth claims away from the Biblical base.

Third, we see in church history the *mission* of the
church. In our own time, at the beginning of this century,

there arose another new error.

For a decade, Walter Rauschenbusch was one of the best-known ministers in America. In 1907, suddenly and unexpectedly, he became a national figure. From then until his death in 1918, Rauschenbusch was greatly in demand as a preacher, lecturer, and writer ; and five important books, as well as a number of smaller pieces, came from his pen. Rauschenbusch was regarded as the central figure in the movement known as the "social gospel," which was influential in American Protestantism in those days. Henry Van Dusen, a "Liberal," and World Councilman (we have already mentioned that many modern Pentecostals accept him as "a charismatic before his time"), has actually classed Rauschenbusch with Jonathan Edwards and Horace Bushnell as one of the most influential men in the thought of the American church.

Walter Rauschenbusch was born in 1861 in Rochester, New York. His German-born father came to this country as a missionary in the middle of the last century; and soon thereafter he left the Lutheran church to enter the Baptist fold. Young Walter was educated in both Germany and America. He was graduated from the Rochester Theological Seminary in 1886. He accepted the pastorate of the Second German Baptist Church in New York's tough West Side, not far from the region popularly known as "Hell's Kitchen." Rauschenbusch's congregation was composed of working people, and he became acutely aware of their difficult struggles against poverty and disease, especially in hard times. Their suffering forced him to confront social problems. As he put it, his social view "did not come from the church. It came from outside."

Christianity and the Social Crisis by Rauschenbusch appeared in the year of the financial panic—1907. His thesis was that "the essential purpose of Christianity was to transform human society into the kingdom of God by regenerating all human relations and reconstituting them in accordance with the will of God." He believed that this purpose had been obscured through the centuries. In another statement he said: "The kingdom of God includes the economic life." In explaining Jesus' idea of the Kingdom, he included too much of his own progressive and evolutionary view and failed to give proper emphasis to essential beliefs, such as the New Birth, and the Second Coming of the Lord Jesus. In stressing the immanence of God, in identifying God so closely with humanity, Rauschenbusch minimized the transcendence, majesty, and sovereignty of God.

It can be easily pointed out that the "social gospel" has continued in opposition to the more fundamental and essential teachings of the message of the Gospel. The Social Gospel was embedded in the liberal teachings that arose at the beginning of the twentieth century. In more recent times, Neo-Pentecostalism has embraced belief in the materialistic benefits of personal prosperity and health as being co-equal in the atonement of Jesus Christ. Much emphasis is being placed on the social, economic, racial, political, and physical benefits of the Christian concepts. These aspects of the "social gospel" involved in Neo-Pentecostalism are somewhat different; yet they share a very important place in their Charismatic gifts. This is simply another indication of the old ecumenism in the new ecumenism.

Fourth, and finally, we come to the church and its *methods*. The modern church is "super" administrative, mechanical, and program conscious. With so many programs in the offing, budget pressures often cause us to act in an unnatural and unscriptural manner in order to come through with the proper finances. An honorable Christian who does not quite measure up to the other ministerial statistics, contests, tricks, and psychological gimmicks, which many times are worldly and untrue in the work of the modern ministry and evangelism, could easily feel intimidated if he did not have the Lord in his heart. More and more churches and schools are becoming involved in bankruptcy, mismanagement of funds, overspending, and other conditions that indicate a need in our institutions for worship and teaching to be measured equally by honor and spiritual integrity.

Another obvious lesson from the past is that the spiritual and moral influence of the church usually wanes in proportion to the church's engrossment with economic, social, material, and political matters of success; and the church becomes institutionalized.

Worldly success is not necessarily success for the Lord. It has always been the *message* of the Gospel that God has honored—in times when the church was without methods and means; when ministers of the Word were in prisons or dungeons; or when the means were enlarged through the scope of finance and facility. We might increase the *crowds* in the church with carnal means, but it does not necessarily mean that we are leading souls to Christ.

The next thing for which God is looking is the *man*. Where are the men of God? Where are the spiritual fathers? This is the gist of Dr. Moody's conversation with Dr. Holmes, of which we spoke in Part I. How the world needs a man of God who has the message from God and who is willing to deliver that message at all costs! The combination we need is a Godly man with a Biblical message and a spiritual stamina. This is still the greatest impetus for all forms of evangelism: the simplicity of person-to-person soulwinning about the Lord Jesus Christ. Evangelism must be evangelically based upon the fundamentals of the Word of God. The end does not *justify* the means; it *dicates* the means.

Even in the spiritual preparation of the man himself there is this same consistency of the principle:

> But ye, beloved, building up yourselves on your most holy faith, praying in the Holy Ghost, Keep yourselves in the love of God, looking for the mercy of our Lord Jesus Christ unto eternal life (Jude 20-21).

These verses employ four verbs. Three are participles—building, praying, looking—and one verb is in the imperative—Keep! The main clause and command is this: "Keep yourself in the love of God." The subject "you" is understood. The subordinate ideas may be time or cause or result or purpose, as they relate to the main verb. Even our *building* ourselves up in the faith, our *praying* in the Holy Ghost, and our *waiting* for the Lord to come are methods and means in serving the Gospel.

The Great Commission presents the true *balance* in these things:

> Go ye therefore, and teach all nations, baptizing them in the name of the Father, and of the Son, and of the Holy Ghost: Teaching them to observe all things whatsoever I have commanded you: and, lo, I am with you alway, even unto the end of the world (Matthew 28:19-20).

The exegesis here firmly fixes the pattern that we are to follow. The main verb is an imperative and could be explained as "disciple-ize" or "make disciples" or "teach." The ideas in the lesser verbs are always inferior to the idea in the main verb in the sentence.

With this in mind, let us view again the Great Commission: The main idea is not "going" but "disciple-izing." Wherever we go, wherever we are, by whatever method or means available, Jesus commands us to make disciples. Soulwinning is not always *doing* ; it could also employ *being*. Peter makes that clear in speaking to Christian wives of unchristian husbands (I Peter 3:1-4).

The Great Commission, for most people, does not imply moving out of the home town. It is when they move—within the home town or other geography—by whatever means or methods they move, they are to evangelize as they were supposed to evangelize before they moved. The subordinate clause and idea is the "going "—as you go, when you go, how you go. The method and means are not to be understood as the most important; the main clause is *disciple-ize*. Keep on with the soulwinning in spite of limited methods and means, or with an enlarged series of methods and means. Here again we see the *message* as the great priority, privilege, and duty. The message *inspires* the man and *reveals* the power of salvation through the Word. The message *prepares* the man for the mission. Without this mission or "vision," the people will perish; but the message saves the perished ones. We need methods and means, but they are subordinate to the main thought of the message of disciple-izing or teaching, and that is the work of the message itself.

The Neo-Pentecostals are very much involved in the matter of methods. Their method speaks more of the power involved in their evangelism—a power of a Charismatic person with their definition of "Spirit-filled."

New Evangelicals speak of methods in still another way; it is the methodology of an unseparated practice of evangelism as well as the emphasis of intellectual dialogue which they feel is a powerful tool of evangelism with those who are the enemies of Christ. They do not realize that even a Christian cannot bargain or dialogue and bring about the conversion of a sinner. Only the Gospel can do that.

Arthur Brisbane gives a good analysis of the scope and power of methods and means in a more political context. A number of evangelical writers of our time have mentioned this. Brisbane says:

> We may sweep the world clean of militarism. We may scrub the world white of autocracy. We may carpet it with democracy and drape it with the flag of republicanism. We may hang on the walls the thrilling pictures of freedom—here the signing of America's Independence, there the thrilling portrait of Joan of Arc, yonder the Magna Charta, and on this side the inspiring picture of Garibaldi. We may spend energy and effort to make the world a paradise itself, where the lion of capitalism can lie down with the proletarian lamb. But if we turn into the splendid room mankind with the same old heart, "deceitful and desperately wicked," we may expect to clean house again and again not many days hence. What we need is a peace conference with the Prince of Peace.

We might well be admonished, as an institutional church, that if we had all the men, missions, means, and methods of the past at our disposal; if we were perfect in

our tools and tapes and tracts; if we were polished,
educated, and psychological in all our dealings with man;
and, if we could execute all our methods and means most
effectively in our evangelism—it would still require the
power of that Bible message and of the Holy Spirit to do
the work that needs to be done to the salvation of the lost
and the safekeeping of the believer. We laud every
honorable means available, but we place all of them on
the altar of spiritual consecration, through the power of
the Holy Spirit, for the proclamation and exaltation of
Christ and His Gospel. All of our motives, methods,
means, and everything else, must be separated and
sanctified; we cannot afford to use that which is carnal
and worldly.

There is no intention in these principles to produce lazy
evangelism or slothful soulwinners. However, we cannot
afford, either, to send the fresh, cool water of the Gospel
through sewer-pipes to slake man's thirst and then allow
him to die in the carnal death of polluted water. His New
Birth must have a pure, spiritual pedigree, but there are
some so-called New Births in our time which are merely
psychological conversions and human reformations.
There is only one "New Birth," and it is easily identi-
fiable, for it is accompanied by a transformed life!

All apostolic *succeedings* since the beginning of
church history reveal the utter futility of any form of
religion that is not built upon the power of the Word of
God. We cannot win souls or have victory over sin without
the supreme acknowledgment and emphasis placed upon
the Message of the Word Itself. Neither Neo-Pentecostalism with its emphasis upon human, experiential
power, nor Neo-Evangelicalism with its emphasis upon
human, intellectual methodology can be substituted for
the power of the Scriptures.

> Should all the forms which men devise
>   Attack my faith with treacherous art;
> I'd call them vanity and lies,
>   And bind the Gospel to my heart.[70]

6

Experiential Compromises of the New Ecumenism

Before we conclude this section on "The Weakness of Human Experience," we need to consider the ecumenical and corporate experience of those who are coming together in this latter part of the twentieth century. The *old* ecumenism is sustained in the *new* ecumenism by the *companions* who have gathered around them. In a manner of speaking, and as far as it concerns recognition of its error, the old ecumenism may have had a black tint to the compromise, by openly *subtracting* from the Word of God and the supernatural, and the new ecumenism of the Neo-Pentecostals, by speaking *positively* for the Holy Spirit and the supernatural, may have a white tint in their compromise; but both ecumenisms wear the gray of erroneous compromise, which is far more deceptive.

Companions in Compromise

When the Classical Pentecostals deny a relationship between themselves and the old ecumenicity, they contradict the facts. There is an ecumenical unity among all ecumenists of the past and the present. Overwhelming evidence supports a singular Neo-Christianity of personalities and movements receiving contributions of error from both old and new ecumenicities. We might describe these personalities and movements as "Companions in Compromise."

An extended quotation from "The Pentecostal Phenomenon" in the 1973 *Britannica Book of the Year* supports a general tendency of this movement with all ecumenists:

> The 1960's movement drew attention to Pentecostalism because of its spread into churches that historically gave little attention to this version of "baptism in the Holy Spirit." These include the Episcopal, the Lutheran, and the Roman Catholic.
>
> Before long a number of denominations were reporting outbreaks of tongue-speaking or other phenomena connected with Pentecostalism. Both on the West Coast and around Minneapolis, Minnesota, the Lutherans were stirred or disturbed over reports of such events in their midst. The American Lutheran Church authorized a study in 1962, and the Lutheran Church—Missouri Synod found it had to deal with the subject after one of its Minnesota congregations divided over the issue of its pastor's involvement.
>
> The Roman Catholic Church, through its long history, had known outbreaks of activities similar to modern Pentecostalism, but Pentecostalism had been a Protestant movement and until the Second Vatican Council (1962-65) it would have been almost inconceivable for Catholics to identify with an expression of Christianity that derived from Protestant influences. The new ecumenical spirit, however, permitted Catholics to acknowledge such debts, to associate with non-Catholics, and to develop a version of charismatic renewal appropriate to Catholicism.[71]

It is obvious that the author of this article interprets Neo-Pentecostalism as a part of the World Ecumenical Movement, having a direct thrust toward the permanent resolve of this unity. The "new ecumenical spirit" is identified from Vatican II and the accompanying fellowships of other groups that are ecumenical in spirit.

In 1966 I was invited to be an observer at the World Congress on Evangelism in Berlin; but I did not attend. Preliminary papers sent to prospective delegates and observers had overtones of an emphasis upon "spirit" and "Holy Spirit." This desire for a "spiritual" Congress was given to the news media with considerable emphasis, and Dr. Billy Graham wrote several letters to the delegates, giving these typical remarks:

> I believe this Congress can have an impact on the entire field of evangelism and missions.

> But I would not try to project what this Congress will say because only God knows that now. It well could be that the Holy Spirit will do something unique, something different, something unusual for those who attend the Congress. I am praying for that.[72]

These words, if spoken in the Biblical sense, would be greatly appreciated. But I do not believe that the Holy Spirit is the author of the modern unity which is being proposed by the ecumenical movements of the day; and if certain presuppositions with different definitions in the meaning of the work of the Holy Spirit, reiterated by the ecumenists, are not founded upon the Biblical base, the conclusions could not be the same.

Brought together in this Berlin Congress was another segment of the ecumenical movement—Neo-Pentecostalism and the Oral Roberts ministry. It was at this Congress that Dr. Graham accepted Roberts' invitation to give the dedication of the newly built Oral Roberts University at Tulsa, Oklahoma.[73] A leading Pentecostal bishop overheard Dr. Graham telling one of his associates that he knew that he would be criticized for accepting the ORU dedication service, but for the sake of unity, he felt that he must accept.

There is a certain sense in which the Holy Spirit does "something unique, something different, something unusual," to quote Dr. Graham. But the modern Ecumenical Movement is not to be interpreted as that "something" which the Holy Spirit has done in a "unique" way for the glory of Christ.

Indisputably, Graham's implications in his letters for the World Congress on Evangelism favor ecumenicity, for previously at Belmont Abbey College, he had said of the great ecumenical revolution in Christendom:

I don't know when it began. Perhaps during World War II
... I think that the emphasis that the late Pope John
brought, the Ecumenical Council of the Bishops in Rome
itself—a council that has had the prayers of all Christendom—herald the present Christian revolution ... The
emphasis in our time may be on the Holy Spirit.
Everywhere people are gathering—Protestants, Catholics
and yes, Jews—to pray together. I know of 114 such groups
on Long Island itself. Is the Holy Spirit in our time doing
something that is beyond any of us?[74]

Again, in an open letter entitled "Separation or
Fellowship," Dr. Graham summoned the Holy Spirit to
justify linking up with religious leaders on which the
Spirit had already pronounced judgment through the
Word of God:

You will be interested to know that I announced here in
San Francisco publicly that I was not sponsored by the
churches, the executive committee or anyone else—that I
have come under the sponsorship of the Holy Spirit ... I
am convinced that we may see the deepest work of the
Holy Spirit in San Francisco that we have ever seen. I am
more convinced than ever that the Holy Spirit is anointing
and blessing these meetings. I have never felt such power
in preaching nor have I sensed the presence of the Holy
Spirit as now.[75]

I ask: If Dr. Graham were not being "sponsored by the
churches" and "the executive committee," what were the
"Liberals" and the ecumenists doing on the platform? We
do not understand the Scripture to teach aggregation of
religionists. We do not believe that the Holy Spirit Who
inspired the Word of God would centuries later anoint this
type of union of personalities. That Dr. Graham "felt such
power" does not compensate for our loyalty to the Word of
God. We have heard of countless Charismatics who have
"felt such power."

A sequel to the foregoing remarks should be inserted at
this point. Addressing a luncheon at the New York
Overseas Press Club in 1976, Graham said that he has

found evidence that the United States may be entering a fourth "Great Awakening" of the Christian witness. Later this message was presented in *Decision* magazine under the title of "The Shaping of America," and for the American bicentennial year. In view of the fact that Dr. Graham definitely places this as the fourth "Awakening" in the comparisons of three previous ones, we are placed in a position of appraising these "Awakenings" in their own light. The three historic "Awakenings" to which he referred are the following:

1. The Great Awakening of 1734-1742, in which God used Jonathan Edwards and George Whitefield.
2. The Great Awakening which came through the revivals of 1800-1801 in Virginia and Kentucky.
3. The Great Awakening of 1857-1859 which followed the launching of the Fulton Street prayer meeting in New York City.

Dr. Graham proceeded to evaluate the religious emphasis in this decade on the basis that church budgets are being met, church attendance has improved, and religion is in the news. He further argued that universities and professional football and baseball teams have prayer efforts and Bible studies. Even the professional golf tour is cited in these groups of religious emphases.

The great question in the heart of the Christian is whether these things attest Biblical evidences of a genuine Bible awakening! In the three awakenings cited by Graham we have the record of what happened under the leadership of the Holy Spirit. There was great conviction *of* sin, and by divine grace, great deliverances *from* sin. Today we are led to believe that the sports world, church budgets, and statistics of church attendance give evidence to the moving of the Holy Spirit upon the ball parks and properties and churches of the nation. Looking back on the bicentennial year—1976—which has passed into history, I seriously doubt that, in truth, we can speak of our spiritual condition as evidence of the moving of the Holy Spirit; for in these same ball parks and church facilities there has been an open manifestation of crime, sin, violence, error, heresy, and apostasy. Does the Holy Spirit direct the actions of these facilities and the false teachings of these churches? What is a Holy Ghost Awakening? Only the Bible has the answer, but we offer a few suggestions which we feel are Scripturally based. There must be

1. The totalitarian authority of the Bible in the meetings.
2. An awakening to the great fundamental teachings dealing with salvation and sin.
3. An awakening to a separated Christian life—away from the life of sin and the apostasy.
4. An awakening to the realization of who the enemy is, where his forces lie, and an identification of his strongholds.
5. An awakening to a strong evangelism with sanctified methods and means.
6. An awakening to a rejection of World Ecumenicity in this age.
7. An awakening to what is truly the Christian life—character rather than Charismatics.

In addition to these *Protestant* "Companions in Compromise," there is also the outreach across the ocean into England by the *Catholic Charismatics*. A typical presentation is headed "Catholic Charismatics 'Come to Age' in Britain at Second National Conference (From Manchester, England)." The report states:

> John O'Connor, chaplain at Hopwood Hall where the gathering was held, said the talks, workshops, and prayer periods had been "stimulating and challenging...."
>
> Mr. O'Connor characterized the conference as an event which provided a "sober and responsible awareness of the need for balance, integration, and deepening" in the charismatic movement.[76]

The Full Gospel Business Men's Fellowship International boasts of more than 2,000 chapters. Their official periodical—*Voice*—has a circulation of well over a million. In March, 1965, this periodical reported a "world-wide revival taken with the glossolalia."[77]

The *Charisma Digest*, formerly published by the FGBMFI, sets forth this typical ecumenical position:

> FGBMFI does not stand on any dogmatic articles of faith. Nor is it composed of trained theologians. It is an international fellowship of Full Gospel laymen, the bulk of whom are businessmen or professional men. That does not indicate a majority of them are not men of letters; but they do not carry theological degrees—and some have made their way up in business only by the grace of God and hard work. There is no denomination or creed ...[78]

There is a definite and public break being made by the Neo-Pentecostal, as well as by all ecumenical groups, with regard to the Fundamentalists and Fundamentalism. Several articles are pertinent to this observation; and since the World Congress of Fundamentalists, in Edinburgh, Scotland, in 1976, there have been further reactions by them. One article— "Charismatics are Warned Against 'Dangers' of Fundamentalism"— stated:

> San Diego—A Jesuit theologian called on Roman Catholic charismatics to beware of "fundamentalists" who are "filled with anger, fire and brimstone," and are preoccupied with the rigid interpretations of Scripture.
>
> But he added, "these people need our help and love, not our judgment."
>
> Donald Gelpi of the Jesuit School of Theology, Berkley, Calif., and author of *Pentecostals: A Theological Viewpoint,* was one of several speakers and worship leaders of the West Coast Regional Conference of the Catholic Charismatic Renewal here. The conference drew 3,500 people from 20 states and five foreign countries.
>
> Mr. Gelpi, who preached at the concluding Mass, said those in the charismatic renewal are being called by God to renew the Church. "He doesn't want prayer groups, He wants Christian communities," he said.[79]

In an article from San Antonio, Texas, the Roman Catholic archdiocese spoke glowingly of the Charismatic movement. William Glynn, who serves as liaison between the archdiocese and the Charismatic groups, envisions

the principal function of the renewal movement "to build
up, and to edify the Body of Christ."[80]

In all of these articles it is the ecumenical *body* to
which they are referring, although they call them
"Christian communities."

Again, we should mention Henry Pitney Van Dusen
who often was applauded by Charismatics, and who was
called, by some, the Charismatic prophet in his time, or
ahead of his time. In the 1950's, Van Dusen served as
president of Union Theological Seminary of New York.
He was one of the men involved in the old ecumenism, and
he sought to bring a Charismatic emphasis to the attention of both Protestants and Catholics.[81] Van Dusen's
emphasis was a bit premature, but his ecumenical spirit
was well known. He was among the first of the old
ecumenists to give a somewhat formal, intellectual
compliment to the Pentecostals. The following remarks
were reported in the *Christian Century*:

> "Fringe sects" we label them, disdainfully, disparaging-
> ly, comfortably, condescendingly. "Sects" they
> undoubtedly are, offshoots from previously prevailing
> churches, as were many of *our* spiritual forebears
> —Baptists and Congregationalists and Methodists and
> Disciples and Friends and the rest; yes, as in the eyes of
> Rome *all* Protestants are "sects."
>
> "Fringe?" On the fringes of what? Of *our* sects, to be sure,
> of ecumenical Protestantism. But on the "fringe" of
> authentic Christianity, of the true Church of Christ? That
> is by no means so certain, especially if the measuring rod
> is kinship of thought and life with original Christianity, to
> which we all go back proudly as progenitor and in some
> sense norm. Many of its marks are strikingly, unmis-
> takably, undeniably reproduced in this "new Christian-
> ity," as they were in historic "sectarian Protestantism" in
> its beginnings:
>
> Spiritual ardor, sometimes but by no means always with
> excessive emotionalism.
>
> Immediate experience of the living Christ, sometimes with
> aberrations.

Intimate and sustaining fellowship, sometimes with excesses.

Leading of the Holy Spirit, sometimes but by no means always with exaggerated claims.

Intense apocalypticism, just like the early church, but hardly more extreme than what is the current vogue in some segments of respectable contemporary ecumenical Protestantism.

Above all, a life-commanding, life-transforming, seven-day-a-week devotion, however limited in outlook, to a living Lord of all life.[82]

It is feared that second- and third-generation leaderships of the Pentecostal denominations were misled by Van Dusen's pretentious compliment. It is a masterpiece of ecumenical words—the ecumenical bait that revealed a desire for courtship between the Ecumenical Movement and the Pentecostals. But no matter how we label them, the words were spoken by a man who never knew the Biblical fundamentals upon the Biblical base. To suppose that the Devil appreciates the true Christian life is to be deceived.

Many denominational leaders accepted Van Dusen's remarks as an indication that the Pentecostals had finally achieved esteem in a world which formerly had despised them.[83] I have heard of Pentecostal leaders who, during the 1950's, spoke with appreciation of Van Dusen's words. To them a new and great day had dawned for the Pentecostals; their persecutions were in the past, and a golden age lay before them. Actually, the "compliment" derived from second-generation leaders who were losing and leaving their last advantages —away from the Biblical base of their heritage in the first-generation leaderships.

When an enemy, such as Henry Pitney Van Dusen, speaks well of us, we should take inventory to see if we have left the legacy of our Biblical fundamentals and spiritual distinctives. Van Dusen's type of enemy is announcing to the world that Pentecostals have left our Biblical legacy, or that he would like to "court us" into the compromise of an ecumenical apostasy. If you will carefully note his words, you will see that Van Dusen not only made juvenile the Pentecostals, but also first-generation Christianity.

While we are dealing with Van Dusen, we should make a connection with Bishop James A. Pike. Pike finally denied the Trinity. His heresy was given public notice as a result of a sermon he preached on August 30, 1964, at Trinity Church, New York City. Yet after his denial, Pike approved "The Community of the Holy Ghost" as an institution of the diocese of California.[84] We wonder what possible reality could be given to this newly formed institution on the Holy Ghost by a man who denied the Trinity. Again it reveals that one can reject the Holy Spirit and yet believe in its contradiction—"Spirit." One of Satan's greatest deceptions is that a person who is in error does not always appear to be in error (II Corinthians 11:13-15). Bishop Pike finally became involved in Spiritualism. His blatant apostate statement of rejection of the Holy Trinity has been well known.[85] However, his whereabouts, since his wanderings over near the Dead Sea, are known no more. Pike's wife, Diane, a spiritualist, claims to have had a vision of his ascension. Yet Pike denied the ascension of our Lord.[86]

In this connection, I quote Roman Catholic Archbishop Joseph T. McGucken, Bishop Pike's guest in the 114th Episcopal Diocesan Convention:

> ... the ecumenical approach must be based on respect for each other's convictions, the desire to know and understand each other's beliefs and commitments ... such dialogue carried on in the spirit of prayer is to be done with the full faith that we will be led by the Holy Spirit ... [87]

Here again the emphasis is upon "Spirit." To many people Pike represents a sort of halfway house toward more recent errors that have led into the ecumenical movement of Neo-Pentecostalism. He was a part of the ecumenical breed and stream (as was Van Dusen), in which "Spirit" is rejected in the contradicting context where "Spirit" also is accepted.

The emphasis upon "spirit" can also be traced back to heathen religions. The late Dr. Donald G. Barnhouse, describing Dr. Samuel M. Shoemaker's book, *With the Holy Spirit and With Fire*, called the book "horrid" in spots, but added:

> The Holy Spirit is found in some measure in every religion, and we must make common cause with Him there...One hears of a resurgence of some of the ancient Eastern faiths. I think we should rejoice in it. Blank unbelief is not such good soil for Christian sowing as loyalty to what truth one knows ... It must be the hope of all Christians that any experience of God's Spirit will eventually lead to faith in Christ. But I firmly believe that this will more likely take place through another faith than in a vacuum.[88]

In this particular concept, even paganism is believed to possess the moving presence of the Holy Spirit, and Dr. Barnhouse expresses preference for a person who embraces an erroneous belief rather than no belief at all.

Not only is there a feeling in our time with regard to the Holy Spirit's involvement in the ancient religions; He is also believed to be involved in Tradition. The Oberlin Consultation of Church Union (COCU) said:

> A new understanding of Tradition is making it increasingly clear that Tradition cannot simply be equated with "the traditions of men"—teachings and practices which obscure or corrupt rather than express the revelation to which the Scriptures witness. By Tradition we understand the whole life of the church, ever guided and nourished by the Holy Spirit, and expressed in its worship, witness, way of life, and its order. As such, Tradition includes both the act of delivery by which the good news is made known and transmitted from one generation to another as well as the teaching and practice handed on from one generation to another.[89]

Tradition, as used here, includes "history of salvation," as well as parallel ingredients of the *Heilsgeschichte* and the Charismatic "experience"; for to COCU, all of this would be a part of the "tradition" which the church has enjoyed and which the Holy Spirit has given to us.

The thinking behind all of this is that there is a belief covering the entire ecumenical spectrum that says that the Holy Spirit is moving in all of these things—through all channels, all means, all religions, all religious personalities, and all aspects of Neo-Christianity. In other words, the Holy Spirit moves through history, experience, ancient religions, tradition, Notre Dame, Vatican II, glossolalia, audible voices, "blessing packs," "burlap," "red strings," and a host of other symbols in our modern century.

This, of course, ties in with the existential philosophy of our time. Tradition is believed to be a part of that existential experience of man, and *his* subjective Christianity led and directed by "Spirit."

The "Companions in Compromise" are getting together. As I have stated before, the year to keep in mind is 1967. In that year Neo-Pentecostalism took off in two new directions. We have presented the outline, and you have observed that 1967 was filled with interactions of other groups. The two new directions were these: a Roman Catholic Pentecostal Movement got underway, and the "Jesus People" emerged.

The "Jesus People" involve a movement which is predominantly Charismatic, though not to the same degree of sophistication as some other Charismatics.[90] William F. Willoughby, Religious News Editor of *The Washington Star*, has done as much reporting on the Jesus People as has any secular newsman. His considered opinion is that a minimum of 70%—and as high as 85%—of the Jesus People are Charismatic, with most of them experiencing glossolalia, as well as, in many cases, other gifts of the Spirit.[91]

I have given extended observations to show that the old and new ecumenism are one. They are coming in together from all avenues of the world as "Companions in Compromise," with an emphasis upon "Spirit." We must admit to being constantly brought to the point of believing that we are bordering on "Spiritualism" in some of these matters; in others, we see the power of demon-force already working.

The apostasy of our day results from the coming together of a wide variety of companions from different backgrounds. Much neutrality and compromise has been invested in this effort in this century to bring about apostasy. From everyday conversations with old friends, to the very sophisticated fellowships of the movements, people are being divided in this struggle away from Scripture and the Biblical base. An educational process is already in force, involving the coming Antichrist, for there had to be a way to bring into union the various—and *seemingly* opposing—apostate pollutions of the past immediate years. We are witnessing this process now through the neo-people. However, God has assured us that good would come of this line of demarcation from His saints. In earlier days a separation was being drawn between the church and the world; today a separation is being made between the institutional, apostate church and the saints of God.

We read with appreciation the words of Paul, as he explains the great reason for the heresies being manifested before us:

> For first of all, when ye come together in the church, I hear that there be divisions among you: and I partly believe it. For there must be also heresies among you, that they which are approved may be made manifest among you (I Corinthians 11:18-19).

"They which are approved" are being "made manifest," and it is my daily prayer that we may be able to view present conditions in the light of God's Word, take a proper stand, and be approved of God before others.

There is a difference between union and unity. True union is dependent upon Biblical unity. Prior to the Day of Pentecost, the Lord Jesus consumed forty days of His resurrection ministry for the sole purpose of uniting His disciples around the Biblical principles of His resurrection and other Scriptures that were needed for the future. The Day of Pentecost did not bring the unity; it

merely revealed that the disciples had been given the
unity from the Lord Jesus in those forty days (Luke 24).
Many Charismatics insist that the Holy Spirit brought
unity *at* Pentecost, in the Baptism of the Spirit. The fact of
the matter is that the unity was brought by the words of
the Lord Jesus *before* Pentecost. There could not have
been a true manifestation of the Holy Spirit in the lives of
the disciples if first there had not been unity around "the
law of Moses, and...the prophets, and...the psalms,"
concerning Christ (Luke 24:27, 44). These were the
Scriptures.

The Classical historian, Vinson Synan, said: "All that
I have seen has convinced me that the Lord has called us
to a new type of unity—an ecumenicity of the Spirit."
Synan persists in the argument that "Spiritual unity
must always precede structural unity," and this is the
reason he desires to erect "Charismatic Bridges" from his
Pentecostal denomination into the Roman Catholic
Charismatic movement. Synan defines "structural
unity" as "doctrinal and structural differences" in the old
ecumenists.[92] No matter what practice the old ecumenists
observed, Christians can have unity only when that unity
is Biblically based. That absolute condition being met,
unity in Christ will prevail.

Why are we plagued with unseparated international
evangelists who purr with the language of "Spirit" and
boast of great power? It is because they have no union in
Scripture and we live near the time of the manifestation of
the coming Antichrist. The "Companions in Compromise" adorn their crusades with rock music, "liberals,"
immodesty, and a philosophy of the age— adding to the
plague instead of promoting the Gospel Cure.

Sometimes the soldier of the Cross is considered a
"bigot." Critics use the word detrimentally, but the origin
of the term is "purity." It is the contraction of two
words—"By God"—and it echoes the day when stalwart
men of God said, "By God's help, I will not recant." There
is an honorable and sacred "bigotry."

Again we refer to words of the Classical Pentecostal

historian, Vinson Synan, with regard to his reaction to his first visit to Notre Dame in June, 1972. We have previously quoted his words, as reported by Willmar Thorkelson of the *Minneapolis Star*. Synan is reported to have said that he rejoiced "at the growth of Catholic Pentecostalism" and that "the Spirit of God told me it was real."[93] This quotation is confirmed by Synan's own article in his denominational periodical:

> Such Catholic figures as the Belgian Cardinal Suenens and the American Bishop Joseph C. McKinney have expressed great interest and approval. The Vatican is being informed about the progress of the movement. Of all the churches that recently have been affected by the Pentecostal Revival, the Catholic Church seems to be the one most open to it.
>
> At this point, the Catholic Pentecostal Movement seems to this observer to be a genuine move of God's Spirit.... [94]

We persist, however, to this experiential approval: "Who is the 'Spirit' that told you, and where is the Biblical authority behind it?"

Undoubtedly, the Second Vatican Council was an important factor in this new direction. Although Dr. Billy Graham gives outstanding credit to Pope John for this new unity, we should keep in mind that Pope John himself had "prayed for a new Pentecost in Roman Catholicism."[95] The Catholic theologian, Hans Kung, speaks of this emphasis as coming four hundred years too late.[96]

Where Are History and Experience Leading Us?

Immediately, history and experience are headed for the time of God's Judgment. Let me illustrate. Prior to the birth of a child, there is movement in the womb of the mother, suggesting that a child will be fully manifest at birth. Likewise, in the womb of politics and religion there is evidence that a child is to be born who will rule the world, temporarily, as Antichrist. Although presently, international evangelists are famous under the courtship of world leaders, the time is soon to come when God's international "witnesses" will be killed by kings and leaders (Revelation 11). This is additional evidence that modern so-called church leaders and some evangelists are popular before world and religious leaders; yet apostasy is the coin by which the purchase is made.

The Millennium and the reign of the King of Kings will be reached after the Tribulation Period concludes. And although all the saints will be raptured prior to that event, the world must enter that Tribulation as the Apostasy of unfaithful, professing Christians and the Ecumenical Movement occasions the descent.

The sovereign will of God is a clear, straight line from the beginning of the fall of man to the present day of apostasy, although at times the line has been dotted and invisible to fallen man. Sometimes God delights in taking a long time to arrive on the visible scene; when He finally arrives, He may seem to many of us to be late. Yet when He arrives—somewhat late to us—He then hides. Scripture and a true sense of spiritual discernment are needed to correctly evaluate His work throughout the years. Sometimes man *follows* the straight line of the sovereign will; more often, however, he *detours* in the direction of his own will. Even then, he is still in the grand will of the One Who controls all things.

Because man has not always chosen the precious will of God as revealed through Jesus Christ and the Word of God, he has deprived himself of the special favor given to those who love God and are the "called" according to His purpose (Romans 8:28). However, the alternatives and possibilities of God are so very great that man cannot make a choice that will remove man and his actions from the whole will of God. That being the case, man's detours always fall within the final will of God.

History and experience, therefore, should never be interpreted by the presupposition that what the Jews have done and what the Church has done (visible— Roman, Unitarian, Pentecostal, denominational) has been a true following and believing of the Biblical base of God's provision and God's will throughout the centuries to the present time. It cannot be proven that the Charismatic is the golden hour, the product of the moving of the Holy Spirit; indeed, the Charismatic stands in error *away from* the Biblical base.

Neither the World Council of Churches, COCU, the old ecumenisms, nor the World Pentecostal movements are presently upon that Bible base; hence they must be rejected as erroneous. If what we are presently seeing is the commencement of the Glory to come, we are in for greater disappointment of what that Glory was meant to be. All through the years, in the mind of God, and according to the Biblical revelation, man has been given his generations in order that he might see and long for the Age to come, not hope for a possible salvage of the Present Age.

We may Biblically set forth the simplistic phrases of the Scripture as follows:

1. "In the beginning ..." (Genesis 1:1a).

2. "And it came to pass, when men began to multiply on the face of the earth ..." (Or, its equivalent; Genesis 6:1a).

3. "And it shall come to pass afterward ..." (Joel 2:28a).

4. "And it shall come to pass in the last days, saith God ..." (Beginning with the first coming of Christ into the world; Acts 2:17a); "... when the fulness of the time was come ..." (Galatians 4:4a).

5. "... Lord Jesus Christ, Who gave himself for our sins, that he might deliver us from this present evil world [age] ..." (Galatians 1:3b-4a; Greek Nestle Text); which is a part of the "last days."

6. "And be not conformed to this world [age] ..." (Romans 12:2a; Greek Nestle Text); which is a part of the "last age."

7. "The age to come" (Matthew 12:32, 39; 24:3; Luke 17:20; Hebrews 6:5); after the passing of the "last days" of this present age.

We can sum up all history under the title, "This Present

Age," which is a time of the manifestations of the will of
the Devil, the will of sinners, and the will of God in
granting to man the opportunity of salvation.

There is nothing in the Bible that indicates that we can
save the world, the age, or history itself. There is no
Heilsgeschichte (history of salvation) or Charismatic
history to indicate it. By the grace of God, souls can be
saved out of the age, but the world itself is not savable. We
have often heard it said at funerals and at other
appropriate places that a good man has left the world a
better place in which to live. That is impossible; the world
never improves. There can be no Reformation without
Regeneration. There can be no renewal or revival unless
the Biblical base has been established. The whole world
(*kosmos;* world system under the usurping authority of
Satan) lieth in the Wicked One (*to poneio;* I John 5:19);
and the Devil is the god of this age (*aionos;* II Corinthians
4:4).

Let us not misinterpret these words as implying
fatalism. Indeed, we have the greatest hope and blessing
of any age—the possibility of seeing the Lord Jesus in the
clouds. We have the assurance that God is in the driver's
seat of history, and that He, in His own way and by His
own exclusive power, shall accomplish the end.

Let us persist in the privilege of this point—"young
men shall see visions" (Acts 2:17). Without doubt, we are
living in the time of the true fulfillment of the
consummation of the ages. We see not only the apostasy,
but also the glorious coming of the Lord Jesus for the
saints. Let us keep the vision!

The Fourfold Vision of a Generation

The Bible has many references regarding a fourfold
vision in a generation. Consider the following words of
Agur, as recorded in Proverbs 30:11-14:

There is a generation that curseth their father, and doth
not bless their mother.

There is a generation that are pure in their own eyes, and
yet is not washed from their filthiness.

There is a generation, O how lofty are their eyes! and their eyelids are lifted up.

There is a generation, whose teeth are as swords, and their jaw teeth as knives, to devour the poor from off the earth, and the needy from among men.

Agur sets forth a fourfold generation, or four generations in a singular principle. He cites four things that bespeak the singular principle, "Give, give," and that are never satisfied (vv. 15, 16); four things that bespeak the singular principle, "too wonderful for me" to fully understand (vv. 18, 19); four things that bespeak the singular principle of being intolerable to bear (vv. 21-23); four things that bespeak the singular principle, "are exceeding wise" (vv. 24-28); and four things which bespeak the singular principle, "are comely" in their manner of carriage and "going" (vv. 29-31).

We should easily see the wisdom of these things, for Agur sets forth a pattern of the influence of four separate actions, four persons, four characteristics, and four observations as viewed in one singular view of time (cf. Amos 1:3, 6, 9, 11, 13; 2:1, 4, 6). The grave, the barren womb, the earth, and the fire bespeak the insatiable longings desiring to be satisfied in a generation. The eagle, the serpent, the ship, and the way of a man with a maid bespeak the wonderful actions in a generation that a man might observe and at which he might marvel. The servant, when he becomes a king; the fool, when he is filled with food; the contentious woman, when she marries a man; and the servant-maid, when she inherits the wealth of her mistress, bespeak the unbearable things in a generation with which we might have to deal. The ant, the coney, the locust, and the spider bespeak perseverance, selection, unity, and determination in a generation in which wisdom is needed. And the lion, the greyhound, the goat, and a king bespeak dignity, swiftness, self-reliance, and majesty—all of which are needed in a generation of trouble and evil.

We can also observe a unity of thought in Agur's four panels of the generation (vv. 11-14):

1. A generation of ungrateful children.
2. A generation of people who were hypocrites.
3. A generation of people who were proud.
4. A generation of people who were cruel.

In every generation of history we find four groups of people coming together in the full expression of the master sin and evil mood of that generation. The prophet Ezekiel gives important appraisal of such a four-panel view in his time (chapter 18):

But if a man be just, and do that which is lawful and right ... (vv. 5-9).
If he beget a son that is a robber, a shedder of blood, and that doeth the like to any one of these things ... (vv. 10-13).
Now, lo, if he beget a son, that seeth all his father's sins which he hath done, and considereth, and doeth not such like ... (vv. 14-20).
But if the wicked will turn from all his sins that he hath committed, and keep all my statutes, and do that which is lawful and right, he shall surely live, he shall not die (vv. 21, 24, 27).

Some commentators have understood Ezekiel's words to mean a literal grandfather (Hezekiah), father (Manasseh), son (Josiah), and children (during Ezekiel's day). Whether or not that is the proper context, we can see the great import of the fourfold groups' influence upon a generation or an age.

In the language of the Pentateuch, during the days of Moses, we find a final illustration of this influence:

Age	Men	Women
1 month-5 years	5 shekels of silver	3 shekels of silver
5-20 years	20 shekels of silver	10 shekels of silver
20-60 years	50 shekels of silver	30 shekels of silver
60 and above	15 shekels of silver	10 shekels of silver

In these values we see the significance of the individual's being placed in the hands of the priest for proper estimation. We must point out a definite distinction in the Pentateuch: (a) The standard of divine *righteousness* has been placed in the authority and leadership of Moses, but (b) the standard of the provision of divine *grace* has been placed in the service and ceremonies of the Priest. Also, it should be pointed out that the God of righteousness is the same as the God of grace; and He will judge man's sin on the scale of His righteousness, and estimate the worth of the individual human instrument on the scales of His grace.

The above list represents the general "estimation" (*erek*; array, order, valuation) set forth for Israel. Vows did not form an integral part of the Old Testament laws; they were entirely a free-will expression of spiritual piety and capacity. Although a vow or dedication by a vow was not commanded, it was presupposed as a manifestation of belief and reverence for God.

Every generation faces urgent need of the four groups of people we have mentioned in order to exalt the Lord Jesus Christ through evangelization and proclamation of evangelical, Biblical truth, as revealed through the Gospel.

We have already noted that within three generations of Pentecostalism there has been a move from the Biblical base to neutrality to compromise. At this time we observe the manifestation of apostasy. The error of every age has been the great progression and mutation from a trend to a tangent and then to a tare. Man will manifest an "error." He will invent a "doctrine" to preserve it. And in turn this turns the hearers into a "way" and a practice of doctrinal error (cf. Balaam: Jude 11; Revelation 2:14; II Peter 2:15, respectively.)

Every generation faces the need of the Whole Vision. This includes:

1. The Prime, Present Vision of Biblical leaderships and teachers, including evangelists, soulwinners, and Christian scholars.

2. The Preparing Vision of Biblical evangelists, soulwinners, and Christian scholars being prepared for later leaderships.

3. The Potential Vision of Biblical children that we must get into our Sunday School, churches, Christian

Day Schools, who will follow the next leaders and teachers, including evangelists, soulwinners, and scholars, who are taught on the Biblical base.

4. The Past Vision of Biblical leaders, teachers, and laymen who have moved away from the Prime Vision in later years who remain to inspire all of the other three groups.

This *Whole* Vision must be viewed as a composite unity working together under the authority of the Bible and the Holy Spirit, through the God-called *Prime* Vision of the leaders God has sent to us. We should point out that this Whole Vision should be manifest through the Prime Vision people (typical: 20-60 years old); for they understand God's Word and the Apostasy in a clearer way than those who have passed away from the Prime Vision, or those younger who have not yet entered into the Prime Vision. Frequently a man, because he has neglected to keep up with the need and the Biblical solution with regard to the decade in which he serves, disqualifies himself from being able to see the vision of the situation.

The Total Vision is needed in all generations, and God issues His calls according to His sovereign selection of those involved in the Vision and in keeping with His Vision of the full spectrum.

Scripture speaks of *pictorial* visions, received as manifestations before physical eyes. Only the pictorial visions recorded *in the Scriptures* are infallible visions. They are selected by the Holy Spirit, and no other pictorial vision—no matter who might experience it— carries with it the authority of infallibility.

The *spiritual* vision of any generation is founded upon the Biblical principles in the Bible as well as upon certain prophetical principles in the Bible, vouchsafed and applicable to each succeeding age. For a Christian to be aware of the purpose of his calling and leadership and witness in his age, a genuine, spiritual discernment is greatly needed in our time. In other words, it is the spiritual vision, upon the Biblical base, that is so urgently needed today. And it is this spiritual vision of which we are speaking at this time.

The Bible clearly defines these spiritual visions, and we offer a simple outline of the principles in this four-panel unity. These Biblical visions, based upon these Biblical principles, apply to every age, and are especially needed in this last age. They are presented in this order: Prime, Prepared, Potential, and Past.

1. Where there is no vision, the people perish ... (Proverbs 29:18).
2. Young men shall see visions ... (Joel 2:28b).
3. For the vision is yet for an appointed time, but at the end it shall speak, and not lie: though it tarry, wait for it; because it will surely come, it will not tarry (Habakkuk 2:3).
4. Your old men shall dream dreams ... (Joel 2:28b).

Simply stated, every generation or age is in dire need of Vision for the proclamation of the Gospel of the Lord Jesus Christ. It is a unified vision in four parts or panels—present, future, young, and past.

First, there is the need of a *present* leadership to see that part or panel of the vision from God's Word that is appropriate for the immediate, the present days—this very decade or score of years. This leadership must serve, lead, preach, witness, instruct, teach, evangelize, and harvest *now!* It must lay hold of God's authority and take a strong stand in defense of the Word of God in the apostasy *right now!* A right-now apostasy is going on, and those who are in the prime places of leadership by the sovereignty of God's appointment must see the immediate and present visions, and obey the Lord accordingly. They are typified in the very costly estimations of the ages of twenty to sixty.

Only a Christian who has been placed in such urgent position by God can know and fulfill such a place and responsibility. Some, because of spiritual sleep, are passing the present responsibility without recognizing it. Others of this very same group are retiring from the fight in the midst of the battle.

The age is divided into these same four parts by the actions of Satan. Agur reminds us of this in his presentation of the "generation." Satan is fighting directly against the *present* leaders who are standing in the gap *right now*! Satan has another kind of attack for the other three groups; but his main attack is upon the *present*, prime leaders of God who are waging the main attack against his present error and immediate strongholds. Without the present vision of the present leaders in Biblical churches, Biblical universities, Bible colleges, Christian Day Schools, and communicable evangelism, the people would perish without the message of the Gospel. Bob Jones University, Greenville, South Carolina, is uniquely an example of a Christian university that has made the transition for three generations (grandfather, father, and son) with the safekeeping of Biblical orthodoxy and evangelism, without changing the Biblical base of authority. There may be others, but they are exceedingly rare.

While the present leaders are on the frontline of the battle, there is a *second* group of younger leaders being prepared for the battle, to take over in a few years the prime vision. They will stand in the prime gap and defense. These young men *shall see* (a little later, in the future) visions appointed by God. They see the battle from a little different perspective, and by the time they become the *present* leadership, there will be some "fresh" strategy or "new" approach to face, upon the Biblical base, that even the present leadership does not fully see.

Typically, this second group represents the ages of five to twenty years. At present they are hiding in preparation with Biblical studies and prayer. They need our prayers and inspiration right now! They do not always see the battle exactly as the present leadership sees it, for they are not at the same point in the vision and perspective as is the present leadership. Often the enemy has used this difference of perspective to set the future leadership against the present leadership, thus frustrating the energies and power and authority needed from both groups in the warfare. In some instances it becomes the occasion for pride, ego, or selfishness from either side of the groups. But we should keep in mind that the prime leaders are there by appointment of the Lord, and not to be appointed. God's authority, as well as God's man, should be respected.

The Message is greater than anything else in this regard, and it is that Message which must unite us. All groups of the Vision must seek nothing less than a total unity around the inerrant and infallible authority of the Word of God. This involves an honorable, verbal, and plenary inspiration view of the Scriptures, and a separated, militant spiritual life. The young and future leaderships must learn at least two things: (1) the truths of the Word of God, bathed in communion and fellowship through prayer and spiritual growth, as well as (2) the most honorable way in which to succeed or replace, personally, the present leadership with love and respect and humility.

Third, there is the unborn and the untaught generation for whom we must also prepare during the present leadership of Christ's Gospel. They are our *potential* resource. There must be Christian education and its various institutions of the Sunday School, Christian Day School, Bible College, Bible Family and Youth Camps, and similar groups through which we might direct the very young. These are they who, by virtue of extreme youth, do not see either the present leadership's vision nor the future leadership's vision. It must be said of them that "the vision is yet for an appointed time." But be sure of this: the vision will come, and indeed will be needed.

Both the present leadership and the future leadership need to be aware of this "potential" group, for success without successor is failure. Or, at least, the future is a failure. The present leadership and the future leadership groups will find their greater spiritual successes and goals in only the long-range perspective and success of the "spiritual offspring" of their witnessing and warfare. Oh, that we could see this, and humbly and willingly give up our own glories and accomplishments in order to glory in the larger and later work of God in the third group, unborn and unprepared.

This third group, typically, in Leviticus, is the group from one month through five years. Do you have a boy in your home or in your Sunday School who is a potential David, Josiah, Daniel, Luther, Calvin, or Wesley? God wants to get hold of that boy for the future. Get the vision to him; do not delay. You need the perspective of his vision which God's Word has for him.

Fourth, there is the age-group sixty and above in the typology of our Leviticus studies. We must be aware of his "dreams." The visions of the young men set forth their burning hearts of *what they would like to do* for the Lord Jesus. The dreams of the old men set forth their burning hearts of *what they have done* for Him. There are potential dangers in this group, too. Older men cannot afford the luxury of being weak, lax, and indifferent about the Vision. Although he has a hard time leaving the position and place of service, the older leader must learn to leave it graciously and as a Christian gentleman. How often have we seen many mighty "cedars" fall in the late years because they were not great enough or humble enough to give way to the present, prime leadership of God's selection. Oh, may God teach us how to conclude our lives and be ready for the "crossing" to Heaven.

All of us have known men who have been a great blessing and a strong, full defense in the days of their *prime* leadership, but who did not do well in making the transition into the realm of *past* leadership. We are not talking about the Lord's men who are placed on the shelf as past leaders; we are referring to a time when a prophet might go "blind," as did several in the Old Testament, but who go blind with dignity. In fact, the blind prophet, Ahijah, could see through the disguise of Jeroboam's wife before she entered the room—even as her feet were walking the path (I Kings 14:1-6). Elisha, when he had fallen sick and was near death, was stronger to shoot the bow and smite the arrows in the warfare against the enemy than was Joash, the king of Israel (II Kings 13:14-19.

We live in a day when similar happenings are coming to pass in a strange way. I know of a Seminary that was considered to be strong on the Biblical base and that took a firm stand in the midst of the generation in which it served. But a president of that Seminary did not know how to pass the torch to another person who could assume the prime place of the generation. A struggle for power developed between him and a denominational leadership which sought to take over the Seminary; yet neither the president nor the denomination had sufficient leadership, on the Biblical base, to really know the mind of God in handling the problem. The result was that the Name of Christ Jesus was shamed and the Word of the Lord was reproached. The president had passed his time of leadership, being no longer the Lord's leader in the prime vision; and the denomination had passed its prime leadership in dealing with the spiritual and moral problems involved. It is doubtful if there is anything there to salvage; if anything is salvaged, it will probably contribute toward the apostasy of the times. A large number of similar situations could be cited among churches, seminaries, and other "former" Christian institutions across the land.

In concluding this section, I wish to quote the words of an elderly minister who, when I was a young minister and launching out into the battle for the Lord, sought to encourage me. He said: "Son, I know that you will see something from God in your time that I did not witness in my time. Although I do not see it, I want you to know that I am aware that you see it, and I am behind you to see your vision through in faithful warfare. Go to it, my son." I trust that to some degree I have, by God's grace, done just what that elderly minister desired of me.

It should be remembered in the language of this Leviticus study that God also estimates the "poor" (Leviticus 27:8). God is not bound by groups of ages and years—neither the 51% majority nor the revolutionary minorities influences. God acts with the individual. There

is something about the care and understanding of the
individual in the Bible that reveals the greatness of God's
grace and the greatness of God's own worth, as well as the
potentiality of the individual "estimation." It is stipulated in Leviticus 27:8:

> But if he be poorer than thy estimation, then he shall
> present himself before the priest, and the priest shall value
> him; according to his ability that vowed shall the priest
> value him.

God has always been free to use the individual—
regardless of age groups or even His usual and desired
procedure. God has often selected, by His sovereign will,
certain individuals who were placed in strategic positions
to carry on the battle for Him. He has had His Spurgeon,
His Whitefield, His Jonathan Edwards; but He has also
had His Sam Jones. There is always the unusual and
unique vision that God plants and estimates in a rare
choice on a peculiar occasion for His glory.

An unknown poet expressed it in these words:

> God sometimes will give me a light
> No other man can see,
> A light that teaches me a way
> That's only shown to me.
> Then shall I follow on although
> All else in darkness be,
> I'd rather let God's will be done
> Than men speak well of me.

All of God's choices are made on the basis of men who
are rooted and grounded in the authority of His Holy
Word.

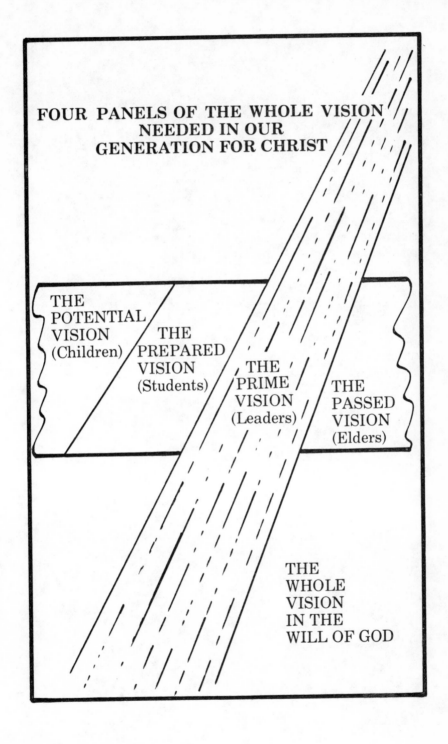

FOUR PANELS OF THE WHOLE VISION
NEEDED IN OUR
GENERATION FOR CHRIST

THE
POTENTIAL
VISION
(Children)

THE
PREPARED
VISION
(Students)

THE
PRIME
VISION
(Leaders)

THE
PASSED
VISION
(Elders)

THE
WHOLE
VISION
IN THE
WILL OF GOD

PART THREE

THE INFALLIBILITY
OF DIVINE REVELATION

7

The Infallibility of Divine Revelation

At this point in history, we have the double advantage of having access to the infallible Word of God, as well as knowing the historical flow of Christianity through nineteen centuries.

By studying Scripture and the Creeds, we can check the eternal verities of the Bible against the historical varieties of practice; we can view God's proclamation of His singular revelation and man's presentation of a fundamental consistency. As Peter says (II Peter 1:16-19), we "have not followed cunningly devised fables," but "a more sure word of prophecy." We have followed "a light that shineth" down through the "dark" places of history to an hour when the voice of the Christian is urgently needed for the time of apostasy.

The Most Magnanimous Benefits Received By Man in History

We rightly believe that God has spoken *once-for-all* to man through certain assets given as the most magnanimous benefits received in history. These assets are:

Revelation, which assures us that God, Himself, has spoken to man through His Holy Word.

Inspiration, which assures us that the Holy Spirit moved upon "holy men" and gave us the Written Word in verbal, plenary authority and accuracy, and in simple, literal, propositional utterance.

Consummation of Scripture, which assures us that God has finalized all truth in the Written Word of sixty-six books, and that we are no longer receiving verbal, plenary revelation in history. This deals with the sufficiency and completeness of revelation in a once-for-all delivery of redemptive truth in history.

Preservation, which assures us that God has maintained the safekeeping of His Revelation down through the centuries, since the original manuscripts, with providential care in a certain lineage of translations to other languages.

Proclamation, which assures us that God has called certain human instruments throughout history to announce His Revelation to the world, and all Christian witnesses, everywhere, to set forth His Word for the hearing, obeying, and believing of His Gospel.

Illumination, which assures us that the Holy Spirit remains ever faithful in keeping the Scriptures alive in all generations through immediate spiritual insight and understanding of Biblical truth.

Interpretation, which assures us that we have received into our own hearts a true and faithful rendering of what is written in the Word of God. Although we do not claim total comprehension of the Bible, we believe that we have received a full realization of the Biblical fundamentals needed for our salvation and safekeeping through faith in the grace and Blood of the Lord Jesus Christ.

The *apologetic Declaration of the Bible,* which assures us that God has always and always will set forth a defense of His Scriptures through certain human instruments, by the power of the Holy Spirit, against the workings of Satan in a particular age. This is in accordance with God's perpetuity of certain Biblical fundamentals which are essential in any age.

The *historic Creeds and Councils,* which, although they are not inspired in the same sense that Scripture is inspired, reveal much that gives external substantiation of the Scriptures as well as to what has been theologically accepted in the historical periods of the Christian Faith. We deeply appreciate the contribution of Creeds and Councils to the overall defense of the fundamental teachings of the Bible, and to the giving of insight into why an age reacts against God as it does.

The words of Philip Schaff describe clearly the involvements of these historical symbols:

> Each symbol bears the impress of its age, and the historical situation out of which it arose.
>
> There is a development in the history of symbols. They assume a more definite shape with the progress of biblical and theological knowledge. They are mile-stones and finger-boards in the history of Christian doctrine. They embody the faith of generations, and the most valuable results of religious controversies. They still shape and regulate the theological thinking and public teaching of the churches of Christendom. They keep alive sectarian strifes and antagonisms, but they reveal also the underlying agreement, and foreshadow the possibility of future harmony.[97]

Faith, the strongest conviction of all, has a desire to utter itself before others. This utterance may be as simple as an informal street testimony for Christ, or as profound as the formal, sacred scholarship. Symbols and creeds never precede faith; they really presuppose faith. Symbols and creeds arise from the saint's inner life, independently of external occasion. As it has been said, "There would have been creeds even if there had been no doctrinal controversies."[98]

In our time, which is an age of apostasy, there has been the intense advancement of a multitudinous neo-crowd of personalities and movements that have stayed in pulpit and pew, vocalizing and advocating "new" concepts for the Christian Church. This advancement has necessitated both the privilege of testimony and the controversy of council to combine energies for a World Congress of Fundamentalists and similar efforts. This is in keeping with the Christian spirit of the past, as Dr. Schaff has reminded us, and the dignity and courage of the present Christian of the twentieth century. We agree with John Fletcher, Vicar of Madeley (1729-1785) that "controversy, though not desirable in itself, yet, properly managed, has a hundred times rescued truth, groaning under the lash of triumphant error."

The word "neo" is from the Greek, meaning that which is *new* in time. There is another Greek word, *kainos*, meaning that which is *new* in quality.[99] It should go without saying that eternal Written Truth will always be new in quality and freshness, but never new in time and commencement. Truth is like its Source—God. It neither begins nor changes:—it is eternal! That which is true is never really new; it is old and eternal.

Absolutes, Hypostatics, Paradoxes, and Systems

God communicated His Revelation propositionally to man. In historic Christianity a personal God creates man, and He communicates to man in the manner in which He has created Him by a natural, verbalized form. Why should God not communicate in verbalized form when He has made man a verbalizing being in thought as well as in communication with other men? Thus, this propositional or logical communication is the mode which is set forth in the Scriptures. God has spoken in a linguistical propositional form of truth concerning Himself, man, history, redemption, and the universe.

To have a propositional revelation, God must speak in absolutes; and to have an infallible truth it must be communicated in absolutes. There is nothing behind or beyond God, for He is absolute; and all absolutes rest upon His character. God's propositional expressions in the form of verbalized absolutes give to man the access to revealed truth from God. This access gives the Christian the nature of proof and an anchor for faith. All true Christians believe in the Biblical absolutes of the centrality of redemptive truth through Jesus Christ.

Certain Hypostatic Unions

When God sets forth certain *absolutes,* they undergird certain *hypostatic* unions as well.

Let us look briefly into the background of this word "hypostatic" (Greek; *hupostasis,* cf. Hebrews 1:3, "substance").

First, let us consider "hupostasis" (Greek; *hupo,* under; *histasthai,* to cause to stand). (a) In the original Nicene use, it is equivalent to *ousia* ("being, person, substance"); but specifically it refers to the unique essence of the Godhead, and, as such, of the three persons of the Trinity—Father, Son, and Holy Spirit. (b) In later use, it has come to mean one of the persons of the Godhead. (c) Also, there is the meaning of the whole personality of Christ as distinguished from His two natures—human and deity.[100]

Second, let us understand "hypostatic." In a general and practical sense, this word is simply the English transliteration of hupostasis. The general meaning, however, is simply that "consisting in one substance there are two whole and complete natures and forces." It is with this particular meaning in mind that I set forth eight hypostatic unions to be found in the Word of God:

1. The hypostatic union as set forth in the dual authorship of the Bible (II Peter 1:20, 21).

2. The hypostatic union as set forth in the reality of the deity and humanity of the Lord Jesus Christ through the incarnation and Virgin Birth (John 1:1, 14; Luke 1:34, 35).

3. The hypostatic union as set forth in the reality of the transcendence and immanence of God (Isaiah 57:15).

4. The hypostatic union as set forth in the reality of a material and immaterial universe (Genesis 1:7; Hebrews 11:1-3).

5. The hypostatic union of the depravity of man and the redemption of man (Romans 3:23; 6:23; I Corinthians 15:3; Romans 6:10).

6. The hypostatic union of the sinfulness of man and the sanctification for man (Romans 7:15-25 and 6:1-14; John 17).

7. The hypostatic union of the "earthen vessel" and the indwelling of the Holy Spirit (II Corinthians 4:7).

8. The hypostatic union of the Objective Word of God and the subjective experience of the Word of God in the believers (John 1:1, 2 and I John 1:1-2; Romans 10:13-15).

It is not the purpose of this chapter to go into *all* of these Biblical unions, or to suggest that this list represents all pertinent references of them in the Word of God. Our purpose is to set forth a definite problem in church history. Though belief in Biblical absolutes and hypostatics is not a simple matter, it does not impede our relationship with the Lord Jesus Christ. Church history furnishes supportive evidence that whenever man overemphasizes one side of a hypostatic union to the neglect of the other, sooner or later error manifests itself. This tendency accounts for many of the heresies with which the Christian church has been plagued down through the centuries.

Our list of eight hypostatic unions sets forth certain Biblical fundamentals and Biblical distinctives which involve the truth of Biblical authority, Christ, man, and the deeper Christian life. All of these are appropriate to our study.

When an individual or a movement has dedicated itself to the full acknowledgment of absolutes involved in these hypostatic unions, in a balanced fulness, there has been a proclamation and defense sounding a clarion call back to the Scriptures and to the essential truths that are needed not only for a man's salvation, but also for a balanced appreciation of all Biblical truth. Faithful men will preach both sides of hypostatic union with the full force of both truths that are involved.

Undoubtedly, the Neo-Pentecostal has over-emphasized the last five of these eight unions mentioned and therefore has brought in error. This has resulted in a spiritual and theological schizophrenia which, in reality, follows because of the same error in Neo-Pente-costalism's overemphasis on "Spirit" in the Godhead. First comes a trend, then a tangent, and finally the breaking away of error from the fundamental hypostatic union, and heresy culminating into apostasy.

Neo-Pentecostalism has overemphasized materialism (the pursuit of prosperity and health) to the grave neglect and erroneous teaching of the true spiritual values of Calvary. The emphasis of Oral Roberts' ministry illustrates this. It is, therefore, a schizophrenia of the fourth union.

Neo-Pentecostalism has undermined the Biblical teaching of the total depravity of man by making super claims of the spiritual power of man himself. Roberts' so-called "power in the right hand," as well as his overemphasis upon "faith" as a force in the life of every man, illustrates this point. In fact, Roberts teaches that "faith" is in every man; and in his earlier years he spoke of this as a counterpart of the sex drive in man.[101] Paul makes it clear that "all men have not faith" (II Thessalonians 3:2). Apparently that which Roberts calls "faith" is nothing more than positive thinking. It is a schizophrenia of the fifth hypostatic union.

Neo-Pentecostalism has exalted spiritual powers of man to a place that neither the Bible promises nor Calvary provides. It is really a neo-sinless perfection, if you please—or possibly more accurately, a neo-super-perfection life. Paul warns us of the dangers of projection into areas and spheres beyond our place (Galatians 1:8; Colossians 2:18-19; II Corinthians 12:7; etc.). In another way, this was the error of the Gnostics. It is seen in the schizophrenia of the sixth union.

Neo-Pentecostalism has insubordinately taught the indwelling of the Holy Spirit to the neglect of a humble acknowledgment of the finite and earthly vessel of the believer. This is seen in the schizophrenia of the seventh union.

Neo-Pentecostalism has existentially inculcated the modern principle of the dialectical interpretation of the Scripture and erroneously accepted the subjective experience of man to the neglect of, and apart from, the inerrant and authoritative Word of God as Objective

Truth. This is seen in the schizophrenia of the eighth union.

The Biblicist dares to take the position of acknowledging the simple, balanced, separated, clear position of the full value of the hypostatic unions of the Bible.

Undoubtedly, everyone is born somewhat off center of the target in his religious background—to say nothing of his being born positively in sin. Some are born in better theological backgrounds and positions than others. Man has suffered not only from total depravity, but also from the mistakes and errors of some of his theological systems. The Bible is the Book above all books, and man must find Christ Jesus as the only Saviour and must find himself in his varied relationships as they might differ from the true authority of the Biblical system. We come from sin to the Saviour. Many of us have had to come also from the perimeter of an immature religious system to the center of Biblical balance in the understanding of truth. If we do not humble ourselves to do this, we shall find ourselves perpetuating ignorance and inventing added error. There is the exodus from sin through the Lord Jesus Christ. There is also the exodus from certain religious systems that have come through history apart from the authority of Biblical truth. There is a certain ignorance that grace covers; there is an erroneous ignorance that God will not allow in any person. This is the impetus of this age of apostasy. Man has followed his own subjective systems and positive sin; and these have wedded together as a neo-force for evil and antichrist in Neo-Christianity.

Understanding the Paradox

Through faith we appropriate the Biblical hypostatics and paradoxes. We may not be able to comprehend the paradox with human wisdom and finite reason; but faith and trust in the inerrancy and authority of the Bible satisfy the need of man in the way that God has ordained, and also set forth the proclamation and defense of Christian truth to a lost and dying world. This is the great purpose and blessing of the paradox. The paradox views the hypostatic from another side; it reveals that the hypostatic union does not contradict itself but is held in paradox in the infinite knowledge of God.

Being in the flesh, we are not far-sighted enough to view the unity of the absolute and the hypostatic as they are in God. Our Sovereign God is as far back as man can see; and thank God, in Him there is absolute truth held in perfect paradox. This is another reason that we must believe that the Gifts of the Holy Spirit are demonstrated from the sovereignty of God rather than from the volition of man.

The Christian declares both doctrines in the Biblical truth of the dual authorship of the Bible by the Holy Spirit and holy men; of the deity and humanity of Jesus Christ; of the transcendence and immanence of God; of the tangible and intangible realities of the universe; of the depravity and redemption of man; of the sinfulness of and sanctification for man; of the earthly humanity of the believer and the indwelling of the Holy Spirit; and of the subjective experience of man under the authority of the Objective Word of God.

There can be no "sinless perfection" doctrine, no super-spirituality doctrine, no Charismatic or glossolalia doctrine, and no new-revelation doctrine as purported by the Charismatics. All true doctrine bows in harmony with the Biblical authority of God's infallible Word. When that is done, propriety and purity of teaching will prevail. Everything else is error!

The Sufficiency of Scripture Versus Extant Revelation

Every garden provided of God has in it a tree of forbidden fruit. Every tabernacle that God erects has a pattern. Every river that God extends has a reed. Every promised land of Canaan has a boundary. Every wall that God erects has a plumbline. Every kingdom that God ordains has a rule of life and a Ruler. And every born-again Christian called of God must live within this authority. It is only as we live within this boundary of truth, revealed by the very Word of God—building according to the pattern, measuring with the reed, laying forth Godliness with the plumbline, and obeying the rule and the Ruler of the kingdom—that we can ever hope to see God in the final redemption beyond the grave.

It is the sad truth of many millenniums that when any creature gets beyond the boundaries of the Word of God, as given and revealed by God, that creature is hopelessly lost.

It is said of some angels that they "kept not their first estate, but left their own habitation," and therefore, are "reserved in everlasting chains under darkness unto the judgment of the great day" (Jude 6).

It is said of man that he left the boundaries as stipulated by the Word of God and did eat of the forbidden fruit (cf. Genesis 2:17 and 3:6).

God has laws. God has boundaries. And those boundaries are set up by the inerrant Word of the living God.

The Grand Coulee Dam, which extends across the Columbia River in the state of Washington, is still considered one of the largest gravity-masonry dams in the world. The dam backs up the waters of the river to form a lake 151 miles long. Ultimately, the water impounded by the Grand Coulee Dam will irrigate nearly a million and a quarter acres of land, besides furnishing about 1,900,000 kilowatts of power.[102] Before the dam was erected, these same waters were the cause of floods, soil erosion, and great loss of property.

How like the Word of God given to mankind. God chose to harness His power through His own Word. His power, if let loose upon the world, would utterly destroy us all; but through His marvelous grace, He has chosen to use His power only through the promises of His Word. Some men argue that belief in the finality of the Bible would *limit* God's power. To the contrary, it harnesses God's power for the most effective benefits possible to mankind. It is this "Grand Coulee" element that illustrates how the

Word of God becomes the mighty "Dam" that secures, reserves, and restrains, through the harnessing power of the promises of God, preventing its becoming an unleashed force of dangerous potentiality in a finite world.

It is at this very point that we must raise another attack against Neo-Pentecostalism. Not only has the Neo-Pentecostal removed himself from the inerrant authority of the Biblical base, but also his interpretation of certain Scriptures precludes the sufficiency of the Bible. We have seen not only that through their "audible voices" and extant revelations they add to the Word of God, but also that their super-spiritualities are managed by an extravagant interpretation of certain passages of Scripture.

For example, one of the leading personalities involved in modern glossolalia movements is Mrs. Frances Hunter. In her book, *The Two Sides of a Coin*, she reveals her personal experience in receiving the gift of speaking in tongues. This quotation illustrates the fallacy of her concept of the glossolalia:

> In that moment of silence with the presence of God so real, someone quietly began to speak beautiful, loving, soothing words in a language I did not understand. It sounded like one or two sentences and that was all. I thought to myself, "That must be tongues, but it's beautiful!"
>
> Instantly there was an interpretation. "The words you have heard from the lips of Frances Hunter are not her words. They are mine. Take heed and obey." The Spirit of God crackled like electricity through the room.

There is no misunderstanding of Mrs. Hunter's words. She is actually informing her reader that she believes that the glossolalia is a means through which God gives new revelation. And her position is true of many other Charismatics in our time: the books are full of similar expressions.

Of course, we have discussed this in our former presentations. The gift of tongues is not the gift of prophecy, and the Corinthian catastrophe (Introduction and Part I, chapter 3) helps us to realize that the leading Corinthians were using the gift of tongues *in error* and gaining certain excesses which were neither the purpose that God had ordained in the glossolalia nor what Paul presented in his own inspired understanding from the Lord of the gift of tongues.

Paul rightly condemned the Corinthians. As we have already explained, the word "unknown" is given by our King James translators in italics, thus announcing that "unknown" tongues are not in the original Greek Text. "Unknown" was supplied by translators who sought to accommodate sense to the English mind. In reality, the glossolalia as presented to Paul by the Holy Spirit was not an unknown tongue; nor was it designed to replace prophecy, revelation, knowledge, and other gifts. In our day, however—as in the time of the Corinthian catastrophe—Charismatics are promoting erroneous glossolalia, thereby giving a false meaning of the glossolalia by claiming a new revelation from God. To confirm this, they even have the presence of God, so-called, authenticated by the sound of "crackled" electricity. Scripture says that the Holy Spirit did not come to "speak of himself," but to glorify Christ and guide the believer into all of the truth of the Scriptures (John 16:13, 14). There is no proper noun, as a name, given to the Holy Spirit. His desire is to glorify the Name of Jesus.

There are three main areas in which the Neo-Pentecostal proceeds without total Biblical authority in his promulgation of doctrine: (1) The Possibilities and Impossibilities of the Word of God; (2) The Completeness and Finality of the Word of God; and (3) The Necessity for the Objective Word of God apart from human subjective experience.

The Possibilities and Impossibilities of the Word

The Neo-Pentecostals give considerable publicity to an extravagant interpretation of a variety of texts announcing that subjective faith makes all things possible with God. Hollywoodism and a carnival atmosphere are often staged to cause the audience to think that the various manifestations of faith, as demonstrated in "a point of contact" as exemplified in the actual touching of the hand upon a material object, puts God and man into a reciprocity to do the impossible, perform a miracle, or even reroute the otherwise ordinary boundaries of God's usual actions with man.

The word "impossible" (Greek; *adunatos; anendektos; aduna*) is used about nine times in the New Testament (Matthew 17:20; 19:26; Mark 10:27; Luke 1:37; 17:1; 18:27; Hebrews 6:4, 18; 11:6). A careful investigation of these passages yields another truth which indicates that God has chosen that some things shall be impossible and that other things shall be possible. Charismatics continually speak of the impossibles as being possible.

Let me illustrate. When Gabriel announced to Mary that her body would cradle the Son of God, she asked, "How shall this be, seeing I know not a man?" Gabriel answered, "For with God nothing shall be impossible" (Luke 1:37).

Our English word *nothing,* often understood, unfortunately, as "zero or all-inclusive as nothing," should be literally understood as "no word" (*ouk rheima*) in the Greek. In the Greek language one word (*rheima*) is used for two English words—"thing" and "word." The King James translators were aware of this, and they used both words in the two adjoining verses. Mary responded, "Be it unto me according to thy word" (Luke 1:38). Because of the Greek arrangement of "thing" and "word," we understand that no thing and no word of God is without power. Elizabeth shares in this understanding, giving confirmation in her words, "And blessed is she that believed: for there shall be a performance of those things which were told her from the Lord." "Those things" told her from the Lord were the "words" spoken to her.

From such an index as this we can see both the *boundlessness* and the *boundaries* of the Word of God.

This simply indicates the possibilities and the impossibilities which God has chosen to perform His power as given in His Word. He has made the decision in His own promises. We cannot limit God, but God limits Himself. We cannot make God boundless, but God makes the boundary for Himself. There is a twofold stipulation: (1) According to His Word, and (2) According to His will (I John 5:14-15).

All of God's words are "sure words" and possible to those to whom He has promised them; but only those words which He has promised in His Word are sure words. The boundlessness of His power lies within the boundaries of His Word; the possibilities lie within, and are surrounded by, the impossibilities of God. God has chosen to perform His power within the boundaries of His Word. It is impossible for God or the Holy Spirit to perform with power apart from the Word of God.

In the list of verses previously mentioned there are several impossibilities which God has declared in His Word:

1. It is impossible for God to lie (Hebrews 6:18).
2. It is impossible for a rich man to get into Heaven on the basis of his riches (Matthew 19:26).
3. It is impossible "but that offences will come" (Luke 17:1).
4. It is impossible to please God without faith (Hebrews 11:6).
5. It is impossible for the apostate to be saved (Hebrews 6:4-6).

But we go back to the basis of the possibilities of the Word of God. "With God no word of God is without power."[103] No word that God has spoken through the Bible is "void" of His power (Isaiah 55:11). The impossibilities of the Word of God give greater strength to the greatness of the possibilities of that same Word from God. The truth is protected by the boundaries of the impossibilities, whereas the possibilities become more sure. It is impossible, therefore, for God to lie. He will not change His Word.

A most practical illustration of a Neo-Pentecostal's viewpoint in this matter (although some would be disappointed in the example) comes from a conversation I had with a typical ecclesiastical leader and preacher in Oklahoma. His subjective faith as well as his experiential interpretation of the Bible is obvious.

This leader was defending his claim that God had spoken to him "audibly" in a garage building. At first he had not had faith that God had truly spoken. After he had prayed, however, he asked God to speak "audibly" a second time, if indeed it had been the Voice of God the first time. This leader did not seem to realize that he was testing his first "voice," which he doubted, with the same "voice" which he did not doubt. Perhaps that is circular reasoning like proving that a dog is chasing a rabbit around a tree because the rabbit is chasing the dog around the tree. My meaning is that it is improper to test a fallacy by a fallacy. You could arrive at no other solution or confirmation than the matter which you doubted. To test a doubt with a doubt would leave one doubly in doubt. Even before the Bible was completed through the New Testament and the Word of God was consummated, Biblical men tested their "fleece" with greater deliberation than the example just given. Both Gideon with his "fleece" and Elijah's testing the fire of his sacrifice with the twelve barrels of water are ample evidence of the observation.

We do not live on the other side of an incomplete, insufficient, and unconsummated revelation. We stand in the sure verities of the inerrant, infallible, and consummated Word of God. We do not need lesser confirmations; we have the *great* confirmation by God's Word and the Holy Spirit through the Scriptures.

It should be noted that the "circular reasoning" of the Oklahoma preacher's audible voice was a retaliation to a sermon I had preached in a Minister's Conference the evening before. My subject had been "The Infallible, Consummated Scriptures," and the more we discussed the matter, the more confident I was that his way was not on the Biblical base. This man argued that God could do anything, that absolutely nothing was impossible in the unlimited possibilities of life. He stated that Jesus Christ could go back through history, get on the Cross again, decide to forget the Atonement, and take back His historical position at Calvary. He furthered his hyperbole of such possibilities by saying that in this present age Jesus Christ could forsake His High Priestly intercession and come down from Heaven and simply forget the entire work of exaltation and session. I would call this "raw Neo-Pentecostalism," and we should not forget that many of their leaders believe and teach these extravagant doctrines, although not always taking them to such conclusions in illustration. Many of them make such extravagant statements as this: "God does nothing but in answer to the power of prayer or the contact of personal faith." The Bible speaks of a God Who does many wonderful things, even through His providence, without our prayers or the exercising of our faith. Who prayed for the sun to rise or the rain to fall today upon our planet? I forgot to do so, and the sad thing about this observation is that too many persons also forget to thank God for His blessings.

It is impossible for God to contradict Himself; He will not do anything that is against that which He has promised to do. In view of the fact that we have been given the precious Word of God, there are no alternatives to indicate that God will accept any violation of that Word. His revelation being complete and final, it is impossible for God to do anything other than what He has *said* that He would do.

God is almighty in His power; but it is also said of Him that He does all things well (cf. Genesis 18:25 and Mark 7:37). The Bible speaks of power from God that could remove a mountain; but we wonder if God would move a mountain on which a Godly widow lives in dutiful residence. The Greek word for "power" (Acts 1:8; *dunamis*) is a word which later would be transliterated into an English word, "dynamite"; yet dynamite came much later through the intellectual resources of Alfred Bernhard Nobel in 1866. It probably is unfortunate that in too many popular sermons we have magnified *dynamite* as the word for the "power of God." The Greek word *dunamis* pleads more for that inherent power, such as coal in a mountain, sap in a tree, or life in an ear of corn. To say the least, it does not simply boast of an explosion that blows a fuse and jumps the boundary and laws which hold it in available resource. All of God's power is harnessed to its greatest potentiality and purpose. There is no loss of power or meaning; God's Word sees to it that the most effective work is done. We marvel at the text of Gabriel to Mary. The Son of God would come through the galaxies in condescension—almighty power implanted in a womb; the inherent potential resource of all salvation rather than the overt explosion of raw or super omnipotence. The glorious Virgin Birth and incarnation were a manifestation of that power!

The Neo-Pentecostal does not seem to understand the purpose of power or the Biblical impossibilities of God. Their erroneous teachings and super-spiritualities go far beyond the Word of God, expending powers in a direction that discharges reckless powers beyond the provisions and purposes of God. The greatest power ever manifested in a human being is the power of a transformed life through the New Birth because of the Blood of the Lord Jesus Christ.

The Completeness and Finality of the Written Word

The Neo-Pentecostals not only teach away from the Biblical base; they also allow a variety of extant revelations to be included in their claims of the Charismatics of the Holy Spirit, so-called.

God is not giving additional revelation today. This means that now He is moving in the hearts of men for the singular proclamation and defense of the *already completed and written Word*. It is necessary, therefore, that we openly defend the fact of the finished work of the Written Scriptures. John refers to the "Spirit of truth" as a divine Unit. We do not view the Bible as a series of incomplete truths, separated, unrelated, or unfinished. We might illustrate this with a pie. A pie is not merely salt, sugar, eggs, flour, butter, flavoring, and fruit. A pie is a whole unit—complete within itself. When we eat pie, we do not insert the fork to eat the sugar, flour, or salt of the pie. That is not pie. We must eat pie itself—all the ingredients blended together. In like manner, we do not go to our pulpits and streets and classrooms and Sunday Schools merely to proclaim an incomplete revelation separated from the finished Word of God.

The Bible includes all of the absolutes, hypostatics, and accompanying paradoxes needed for the full revelation of God to man. We are believers in the *both/and* of all the words of Scripture, rather than the modern situational acceptance of *either/or* in parts of the Scripture, which may be added to or taken from in further *neo* visions, dreams, or voices. Either the Bible is the complete, inerrant, infallible, final, Voice of God, or the matter remains open for further revelations. There must be some point in history at which God concludes His revelation to man; otherwise, certain truths would remain open indefinitely from the whole Word of God. It should be further understood that although there are some Neo-Pentecostals who would not be bold enough to actually speak of their impressions, demonstrations, and feelings, as equal to the Bible itself, their liberties in the importance of these things are taken too far because they do not speak from the Biblical base as the totalitarian authority of their lives.

In earlier days the Modernist *deleted* parts of Scripture, claiming that the Bible merely *contained* the Word of God. They equally doubted the supernatural elements of the Bible (the miracles, prophecies, etc.). But the Neo-Pentecostal, with his super-spiritualities breaking forth into Charismatic chatter, boasts too often of *additional* revelations, via visions, dreams, voices, impressions, demonstrations, and other experiences, thus implying and actually concluding that the Bible is insufficient. Some Pentecostals have told me that the Bible is often archaic and out-of-date, that it must be made relevant to the age, and that it is insufficient in its principles and prophecies.

In view of the fact that the modern Neo-Pentecostal is not grounded on the Biblical base, extant revelations of all kinds easily appear. Romanism has always been away from the Biblical base, accepting the validity of encyclicals, popes, "ex-cathedra" voice, and tradition as equal to the Scriptures.

The claim or allowance of a "new" revelation gives another deep insight into the error of the Neo-Pentecostal. It is just as dangerous to *add to* the Word of God as it is to *subtract from* the Word of God. Both are a part of the ecumenical movement against Christ and His Word.

Extant Revelations

These include:

1. The *Koran* of 694 A.D., and 350 million people followed it.

2. The *Book of Mormon* of 1830, and there has followed an increasing membership until this day.

3. *The Great Controversy* of the Seventh Day Adventists, with revelation claims extant to the Bible dating from 1843.

4. The *Communist Manifesto of Karl Marx* of 1848, and more than half the world is under its political domination.

5. The *Science and Health With Key to the Scriptures* by Mary Baker Eddy in 1875, and by 1921 the birth of Christian Science, which is neither Christian nor scientific.

6. The *Quotations from Chairman Mao Tse-Tung*, in 1893, and 900 million to follow the Mao cult.

On a study tour reaching into the interior of Turkey, in 1969, at the familiar place of the Biblical Iconium (now Konya), we found among the very conservative Mohammedan priests a belief in new-revelations that would often come from their assembly in the Mosque for meditation, when the cult of Mevlana followers would get themselves worked up into a trance through the implementation of the oriental flute. Our instructor told us that these people, during the moments of "spiritual trance," would speak "unutterable" things. It would be hard to fully realize the meaning of "trance," "unutterable," and "spiritual." But we know that none of these matters stand upon the Biblical base. It is our firm opinion that a day will come when a common denominator of an international religion will be identified with an apostate glossolalia of speech in some form. A profusion of the occult tetragrammatons and utterances have been with the occult for years. It will return.

The Bible is our only Divine Revelation: whether it is Apocrypha, Jewish Mishna, Talmud, or Targum; Roman Catholic encyclical or "ex-cathedra" voice; Pentecostal, pope, dream, vision, audible voice, poltergeist, four-leaf clover, rabbit's foot, *ad infinitum*, we cannot accept it as the power, authority, and Voice of God. There is but one complete and inerrant Word of God. We believe in the leading of the Holy Spirit, sanctified impressions, and spiritual insights on the Biblical base; but we lay these at the altar of Scripture. They must bow as less authoritative than and unequal to the Word of God. During the Protestant Reformation and succeeding days, a Latin phrase was carried around the world. It was *homo unius libri*—"a man of one book." This phrase represented the burning hearts of the reformers who were men of one Book—the Bible.

Contrary to popular opinion, the Devil does not want to be understood, primarily, as a rogue and a rascal. He desires to be "the shining one" (Genesis 3:1, *nachash*, serpent). His greater aim is to be "like the most high" (Isaiah 14:14). This he approximates to its grandest intent when he comes in the guise of the Word of God—subtracting from, adding to, or perverting the Word.

In the Garden of Eden, Satan advanced the very same

principles to Eve.

Now the serpent was more subtil than any beast of the field which the Lord God had made. And he said unto the woman, Yea, hath God said, Ye shall not eat of every tree of the garden? (Genesis 3:1).

Satan questions the Word of God before Eve, and in the final analysis Eve also questions God's Word. She commences to set forth—back in the beginning—a new concept. In that first sin are three false reactions against the Word of God:

1. Eve *subtracts* from the Word of God.

And the Lord God commanded the man, saying, Of every tree of the garden thou mayest freely eat. . . (Genesis 2:16).

Eve *deletes* the word "freely" from her later incomplete quotation to the Serpent (Genesis 3:2-3). It is common, even to this day, that people leave the *free* grace of God out of their interpretations of God's Word. Eve did not seem to be attracted either by the fact that she might "freely eat" of all the other trees, or the wisdom of refraining from the forbidden one. She ignored the other gracious benefits which God had provided.

2. Eve *adds* to the Word of God. This might seem to be as incidental as the previous one; nevertheless, Eve adds, "neither shall ye touch it" (Genesis 3:3b). God had not spoken that phrase. In fact, everything indicated that His creatures might "freely" touch anything in the Garden. It was not the environment that was evil, nor even the tree itself. The sin was disobedience to the Word of God.

3. Eve *perverts* the Word of God. It was Eve's basic attitude toward God that caused her to subtract and add to the Word as mentioned before. It is obvious, however, that running throughout the conversation between the Serpent and Eve, there was a mutual spirit growing to pervert what God had originally said. Eve exemplifies a critical spirit, away from the Biblical base, toward God's Word. You can read between the lines here; it is heavily freighted with the defense of self against God. She seems to be offended by what God had said. Only one attitude could be given here as a result of these things: she would

deny God's Word entirely.

At this point we might offer several formal viewpoints of more recent history concerning the matter of totalitarian acceptance of the Bible.

They ignore God's Word, passively. (Heathen)
They deny God's Word, actively. (Infidel)
They subtract God's Word, partially. (Modernist)
They add to God's Word, extantly. (Neo-Pentecostal)
They pervert God's Word, originally. (Neo-Orthodox)
They practice God's Word, situationally.
(Neo-Evangelical)
They believe God's Word, completely.
(Fundamentalist)

The Spirit Behind the Words of Men

The Britannica Encyclopaedia has published *The Great Books of the Western World* in fifty-four volumes. It includes the classical writings of men for thirty centuries. Volume One introduces the entire, massive account under the title, "The Great Conversation." Thus, the words of the genius of men have set forth their singular conversation around the fields of philosophy, history, religion, art, and science. The words are spoken from the hearts of men born in sin, ever searching, longing, and often achieving their thoughts of knowledge upon truths drawn from creation and nature—but upon the authority and interpretation of a human base.

Many of these things have been found to be hopeful, proper, genuine, and partially true, as viewed in the light of the whole Word of God. Paul, in Romans, chapter one, speaks of man, through natural revelation, being able to find and know God's "eternal power and Godhead." However, Paul also taught that the infallible Biblical revelation was found only through the words of Scripture (cf. Romans 1:18-32 & I Corinthians 2:1-14).

Has there been behind the words of men, away from the Biblical base, down through history since the Fall a spirit that the Devil has hoped to use against mankind? Although the individual may not have been altogether conscious of it, has there been an inspiration and a power that has longed for a time when it could completely counterfeit or counteract the Word of God for a final deception? Is the time in which we presently live, this time of increasing apostasy, a time to deceive the whole earth except for the saints who follow the authority of Scripture on the Biblical base?

We do not desire to strain a point with oversimplification, but should we not consider a tremendous observation in history from *The Great Conversation?*[104]

There have been four great periods in history when the genius of mankind brought into existence his greatest written words of art, religion, philosophy, history, and science. Technology, science, religion, art—all of these have been the most powerful forces of influence in the progress of mankind in his worldly pursuits and flights *away from God.* Only the Bible has exerted a greater influence. Let us briefly note these historical panels:

1
The Age of the Pericles or Greek Period
(450-400 B.C.?)

Drama in this period was manifested through Sophocles, Euripides, Aristophanes, Cratius, and Eupolis; history through Hellanicus, Herodotus, and Thucydides; oratory through Antiphon, Andocides, and Lysias; philosophy through Anaxogoras, Parmenides, and Empedocles; and lyric verse—a height of immortal literature alive today—through Pinder, Bacchylides, and Timotheus.

2
The Latin Period (70-20 B.C.?)

Although much of the drama and history perished in this period, it had a powerful influence in its day. This is also the Augustan period of Latin literature. The names of Sisenna in history; Vitruvius in architecture; Cicero, the subject in essays; Tibullus, Propertius and the fables of Phaedrus; Lucretius, Catullus, Vergil and Horace in verse, survived their times.

3
The Elizabethan Age of the English
(1580-1630 A.D.?)

In the field of literature there are the names of Bacon,
Hooker, Lyly, Bishop Andrewes, Sidney, Raleigh, and
Hakluyt with prose; Spenser, Davies, Crashaw and
others in poetry; and Ben Jonson, Beaumont,
Shakespeare and others in drama. The English Period
was also the time for many translations of Homer, Pliny,
and Plutarch; with Ariosto, Tasso, and Montaigne.

4
The French Period (1636-1686 A.D.?)

This period reached its peak under Louis Quatorze.
There was the prose of Descartes and Pascal; the verse of
Boileau and La Fontaine; the romances of Mademoiselle
de Scudery and Cyrano de Bergerac; and the drama of
Corneille, Racine, Quinault, Regnard, and Moliere.

Although greatness has often been seen and earnest
benefits received through the various aspects of these
contributions, did they not come into history in unique
periods?

The Age of Pericles came toward the close of the Old
Testament revelation; it arose in prominence during the
period after the last prophet of God, Malachi. Was the
Devil hopeful that these written expressions of human
genius would get the mind and steal the heart away from
the revelation of the Old Testament? Would this assist in
preparing man for the rejection of the revelation of the
Messiah, the Lord Jesus, in His First Advent? We are
confident that it contributed a large part in the rejection
of Christ through the various schools and scholars of that
day. To our own time, it has been a mystery why Socrates,
Plato, and Aristotle did not mention the writings of
Moses. The omission seems most unnatural.

The Latin Period came immediately before the
Incarnation and Virgin Birth of the Lord Jesus Christ.
Was the Devil hopeful again that these written
expressions would infiltrate the Gospel Message and
pervert the Truth of the Gospel? We saw earlier the

influence of the Stoic and the Epicurean, which were later developments of the influence of Socrates and Plato. This Stoic and Epicurean influence is seen adjacent to the New Testament community (Acts 17:18). Later, during the times of the Patristic Period (the early Church Fathers), we would see the occasion of these things in the allegorizing and philosophizing of the Word of God.

The Elizabethan Age of the English assisted the Christian world in the written English translation of the King James Version of the Bible, although it should be remembered that this particular style of English had been dead for forty or fifty years. At the same time, this period occasioned the opportunity of skepticism and the Enlightenment. This finally led to influences which later came out of the French Period. We are fully aware of the tragedy of the French writers who actually gave birth to formal atheism and agnosticism, as well as a variety of other forms of infidelity.

One of the great needs of the Protestant Reformation, so effectively rendered by the reformers, was to cut asunder the influences of the past and get back to the Biblical base without these philosophical influences upon them. Both Augustine and Aquinas considered Greek philosophy of great importance; and the Ptolemaic theory of the universe (the Geocentric Theory) gave way, which was a radical departure from the thinking of the time and of the Roman Church, and was revolutionized by the coming of Copernicus (the Heliocentric Theory) and Galileo.

Are we presently entering into a fifth and final period of the multiplicity of beliefs and writings from the hearts and pens of religious new-revelationists? Are we to see a proliferation from the Neo-Christian world and the cults of extant revelation-concepts?

There are literally tons of printed matter currently being shipped around the world. Neo-Pentecostalism and Roman Catholic Charismatics are a part of that proliferation of neo-thought away from the Biblical base; and it must be acknowledged that there is a growing similarity between the Charismatics, the cults, and the occult. There is a revival among us of the ancient Babylonian, Egyptian, Hindu, and other mystery religions of the past. Transcendental meditation, yoga, mysticism, and Charismatics have a great similarity, and we believe that ultimately they will consolidate into one religion. The science of physics (matter) is giving way to the science of spiritualism (mind, ESP, etc.).

Since the days of Rosicrucianism (the 13th and 17th century, but greatly acclaimed again in the 19th and 20th centuries), the School of Unity (1814-36?), Mormonism (1823?), the Seventh-Day Adventist (1843-44?), Christian Science (1844?), Spiritism (1850-72?), Jehovah's Witnesses (1914),—this harvest of tares has grown—and finally, the most deceiving situation of all—a Neo-Christianity away from the Biblical base. Neo-Christianity is more deceiving because it has more truth in its error.

This could be illustrated in the label and contents of a bottle of poison. Law demands the manufacturer of poison to add a label on which is the word "POISON" or the sign of a skull-and-crossbones. If a person should exchange the "Poison" for a beautiful label etched around the border with colorful flowers and bearing the title "Scent of Peppermint," the contents of that bottle would be more dangerous. That is the condition of Neo-Christianity. The title on the new label is "Holy Spirit." Many writings are proceeding from Neo-Pentecostals and Roman Catholic Charismatics, and the multiplicity of persons involved are endeavoring to bring a so-called renewal, reform, and awakening in the name of "Spirit." Where are the great fundamentals upon which we have always rested in the past—true awakenings from the Lord? They are not in Neo-Christianity. From the ecumenicities of "Liberalism," Vatican II, Pentecostal personalities, Romanism, and a distorted interpretation of history we hear the myriad sounds and voices of Neo-Orthodoxy, Neo-Evangelicalism, Neo-Morality, and Neo-Pentecostalism. If it were not for the Word of God, it would

be a frightening view of these days, with definite overtones of Antichrist.

> And the king shall do according to his will; and he shall
> exalt himself, and magnify himself above every god, and
> shall speak marvellous things against the God of gods,
> and shall prosper till the indignation be accomplished: for
> that that is determined shall be done. Neither shall he
> regard the God of his fathers, nor the desire of women, nor
> regard any god: for he shall magnify himself above all.
> But in his estate shall he honour the God of forces: and a
> god whom his fathers knew not shall he honour with gold,
> and silver, and with precious stones, and pleasant things
> (Daniel 11:36-38).

The Necessity for the Objective Word of God

Neo-Pentecostalism is existential in its philosophy, as
we have already noted in the example of Oral Roberts and
the influence of Paul Tillich, and his writings, when
Roberts went to the Methodist Church. Involved in
existentialism is the popular battle between objective and
subjective truth.

The influence of existentialism and its interaction
with orthodoxy has had a far-reaching effect upon the
church and the world. The spearhead of this *new*
philosophical approach was Soren Kierkegaard (1813-
1855), who entered the University of Copenhagen at the
age of seventeen. One of the towering figures of the
intellectual world at that time was Georg Hegel (1770-
1831) who is considered the father of existentialism in his
presentation of the thesis, antithesis, and synthesis.

Abstract speculation or reason could never find God,
Kierkegaard affirmed, because there is an "indefinite
qualitative difference" between time (man's realm) and
eternity (God's realm). Kierkegaard believed that finite
mankind is incapable of knowing the divine, infinite,
transcendent God unless God breaks in upon man by
spanning the gulf. According to Kierkegaard, God did
take the initiative and reveal Himself through a
continuous series of crises. At each "encounter" (crisis) or
"confrontation" man is faced with an *either/or:* either he

yields his whole being to God, or he bears the responsibility of rejecting God's claim on him. Knowledge comes at this moment of confrontation—it can never come from or through human reason.[105]

This contrast between objectivity and subjectivity was basic to all of Kierkegaard's thought. His definition of essential truth (the truth that is essentially related to existence) is as follows:

> When the question of truth is raised in an objective manner, reflection is directed objectively to the truth, as an object to which the knower is related. Reflection is not forced upon relationship, however, but upon the question of whether it is the truth to which the knower is related. If only the object to which he is related is truth, the subject is accounted to be in the truth. When the question of the truth is raised subjectively, reflection is directed subjectively to the nature of the individual's relationship; if only the mode of this relationship is in the truth, the individual is in the truth even if he should happen to be thus related to what is not true.[106]

These words boil down to the fact that behind this matter is a grave error which denies the objective Word of God, believing the "gulf" hinders man from having such access to God. God created a verbalized creature and also revealed His Word in a verbalized, propositionally logical way. The Word of God is God's own revelation. If it is kept closed on a shelf, it remains the infallible Word, objectively. If no one had ever been born again, the Bible would still be the Word of God, objectively. It does not take the subjective "encounter" or "crisis" of the involvement of man for the Bible to *become* the Word of God. However, man is honored in that he might subjectively participate in God's grace and Word, and that grace may become experientially a subjective part of that man's life.

Oral Roberts lauds the names of Hartshorne, Ogden, Hordein, Outler, and Tillich who influenced his decision in going into the Methodist Church. [107] We would be hard pressed to find a more influential American existentialist than Paul Tillich.

Neo-Pentecostalism incorporates the existential principle of subjectivity in their fallacies and weaknesses of the witness of human experience, which we discussed earlier; and it is clear that their "Companions in Compromise" are working from that base of the *interpretation* of Scripture as well.

8

Neo-Pentecostalism:
A Point of Departure
A Place of Achievement

We live in a peculiar hour in church history. It is an eschatological time not to be managed by dialogue with the new ecumenism, but to render a defense for the Gospel of Christ. It is not the time of spiritual awakening, renewal, or reform; it is a time of falling away and decline. It is the Age of Apostasy.

Archbishop Trench gives this definition of an age:

> All that floating mass of thoughts, opinions, maxims, speculations, hopes, impulses, aims, aspirations, at any time current in the world, which it may be impossible to seize and accurately define, but which constitutes a most real and effective power, being the moral or immoral atmosphere which at every moment of our lives we inhale, again inevitably to exhale.[108]

The age in which we live carries with it all the outward characteristics of any other age; but involved also is an inward falling away of the institutional church, marking it as a more peculiar age. The words of Martin Luther enlighten our understanding with regard to the proper position to be maintained at such a time:

> If I profess with loudest voice and clearest exposition every portion of the truth of God except precisely that little point which the world and the Devil are at that moment attacking, I am not confessing Christ. Where the battle rages, there the loyalty of the soldier is proved, and to be

steady on all the battlefield besides, is mere fight and disgrace if he flinches at that point.[109]

The Point of Departure in the Error of Neo-Pentecostalism

Two specific areas have become the point of departure into the error of Neo-Pentecostalism: (1) The overemphasis upon "Spirit" to the neglect of the balanced view of the Trinitarian Godhead, and (2) the claim of additional light and/or revelation from subjective, human experience in the twentieth century so-called awakening.

Having already discussed, at length, the first point, we now present the second point. The Bible clearly teaches that God's Written Word has been consummated, and the following internal evidence of the Bible is a typical part of that conclusion:

1. The Bible admonishes man not to subtract from or add to the Word of God (Deuteronomy 4:2; Proverbs 30:5-6; Revelation 22:18-19).

2. The Bible declares that Christ is the Word (Logos), *in the singular,* demanding a consummation, as a unit, rather than an unending continuation of words; and the Holy Spirit is the "Spirit of Truth," *in the singular,* demanding a consummation rather than an unending series of truths (John 1:1-14; 14:17; 16:13; Hebrews 3:7).

3. Jesus promised that the Holy Spirit would lead and guide the disciples "into all truth" (John 16:13), which could not have meant that the disciples would receive total comprehension of all truth. To guide into all truth simply meant the completing of all truth in the full revelation of the Written Word. Our Lord's coming in the flesh brought to man the fulness of grace and truth (John 1:14).

4. The coming of Christ into the world is declared to be the "last days" when God would speak through His Son as a final revelation to man (Hebrews 1:1-3). This placed all other credentials of revelation in a secondary sense. Jesus Christ, by His coming to earth, completed revelation.

5. The aorist tense of the Greek, in its unique punctiliar potency, reveals that revelation has come in a *once-for-all* delivery to the saints (cf. John 1:18, "declared"; Hebrews 1:1, "spake"; Hebrews 1:2, "spoken"; Jude 3, "once delivered").

6. Man could not speak of "the faith" as the Scriptures reveal it—a divine Unity—if the revelation were incomplete (Luke 18:8, "the faith," Nestle Text; Jude 3, "the faith," KJV).

7. The Bible reveals that Scripture is both *the* final authority and final *in* its authority. Abraham said to the Rich Man in Hell that man would not be persuaded, genuinely, if he were not persuaded by the Word of God (Luke 16:29-31). Jesus met the Devil and his temptations with Scripture alone (Luke 4:1-13). This is the simple Biblical pattern in all instances.

8. The perfect tense in the Greek New Testament reveals the grammatical fact that God's Word *is* "written" (Matthew 4:4, 7, 10). This sets forth, grammatically, that the Word of God has been completely written (past tense) and is presently and permanently on record as the truth. The Bible says, "For ever, O Lord, thy word is settled in heaven" (Psalm 119:89).

9. The Bible makes it clear that the sign, the wonder, the miracle, the dream, or the experience, is not the conclusive criteria for truth or the true prophet (Deuteronomy 13:1-3; Job 4:12-17; 7:13-15; Jeremiah 23:28-30; Numbers 12:5-9; etc.). The only criterion for truth is the Word of God.

10. The Bible specifically warns that in the last days a claim will be made by false prophets and false christs, saying, "Lo, here is Christ" (Matthew 24:23), which appeals to the seeing of the eye, and "Behold, he is in the desert," or "behold, he is in the secret chambers" (Matthew 24:26), which appeals to the hearing of a voice. The believer is instructed to "believe it not" (vv. 23, 26). Apparently, that which is mentioned concerning the "secret chambers" has reference to some "new" revelation, so-called.

11. The Bible specifically warns believers that in the last days there will come the manifestation of a great claim in the "great signs" and wonders and miracles, which will be a part of the coming of Antichrist (Matthew 7:21-23; Revelation 13:13-14; II Corinthians 11:13-15; II Thessalonians 2:9-10). The "great signs" (Matthew 24:24) should be distinguished from the more "lowly sign" (Luke 2:12) and "the sign" (Matthew 12:39-40), of the death and resurrection of the Lord Jesus Christ.

12. The Bible specifically warns believers that in the last days there will be teachings projected that will deceive and lead people away from "the faith" (I Timothy 4:1) of Scripture, "ever learning, and never able to come to the knowledge of truth" (II Timothy 3:7). It prophesies that some will leave "the faith" and not come to "the truth." Paul furthers the thought with the urgency that because they "received not the love of the truth" and "believed not the truth," God would send them "strong delusion" so that they would believe a "lie" (II Thessalonians 2:9-12). This is a most important point to Christians in their persistence for the inerrancy and authority of the Word of God in these days.

13. The last three persons to see the glorified Christ after His ascension (as recorded in Scripture) were Stephen, Paul, and John. Stephen, in the hour of his martyrdom, saw our Lord "standing on the right hand of God" (Acts 7:56); Paul saw Him in a vision and conversed with Him on the Damascus Road (Acts 9:5), at Corinth (Acts 18:9), and at Jerusalem (Acts 23:11); and John saw the Christ, glorified, on the Island of Patmos when he received the prophecy of the Book of Revelation (chs. 1, 2, 3, etc.).

We do not believe that since the times of these incidents anyone has actually seen the glorified Body of Christ or heard the audible Voice of God (cf. I John 1:1-3; II Peter 1:16-21). In fact, Peter states that we have a "more sure word of prophecy" than they had on the other side of the unfinished Word of God when they were eyewitnesses on the Mount of Transfiguration.

The next time man is to see Christ will be in the clouds (I Thessalonians 4:17 and Revelation 1:7).This must be kept in harmony with the fact that "this same Jesus, which is taken up from you into heaven, shall so come in like manner as ye have seen him go into heaven" (Acts 1:11 and Zechariah 14:4), which will be after His appearance in the air—when He shall return to the earth on the Mount of Olives.

The order of eschatological events is not the all-decisive point by the author. I simply establish what the Bible says about our Lord's appearance. It is true: Christ will return in the manner that is foretold in Scripture.

The Place of Ecumenical Achievement in the Error of Neo-Pentecostalism

In keeping with our somewhat detailed presentation of the different areas complementing each other in the new ecumenism, it seems fitting to enumerate in simple outline the various forces which have united to achieve total ecumenicity in the apostasy of the 1970's.We believe that the burden of proof, as confirmed by the evidences presented, should at least give the reader another side of Neo-Pentecostalism, as viewed by a former Pentecostal, as well as the total Neo-Christianity, which is not so abundantly spoken and written by Pentecostals. Having spent twenty-four years in Pentecostalism, and having extended refutation and controversy throughout all those years, my own heart has come to an unprecedented concern with regard to the trend throughout Pentecostalism and the world in these Charismatic heresies.

It should be kept in mind, of course, that the Charismatics themselves describe their movement as an ecumenical one. Rev. Larry Christenson, a Lutheran Charismatic pastor and author, in one of the main messages delivered in the recent Kansas City Charismatic Conference (1977), actually confessed: "Where the ecumenical influence is restricted, the charismatic movement shrivels up."[110] The involvement of ecumenical achievement in the error of Neo-Pentecostalism stems from a number of actions and forces. Contributing forces are these:

1. The move of the second-generation Pentecostal denominational leaders to neutrality away from the Biblical base of the first-generation leaders.

2. The move of the third-generation Pentecostal denominational leaders to compromise away from the Biblical base and involving themselves with Neo-Pentecostals and Roman Catholic Charismatics in erroneous situations of Pentecostal personalities and places, such as Notre Dame.

3. The move of Romanism in her apostasy to Charismatics, and the ecumenical positions of Pope John and Vatican II toward the reception of Neo-Pentecostalism away from the Biblical base.

4. The move of liberal, main-line denominations—such as Episcopalians, Lutherans, Baptists, and to a lesser degree some others, including Methodists, Congregationalists, and Presbyterians (at the first)—to the error of Neo-Pentecostalism.

5. The move of second- and third-generation Pentecostal denominational leaders to affiliate fellowships with Chilean Pentecostals who were members of the World Council of Churches.

6. The presence of earlier "Liberals," like Henry Van Dusen who was a leader of old ecumenism, but who presently is lauded by certain Neo-Pentecostals as a forerunner and endorser of their movements.

7. The presence of earlier Pentecostals, such as David J. Du Plessis who has been so instrumental in bringing Pentecostal acceptability to the World Council of Churches and the Vatican, as well as having personally accepted papal infallibility.

8. The endorsement of such Neo-Evangelicals as Billy Graham, by dedication of the Oral Roberts University, a Neo-Pentecostal institution.

9. The move of Neo-Evangelicals away from the Biblical base in their methodology, which has destroyed

Biblical separation between the truth and error of sponsorships in their cooperative efforts of evangelism.

10. The successful expansion of the Full Gospel Business Men's Fellowship International across all denominations and movements, bringing together an opportunity for the new ecumenism.

11. The overwhelming success of independent Pentecostal personalities, such as Oral Roberts, who have espoused Neo-Pentecostalism to the various ecumenical movements of the world.

12. The inculcation of the very popular principle of existentialism, so prominently involved in Neo-Orthodoxy, as a principle upon which Neo-Pentecostalism speaks both from denominational leaderships and modern Pentecostal personalities.

13. The adoption of an untenable presupposition for the interpretation of history in order that a conclusion might be drawn concerning the modern Pentecostal phenomenon as a moving of the Holy Spirit and an Awakening, rather than the fulfillment of the Biblical prophecy of the coming Apostasy.

14. The successful actions of certain youth movements, such as Teen Challenge and the Jesus People, who have brought an erroneous interpretation of certain liberties of the Gospel.

15. The general apathy and gravitation of denominations toward unity above truth, peace above sacrifice, progress above stability, success above spirituality, statistics above principles, and Charismatics above character.

16. A united rejection of Fundamentalism, although the ecumenical spirit, so-called, of love and peace is the heartbeat of their movement of Pentecostalism.

Undoubtedly, Neo-Pentecostalism will add the largest ingredient to future ecumenical movement. Indeed, world unity has long hungered for this ingredient of "Spirit." The most dangerous conclusion to be drawn, after the shift from neutrality, compromise, and apostasy, is "Spiritualism" itself. The occult is among them.

Final Pentecostal Echoes From the Past

All of these observations reveal that there is only one ecumenicity now. This is best noted in the words of Rev. Ralph Martin, a pioneer in the Catholic Charismatic movement, working with Roman Catholic Cardinal Leon Joseph Suenens in Brussels. Martin was one of the main speakers at the 1977 Kansas City Charismatic Conference, and he was introduced as "a young man who has the gift of prophecy." He says:

> Pope John XXIII prayed the prayer for renewal in the Roman Catholic church after reading *The Cross and The Switchblade, They Spoke With Other Tongues,* and other books, Martin informed the crowd. "God uses you, the Classical Pentecostals and Protestants, to answer that prayer! God is uniting His blessed body ... I assure you your Catholic brothers and sisters are with you all the way until God completes His purpose!"[111]

An interesting series of biographies could be written on the lives of certain men who are involved in this unity of the Classical Pentecostals, Neo-Pentecostals, and Roman Catholic Charismatics. I refer to biographies that would reveal the influences which dominated the lives of these personalities and finally led them to overthrow Christian Faith and Biblical identity. There is Karl Barth, with his ingredient of dialectical existentialism; Billy Graham and his unseparated methodology; Oral Roberts and his singular independence of new-revelationism; Dennis Bennett and his first Protestant Pentecostalism; Vinson Synan and his presupposition of interpretive Pentecostal and church history; Cardinal Suenens and his key position in Vatican Council II and the Catholic Charismatic circles; and David Du Plessis and his connections with the World Council of Churches and the Vatican, through the Roman Catholic Pentecostal dialogues, Assemblies of God and Church of God at Lee College.

Pentecostalism's point of departure and the place of achievement in Neo-Pentecostalism stirs old chords and echoes of personalities and forces in the Pentecostal

denominations that should be considered in our appraisal
of the modern Charismatics.

As we have mentioned earlier, the Classical
Pentecostal set the prime mood for the Pentecostal
denominations and their involvement in Neo-
Pentecostalism and the Roman Catholic Charismatics.
The Classical Pentecostal originated early in Pentecostal
history, and is identified with Charles Fox Parham's
Bible School in Topeka, Kansas, and with the primarily
black revival in Azusa, California. The mood of the
Pentecostal denominations at that point in history was
definitely that of the Classical Pentecostal, rather than
the Old-Line or Traditional Pentecostal.

To achieve this place in Neo-Pentecostalism there was
a definite point of departure from the Biblical base
identified with some of the early Pentecostals. And a final
presentation of the denominational picture, from a
Pentecostal's background, will further our understanding of the problems involved.

David Du Plessis was born in 1905, near Cape Town at
a place called Twenty-four Rivers, South Africa, a
commune of Christian believers that grew out of a revival
that was led by a Norwegian evangelist. Du Plessis was
the eldest son of parents who were descendants of the
French Huguenots. Although his father was Dutch
Reformed in immediate background, he invited a
Pentecostal minister to come and pray for his sick
grandfather; and out of this experience, Pentecostalism
came to their home. David Du Plessis records that his own
conversion occurred at the age of eleven. Thus, he grew up
in a Pentecostal home and became a minister and general
secretary of the Apostolic Faith Mission, a Pentecostal
group in Johannesburg, South Africa.

In 1936, during one of Du Plessis' mornings at the
mission office, Smith Wigglesworth, British evangelist,
bolted into the room, pushed Du Plessis against the wall,
and in his booming voice prophesied, in part:

> I have been sent by the Lord to tell you what He has shown
> me this morning ... Through the old-line denominations

will come a revival that will eclipse anything we have known throughout history. No such things have happened in times past as will happen when this begins ... It will eclipse the present-day, twentieth-century Pentecostal revival that already is a marvel to the world, with its strong opposition from the established church. But this same blessing will become acceptable to the churches and they will go on with this message and this experience beyond what the Pentecostals have achieved. You will live to see this work grow to such dimensions that the Pentecostal movement itself will be a light thing in comparison with what God will do through the old churches. There will be tremendous gatherings of people, unlike anything we've seen, and great leaders will change their attitude and accept not only the message but also the blessing...Then the Lord said to me that I am to give you warning that He is going to use you in this movement. You will have a very prominent part...One final word, the last word the Lord gave me for you: All He requires of you is that you be humble and faithful under all circumstances. If you remain humble, and faithful, you will live to see the whole fulfilled.[112]

About three weeks after this "prophecy," Du Plessis received from the general secretary of the Assemblies of God an invitation to speak at the denomination's general council in Memphis, Tennessee. Before he would accept the invitation, Du Plessis made a trip to Cape Town to consult with Smith Wigglesworth. Wigglesworth said: "I told you the Lord is going to prepare you for this great move. This is just one of the steps."[113] The trip to Memphis placed Du Plessis under the auspices of the Assemblies of God, and in time he also gained a Bible professorship at the Church of God school—Lee College, Cleveland, Tennessee. Du Plessis retained his papers with the Apostolic Faith Mission; but by the time of the 1952 Pentecostal World Conference, which largely is credited to his planning, Du Plessis had begun to sever his relationship with the Pentecostal denominations named above. By 1955 it was obvious that strained relationships existed between Du Plessis and these denominations, for he notes that he did not receive an invitation to the 1955 Pentecostal World Conference in Stockholm. According to Du Plessis, his "official relationship with the Pentecostal groups underwent a gradual decline through the fifties and into the sixties." To explain this decline he quoted the words of a Pentecostal: "You are so interested in the ecumenical movement in the liberal churches; you seem obsessed by it. And the other thing is that you are too interested in the Pentecostal independents."[114] During those years, he had been working with the World Council of Churches, a connection that had commenced through the friendship of Dr. John A. Mackay, president of Princeton Theological Seminary, by an immediate visit to the World Council Headquarters, and finally a visit to the International Missionary Council in Germany, 1952.

In 1962, Du Plessis received from his wife, by phone, this message: "David, what in the world is happening? ... We've just received a letter from Springfield (the Assemblies of God headquarters) and they've disfellowshiped you. They've withdrawn your credentials, your recognition. I thought it was settled, but now you're out."[115] Prior to that notice in 1962, Du Plessis had lectured on Pentecostal issues at Princeton Seminary; at the Evangelical Congregational School of Theology in Myerstown, Pennsylvania; at Yale Divinity School in New Haven, Connecticut; at Union Theological Seminary in New York; at the Ecumenical Institute of the World Council of Churches at Chateau de Bossey in Switzerland; and at the Perkins School of Theology at Southern Methodist University in Dallas, Texas. The impressive list continues until he reaches the goal of the Wigglesworth "prophecy" and becomes one of the participants in the Roman Catholic-Pentecostal dialogue in Schloss Craheim, June 1974. He was co-chairman with Dr. Kilian McDonnell, and agrees: "God still honours the Pope as the head of the Church. Papal infallibility is exactly what God used to bring about renewal in the Roman Catholic Church and that renewal is now shaking the world."

Extended detail has been given of Du Plessis simply because of the presupposition of his entire lifetime of work in Pentecostalism. That presupposition, which began in 1936 and followed his every action through all the years of his ministry, was based upon his acceptance of Smith Wigglesworth's "prophecy" for his life. Where is the *Biblical* authority of the life and calling of this man? How can a man devote his entire life to the hope and fulfillment of a *human* "prophecy," so-called, under a Pentecostal spasm of Charismatic power? Yet great numbers have made such claims—that a person could give his life to perpetuate a self-centered "prophecy" in the compromise of the Biblical message for the World Council of Churches and Romanism. There has to be a certain determination in any man who would give his entire life for the preservation and fulfillment of such a purpose. It reminds us of the presupposition that was adopted by Vinson Synan in his interpretation of history and Roman Catholic writers. In the case of Du Plessis, there was the "prophecy"; in the case of Synan, there was history and Romanism.

After the five-year dialogue-hopes (1972-1977) established and confirmed by the Vatican, the Du Plessis-McDonnell chairmanships brought the pointed need to make effective all that they sought in their many discussions. We can see it best in the words of Du Plessis:

> But there was a growing desire on the part of the group at the Vatican for a new five-year cycle. Quite to my surprise, the Catholic brethren spoke of a special need to pursue dialogue with the classical, more experienced Pentecostal brethren. "We have dealt fully with theological and psychological issues," they said. "Now we must deal with practical issues. These can only be discussed with men of ripe experience."

> There was a feeling that the mixing of Pentecostals and charismatics from the historic churches unto one team had been extremely useful in the first stages but that the mix had ultimately resulted in a certain ambiguity. "If there were more classical Pentecostals from the big

churches," the Catholics said, "the Pentecostal participants could feel and act more as one body in the discussions." They pressed especially hard for representatives from the Third World Pentecostal churches.

They recognized that the established Pentecostal
churches had much to share in terms of church operation,
missionary work in all lands, persecution, steadfastness
through three-quarters of a century, and ecclesiastical
approaches ...[116]

The amazing thing about this is that eventually the
very denomination that had dismissed David Du Plessis
would come around to his point of view and accept his
interest "in the ecumenical movement in the liberal
churches." David Du Plessis says:

My relationships with my classical Pentecostal brethren
continued to improve as the years passed by and true
ecumenism was seen. The Lord did some powerful work in
all of us. One of the most moving events from my point of
view was the issuance of a "Charismatic Study Report" by
the executive presbytery of the Assemblies of God. It
hailed "the winds of the Spirit" that are "blowing freely
outside the normally recognized Pentecostal bodies."

"The Assemblies of God wishes to identify with what God
is doing," it declared, a bold and courageous statement
that thrilled the hearts of millions and, I know beyond
doubt, brought a joyful smile to the face of our Lord
Jesus.[117]

Thus, once again we view the third-generation
Classical Pentecostal position reiterated in the
"Charismatic Study Report" of the largest Pentecostal
denomination in the world—the Assemblies of God. This
report was presented in the keynote rally, August 14,
1972. We quote it in its entire printed text:

There is thrilling evidence that God is moving mightily by
His Spirit throughout all the earth. The winds of the Spirit
are blowing freely outside the normally recognized
Pentecostal Body. This is the time of the greater
fulfillment of Joel's prophecy. Thousands of people have
prayed for years that this would come to pass. The coming

of the Holy Spirit upon so many in such a broad sweep of the church world is God's way of counteracting the liberalism, secularism, humanism, and occultism that plagues our present day society.

Marks of genuine moving of the Holy Spirit include the following:

1. Emphasis on worship in spirit and truth of almighty God.
2. Recognition of the person of Christ—His deity, His incarnation and His redemptive work.
3. Recognition of the authority of the hunger for the Word of God.
4. Emphasis of the person and work of the Holy Spirit.
5. Emphasis of the Second Coming of Christ.
6. Emphasis on prayer for the sick.
7. Emphasis on sharing Christ in witnessing and evangelism.

The Assemblies of God wishes to identify with what God is doing in the world today. We recognize that no existing organization fully represents the body of Christ. Neither do we believe that for all true Christians—whether Pentecostal in doctrine and practice or not—to align themselves with an existing organization or a new one, will bring the unity of the Spirit. We do believe in the institution of the church. We trust the Holy Spirit to bring the members of Christ's body into a true unity of the Spirit. If there is yet a truth to be revealed to the church, it is the essential unity of the body of Christ, which transcends but does not destroy existing organizational bounds.

The Assemblies of God does not place approval on that which is manifestly not scriptural in doctrine or conduct. But neither do we categorically condemn everything that does not totally or immediately conform to our standards. No genuine spiritual movement in church history has been completely free of problems or above criticism. The Pentecostal movement of this century has experienced its problems relating both to doctrine and conduct. Spiritual maturity leads to a balanced life which will bear the fruit of the spirit while displaying the gifts of the spirit.

We place our trust in God to bring His plan about as He pleases in His sovereign will. It is important that we find

our way in a sound scriptural path, avoiding the extremes
of an ecumenism that compromises scriptural principles
and an exclusivism that excludes true Christians.[118]

This is a masterpiece of words. It reveals how a third-
generation people can once again fellowship a man, such
as Du Plessis, whom formerly they had dismissed. It is a
first-class presentation of the thought pattern of the
modern, institutional church. Many times in earlier
church history similar ecclesiastical logistics existed. In
reality, no positive position is taken in this "Charismatic
Study Report," as far as an actual conflict with Neo-
Pentecostalism is concerned. No error is really mentioned; no Biblical separation is made; and no personality is identified. The document simply leaves to the
individual the decision with regard to all conclusions,
appraisals, and acknowledgments of error and the
apostasy in the modern Pentecostal spectrum. According
to Scripture, God intended his ministers to take a stand
and give a definite Biblical position concerning sin and
error to His people, in all generations.

There are really no absolutes set forth in the
boundaries of error or truth, although truth is certainly
appreciated in its own right. What can the listener to this
report do but continue in ignorance and wonderment with
regard to that which is indeed erroneous or true? This
neutrality leads to compromise, and compromise leads to
apostasy.

In the first paragraph of "The Charismatic Study
Report" the present age is oozing with the "thrilling"
evidence that God is moving by His Spirit. Du Plessis
acknowledges this. Yet in the last paragraph they are
concerned with some "extremes" which are never
identified. In the midst of this typical denominational
schizophrenia, one feels compelled to ask: "Are the
thrilling evidences a part of the ecumenical excesses and
extremes? And do the thrilling evidences include the
ecumenical forces existing in the world at this time?" Du
Plessis is encouraged to believe that.

Where do these words fit into the Biblical pronouncement of the apostasy? No doubt, if Jesus tarries, we shall see, in the light of the new ecumenism, what this ecclesiastical dialogue really means.

Another ecclesiastical leader in the Pentecostal Holiness Church—Bernard Underwood—says:

> There can be little doubt in the mind of any discerning Christian that God is doing some wonderful things among both Protestant and Catholic people to bring them into the knowledge of the fullness and ministry of the Holy Spirit. There have been many significant and scriptural testimonies to this move of the Spirit.
>
> The dangers are in two opposite directions. The first is the temptation to "write off" all such testimonies as false because of certain manifestations of error in this movement. But if one follows this direction he would have to reject the entire pentecostal movement—even the early twentieth century revival that gave birth to the Pentecostal Holiness Church.
>
> The second temptation is just as dangerous. It is the temptation to accept everything now being proclaimed in charismatic circles as the revelation of truth. It is essential that true believers exercise sound, scriptural judgment on every doctrine being propounded in this complex "charismatic movement" of the latter half of the twentieth century.[119]

Thus the synthesis continues. Underwood, a second-generation Pentecostal, does not distinguish between his own first-generation denominational leaders and the modern Pentecostal movement. Once again we see a paragraph that is dedicated to the endorsement, and then a paragraph that discredits complete endorsement. Underwood employs the usual ecclesiastical logic, taking no position to help those in need of Biblical light amidst the compromise of his own situation.

A plea goes from my own heart to the reader. This is a time in which you, as an individual Christian, should exercise wisdom in dealing with Pentecostals. At the grass roots you might find a minority—and only a minority—of ministers and members who are dedicated to the Biblical base, the fundamental principles of the

Gospel, and a separated, holy life. A number of Christian Day School principals have written me with commendation and appreciation for teachers of this background and with this kind of standard. I know a number of laymen and ministers who are genuine Christians and are not a part of the second-generation neutrality or the third-generation compromises. These men of God take a commendable stand against Neo-Pentecostalism and the Roman Catholic Charismatics. I believe that if Jesus tarries, there will have to be an exodus of many of these men from their denominations, for I foresee no return of Pentecostal leaders to the Biblical base. It is my personal opinion that the Pentecostal leaders are to blame for the compromises, and that they will continue to lead the people into the error of Neo-Pentecostalism. The words of the prophet Isaiah are appropriate in this regard:

> Therefore the Lord will cut off from Israel head and tail, branch and rush, in one day. The ancient and honourable, he is the head; and the prophet that teacheth lies, he is the tail. For the leaders of this people cause them to err; and they that are led of them are destroyed (Isaiah 9:14-16).

Pentecostal echoes of the first-generation people are fading away. Soon there will be no more voices of those who preached and lived on the Biblical base. Others who respected that message will either compromise their positions, or they will be excommunicated from the denominational leaderships and large churches. In fact, I do not know of a true Bible man in any large Pentecostal church.

G. F. Taylor, a first-generation leader in the Pentecostal Holiness Church, in his book entitled *The Rainbow*, presented a sermon on the subject, "Many Antichrists." This sermon was printed in 1924, only thirteen years after the birth of Taylor's denomination. An extended quotation reveals certain final echoes from the heart and thinking of at least some of those early Pentecostal men. The message stands on the Biblical base, and is a part of the true gift of preaching that the

Bible lays down for God's ministers. Taylor says:

> The spirit of antichrist is the spirit of deception. It can gain ground only as it deceives the people. It can not thrive where it is unveiled. Paul speaks of "the mystery of iniquity" working already. The word "mystery" means something that is covered, something that works in the dark. The "mystery of iniquity" is not that iniquity that is open to every eye, but it is that which comes under the garb of religion. That is why it is called "the mystery."
>
> Glancing at the religions of the world, the Pentecostal people will take most all of them to be antichristian. Yes, but those who accept those religions do so with as much sincerity as we accept ours. Many of the adherents of those religions are more deeply settled in their doctrines than we are in ours. You see, the spirit of antichrist has captured them completely. The antichrist that they worship exactly answers to their ideas of the true Christ. Their prophets and teachers must correspond to their ideas of religion. There are many antichrists among them, but all antichrists that appear to them, and exert an influence over them, are such as conform to their ideas of true religion. Otherwise, they could have no influence over them.
>
> Coming to the Christian religions, we find two great branches of the Christian Church—Catholics and Protestants. We would put the Catholics as antichristian at once. Yes, in order for antichrist to appeal to a Catholic, he has to be a Catholic himself. Take the branches of the Protestant Church, and we would term the most of them antichristian. Yet, in order for any antichrist to exercise much influence over a Protestant, he must be at least a Protestant, and generally of the same denomination. In other words, no antichrist can persuade and lead us much unless he is of the same belief with us. A Baptist antichrist can not do much with a Methodist, a Quaker antichrist can not do much with a Campbellite, and so on. The antichrist that deceives us must be our idea of a true Baptist, Methodist, Quaker, Campbellite, etc.. This does not mean that all Baptists, Methodists, Quakers, Campbellites, etc., are antichrists. In all of these, there are those who belong to Christ, but the spirit of antichrist has surely crept into all of them. He there agrees with all their doctrines, and appears to be as true a Baptist, Methodist, etc., as the case

may be, as can be found in their ranks.

Let us not suppose that our own church can escape. It makes no difference how hard we try to keep the spirit of antichrist out, it will come in. It will not come into our midst under the same profession that it enters others. It must come to us professing everything that we profess. It must come too with great power to deceive—not power to deceive others, but power to deceive us. There have been many who have come to us with the wrong spirit, who have been rejected; but the spirit of antichrist will find a foot-hold among us when he comes with the right spirit, so far as we are able to tell. Any system of religion will reject a man whose spirit does not conform to their ideas of religion. An antichrist can do nothing with us until he can conform to our spirit and ways. Rest assured that he is able to do it. Yea, he is among us now I fear. How are we to locate him? How can we recognize him?

First of all, we must keep close to Jesus ourselves. We must not allow ourselves to be attracted by human forces. Let the drawing power of the cross keep us lifted above the curse of this world. Let nothing take our attention but Jesus. Read the Word, and spend much time in prayer. By thus employing our thoughts, we will be given discernment, and God will help us to determine the false from the true.

It is said of Antichrist that his "coming is after the working of Satan with all power and signs and lying wonders, and with all deceivableness of unrighteousness in them that perish." Many antichrists are like the final Antichrist. The nearer we draw to God, the greater the signs that follow them that believe. We Pentecostal people are easily attracted by signs and wonders. Hence, there are many who will be deceived by the spirit of antichrist. Notice that the above quotation says, *all power and signs.* Jesus said, "False Christs and false prophets shall rise, and shall show signs and wonders, to seduce, if it were possible, even the elect." (Mark 13:22) One prevailing characteristic of the antichrist spirit is, to show signs and wonders. Sometimes an antichrist will have greater meetings than any one else. The final Antichrist once lived on earth; he is now dead; but he will ascend out of hell. (Revelation 17:8.) The antichrist that appeals to us is the man who once had the experience that we have, then lost grace out of his heart, and yet continues as though he has all the religion he ever had. Such men have had the manifestation of the Holy Spirit; but after He is gone, they manipulate their powers in such a way as to appear to possess still all the power of the Holy Ghost. This antichrist is in the Pentecostal movement. His coming is with all power and signs. He seems to possess every quality of a Baptized believer, and it is thus he works with all deceivableness. No other antichrist could appeal to the Pentecostal people. This spirit is among us, it is very powerful, and it takes grace to stand firm against it. Many will be deceived by it, but we must pray for them, and do what we can to show them the better way.

You can thus see how that the "many antichrists" touch every class of people on the face of the earth. They are in every government and in every circle of religion. In many religious circles this spirit is in control. It finds its way into the assemblies of the most spiritual people on earth. It behooves us to watch and pray, lest we enter into temptation. May God save us all from its snare.[120]

To me, this is true spiritual discernment and Biblical insight by a man who preached from the Biblical base. In third-generation Pentecostal preachers you do not find such insight and such spiritual discernment. I repeat that this message was delivered within thirteen years of the organization of Taylor's denomination, the Pentecostal Holiness Church; and it is almost staggering to read it in the late seventies, and see in the words such insight and truth. G.F. Taylor is said to have read the Bible through *four times a year.*

In those same early years of first-generation preachers, there were some exceptional laymen. One of these laymen was my teacher for three years in the National Pentecostal Holiness Church, Washington, D.C. His name was A. E. Robinson, and he was a close friend of Bishop J. H. King, also of the Pentecostal Holiness Church. Robinson was on the Biblical base; prior to his death in 1950, he had read the Old Testament more than 100 times and the New Testament more than 200 times.

In his little publication, *A Layman and the Book*, first published in 1936, Robinson speaks of certain dangers in his beloved denomination. I quote from chapter 25— "Youth and Our Future as a Church";

> Now let me say to you, young people, you should do better than we older ones have done. It is true some of us went through tough times on many occasions, but that is water under the bridge, and we are not having it so bad now. We expect you to do better than we have, even in the matter of doctrinal teaching and experience. When Pentecost first came our way we formed a lot of ideas that were not exactly sound or Scriptural, and we had to revise our ways of thinking and acting. You have been left a heritage of good literature which we did not have, and you will not be called upon to outgrow and outlive some of the fanciful things we did in the early days of the Pentecostal revival which afterward proved to be dangerous and destructive. For instance, we felt that we must be "led of the Spirit," and some even went so far as to try to lead others farther than the Word of God warranted, with most unfortunate results. However, we finally got over that hurdle and decided that our "leadings" must be strictly in accordance with God's Word, and not merely our own hasty impressions . . . [121]

In the 1953 General Conference of the Pentecostal Holiness Church at Memphis, Tennessee, an era of a people endeavoring to maintain an identity on the Biblical base came somewhat formally to a close in the Pentecostal Holiness denomination. It approximates a similar trend among many of the Pentecostal denominations at that time. In this Conference one group—a minority —heard a timely sermon by the late Bishop T. A. Melton. It was entitled, "If the Foundations Be Destroyed." The other group, a majority, was led by the preaching of the increasingly popular Neo-Pentecostal, Oral Roberts.

In one of his 1950 campaigns held prior to the Memphis Conference, Roberts reiterated an experience he claimed to have had in his hotel room prior to the evening service. I relate the story, as I recall it:

Roberts was ready to go to the services, and he told the Lord that he did not feel His power, which usually was demonstrated in the healing line through his right hand. Roberts informed God that because he did not feel the usual manifestation of power, he would not go to the meeting and preach. As Roberts started to remove his tie and shoes to stay in the room, God saw that he meant business about the power; and He demonstrated His power upon him. "Feeling the power" again, Roberts went to the service to preach. Roberts gave this illustration, hoping to boost people's faith. He made the point that "you must mean business with God if you are going to get His power." The audience went wild in joyous response to Roberts' testimony. Eventually Roberts left his denomination, but his philosophy remained.

In the late sixties—with Du Plessis inside the World Council of Churches and the Vatican, Graham in the ecumenicity of World Evangelism's methodology, and Barth, Brunner, Bultmann, and others having brought to the front of modern ecumenism the philosophy of existentialism—the leaderships of the third-generation Pentecostal denominations advanced the teachings of Roberts and others like him, and called it an Awakening. Also influential in the earlier days were such men as William Branham and A. A. Allen who used magic oils and claims of angels hovering over their congregations to inspire their preaching, giving them words to preach other than the very Word of God. These men actually informed their congregations that they could not preach unless the angel was present in the audience. This parallels the "familiar spirits" of the Old Testament and "control spirits" of the twentieth century in the occult.

Later development of Neo-Pentecostalism and Roman Catholic Charismatics would lead the movement away from the raw Pentecostalism of the past into a more sophisticated and prestigious movement sanctioned and assisted by the Classical Pentecostals and their leaderships of the denominations of Pentecostalism. And there is no doubt in my mind that as Elvis Presley credited a certain ingredient in his "rock" music to his Pentecostal background, so today we are viewing the prostitution of certain truths learned in the first-generation Biblical base in a sellout to the apostate ecumenicity of Neo-Christianity.

It seems appropriate at this point to deliver a personal burden of testimony by relating an untold story of my own experience which I believe is a part of a larger story in the matter of the birth of the Roman Catholic Charismatics:

While pastoring the National Pentecostal Holiness Church in Washington, D.C., in 1965, I was requested to give lectures on the "Glossolalia" at the Roman Catholic University there. This invitation was extended to me by the priest-teacher, David Bowman, and the class that was designated for these lectures was entitled, "Our Separated Brethren." I realized that this class was dedicated by the Catholics to me.

I responded to this invitation only after agony of soul and prayer. I made it clear to the teacher that I could not come and speak solely on the subject of the "glossolalia," for I did not believe that it was essential to salvation, or that a person should *seek* tongues.

After considerable discussion by telephone and personal interviews in his office, I agreed to deal with the Biblical phenomenon of the "glossolalia" *after* I had presented the genuine Gospel of the Lord Jesus Christ and the doctrine taught by Martin Luther concerning justification by faith. Finally, the teacher agreed to my stipulations, and it was clear that I was not coming as a believer in Catholicism.

I was determined to present the glorious Gospel of the Lord Jesus Christ in the ornamental chapel in the neighborhood in which I had grown up as a boy. It seemed imperative for me to announce ahead of time that I was establishing a beachhead on enemy territory, and I wanted to be right in my relationship with the Lord Jesus in this age of ecumenicity and apostasy.

Although at the beginning there was some levity, and

ridicule, the Holy Spirit and the Word of God brought serious consideration to the Gospel in that chapel. As I began to deal with the holy and separated life of the Christian, I realized the specific import of what I was there to say. A nun in the audience interrupted my lecture to inquire further about this kind of Christian life through the Blood of Jesus, and she confessed aloud that her reason for becoming a nun had been the searching for a clean, separated life.

At the end of the message when I extended an invitation to Christ, a large number came for prayer, though only a few actually followed through and accepted Christ. Some of the converts left the priesthood and began to attend my church in Washington.

Several nuns and young priests explained to me that in all of the Roman Catholic institutions across the nation similar lectures were being given, and notes and tapes were being made for a Vatican appraisal of the modern "Pentecostal phenomenon." In spite of several critical reactions—some of which came to my office in correspondence—I was contacted later to suggest other persons to speak in similar seminars at Loyola University. In my response I made it clear that to be involved in this type of ministry would seriously impair Biblical separation.

This incident revealed to me that there would be a Roman Catholic inculcation of the "Pentecostal phenomenon" to an increasing extent—even beyond the previous overtones of Vatican II, Pope John, and the Charismatic interest from the 1960's. I was not surprised later to learn of "Pentecostal Dialogues" and the five-year study between the Vatican and the Pentecostals. It was my firm conviction that this Roman Catholic innovation of the "Pentecostal" and the "Charismatic" was in keeping with the history of their erroneous claims of the supernatural, the miracle, the sign, and the wonder, as well as a confirmation that the third-generation Pentecostals were on the verge of a great compromise. In only six years, I would stand before more than a dozen Pentecostals whom I had known, and be betrayed and condemned for my Biblical teachings and Biblical separation. I proceeded, however, to preach openly against Neo-Pentecostalism and the Roman Catholic involvement.

The Scriptures: Neither Bound Nor Broken

The great protecting paradox of Scripture lies in the security of a balanced appreciation for the whole of the Bible. We can see this balance in the following: (1) The Word of God is not bound (II Timothy 2:8-9), and (2) the Word of God cannot be broken (John 10:35b). In the former, we see the wonderful *liberty* to be found in the Word of God; in the latter, we see the wonderful *limit* to be found in the Word of God. One of the greatest needs of Christians in these growing movements of the apostasy is to maintain a spiritual balance in the Biblical truths that are being perverted in Neo-Pentecostalism. There is the danger of turning from the true, Biblical teachings of the Holy Spirit and from the anointing we need upon our lives by the Holy Spirit.

A story is told of a fish family in which the mother advised her three babies about three alternatives of life. "First," she said, "do not swim in the deep; second, do not swim in the shallows; and third, swim just right." Two of her children reasoned, "Water is water, and every fish must swim; so why bother about the particulars? Besides, whoever heard of a fish that drowned?" The result was that the first fish died, scorched in the shallows; the second fish died, devoured in the deep; but the third fish swam—just right.

Speaking from the Biblical base, there are three alternatives in our modern world. Shall we live in the shallows, in the deep, or just right? Shall we live in the *neutral,* the *broad,* or the *balance* of Biblical Truth?

To be *neutral* in the issues of life is to be against the Son of God. He said, "He that is not with me is against me; and he that gathereth not with me scattereth abroad" (Matthew 12:30).

To be *broad*—all-inclusive of everything and everybody, without discrimination of truth—is equally wrong; for Jesus also said, "No man can serve two masters: for either he will hate the one, and love the other; or else he will hold to the one, and despise the other" (Matthew 6:24a).

There are waters in which to live and survive—waters that are safe, in a *balanced* way; and in this twentieth century we must be careful to honor Biblical balance.

This balance is not in the realm of personality: who would be the criterion of such measurement among men? It is not in intellect, wealth, heredity, environment, personal circumstance, or even in man or man's experience. True balance is found only when man is in his proper place—at the Cross of Calvary—living an uncompromising life (not neutral) and a separated life (not broadminded), with definite, Biblical boundaries.

To avoid the shallows of neutrality, the Christian must take a stand in the center of Biblical fundamentals as expressed in the eternal, inerrant Word of God. We are not talking about the usual "middle-of-the-roader"; he is too broad.

To avoid the deep waters of universal appeal and undefined loves, the Christian must abide in the disciplines and dedications of a separated life. We dare not lose our balance, on the one hand, by omitting the balm of Biblical compassion *for* all men, nor, on the other hand, by omitting the urgencies of becoming involved in a contemporary, universal world *to* all men.

Also, we maintain balance and integrity by witnessing and practicing unschizophrenic unity of genuineness. God spoke of Ephraim as "a cake not turned" (Hosea 7:8b); but the Shulamite (Song of Solomon 6:13) possessed all her teeth—the upper balanced with the lower, clean and white (Song of Solomon 4:2; 6:6); and the Four Living Creatures of Revelation (4:6) were "full of eyes before and behind." What a balance!

Someone might say in the manner of the two dead fish, "To be in the church is to be a Christian; why bother with the particulars and be technical and theological and doctrinal?" The answer is this: it takes Biblical particulars to be Biblically balanced.

As we advance the fundamentals of the Faith, we must always maintain a balance of truth in order to avoid the schizophrenia of the Neo-Pentecostalism; but we must also keep faith with *all* truth that the Bible presents—yes, even in pneumatology.

It has been a particular blessing to me during these years of personal involvement in the controversy with Pentecostals, that the Holy Spirit has been with me. It has led me to a great respect for the Holy Spirit and for His work in my life; and not for the world would I want to do anything to grieve or quench the Holy Spirit. I say this because I would not want anyone to conclude that I am against the Holy Spirit, or that because of the controversy over the heresy that is connected with teachings about Him, He has become a lesser influence in my life. I thank God for the deep concern He has placed in my heart for balance. I have often felt that there was a danger in others I have met who would not maintain a daily communion with God through the power of the Holy Spirit.

9

Biblical Fundamentals and Distinctives

At the World Congress of Fundamentalism which met in Edinburgh, Scotland, in June 1976, the following statement was made to define the position of Fundamentalism in this age of apostasy.

> The Fundamentalist believes in a worldwide testimony to the inspiration, inerrancy, and authority of the Bible, exposing the unscriptural nature of "Neo-Evangelicalism," "Neo-Orthodoxy," "Neo-Pentecostalism," the modern Charismatic movement, and the cults and false religions which characterize the apostasy of our day.[122]

The main burden of Fundamentalism is to be understood upon the Biblical base, proclaiming the absolutes of the central message of the Gospel of the Lord Jesus Christ. No other movement stresses this point more than do the Fundamentalists.

I am not a pedigreed Fundamentalist. Some Fundamentalists, no doubt, would be reluctant to invite my fellowship and ministry. My background probably precludes their understanding of what has happened through the years of my ministry, as well as the position of my dear father as a bishop in a Pentecostal denomination. In the historical sense of the word, my Biblical position lies with Fundamentalism; but I would not give a blanket-endorsement of *all* who identify themselves with Fundamentalists.

Some of my closest friends are spiritual and Biblical giants in Fundamentalism. I do not intend to betray those friendships, nor do I desire to lose them. I shall always treasure one of the greatest invitations of my life-time—that of presenting a paper on "The Funda-mentalist and Neo-Pentecostalism," at the World Congress of Fundamentalists. I believe that there are principles of Fundamentalism which have been compromised and prostituted by the modern movements of Neo-Christianity. Yet I am also aware that there are inherent weaknesses and errors in what Dr. Rodney Bell (Pastor, Tabernacle Baptist Church, Virginia Beach, Virginia) has identified as Pseudo-Fundamentalists. But in the final analysis of man's dealings with the genuine and the counterfeit, there are no movements, no nations, no churches, and no organizations, that are without their hypocrites. But the principles of Fundamentalism stand on a firm Biblical base.

Critics from both sides of the contemporary theologi-cal spectrum speak for and against Fundamentalism. Perry Miller presents one side:

> Here, I would contend, is the beginning of the division which later in the century became the fatal cleavage between what, for short-hand purposes, we may call Fundamentalism and all the many forms of liberalism that found support for a genteel theism in evolution and in the "Higher Criticism." The line of battle was not so clear in 1850 as in 1900 only because the revivalists were still too busy fighting bees while the naturalists were still too vague or too little interested in ideas to lay down an open defiance of the dominant orthodoxy.[123]

That Perry Miller did not see the Biblical base upon which Fundamentalism stood in those early days is obvious. We would take a much more appreciative position in our gratitude toward Fundamentalists' stand for the Christian Faith in the beginning of this twentieth century. They were a courageous group, and to them we are indebted for the Biblical and spiritual success of the Gospel and evangelism. Although many of the Biblical institutions that were started have gone off into some aspect of Neo-Christianity in our time, some remain true, and the Word of God remains steadfast.

Another historian has written about the early days when Fundamentalism assisted the message of the Word of God in a more conservative tone:

> Religion and philosophy in the 19th century were greatly affected by biblical criticism and modernism. Under the leadership of Voltaire, a school of philosophers and critics developed which taught that a large part of the Bible is unaccurate. The most famous of these critics was Renan, who stated in his biographies of Christ that He was but a mere man and that both the New Testament and the Old Testament contained numerous myths and legends.
>
> Both Modernism and socialism resulted in much skepticism among the masses of the people. Consequently, they began to desert church services, and they lost interest in religion.[124]

From a number of Protestant denominations in the early days of the twentieth century came men who have strengthened our hearts in the fight against Modernism. Among them were J. Frank Norris, William B. Riley, Thomas T. Shields, Bob Jones, Sr., L. W. Munhall, H. C. Morrison, Bob Shuler, J. Gresham Machen, Robert Dick Wilson, Harry A. Ironside, Billy Sunday, Harry Rimmer, R. A. Torrey, and many others. These men have left a rich treasure in their sermons, lectures, and Biblical messages.

Dr. George W. Dollar, in *A History of Fundamentalism*, which deals with the history and some of the personalities of Fundamentalism, gives this definition of the movement:

> Historic Fundamentalism is the literal exposition of all the affirmations and attitudes of the Bible and the militant exposure of all non-Biblical affirmations and attitudes.[125]

No one would be more quick to react about the Fundamentalists than those within Fundamentalism. I have heard, on a number of public and private occasions, their

own acknowledgment of certain inconsistencies and
weaknesses. It should be remembered, too, that the media
quite often, and erroneously so, identifies certain sects,
such as the Moonies, with Fundamentalism.

Plagued But Panoplied Fundamentalists

The Great Awakening of 1734-1742, in which God used
Jonathan Edwards and George Whitefield; the Great
Awakening of 1800-1801, particularly in Virginia and
Kentucky; and the Great Awakening of 1857-1859 were
sparked from the living realities of the Word of God.

But the nineteenth century closed, and the twentieth
century began, with a foe that was met fully from the
Biblical base by only the Fundamentalists. Some of the
first-generation Pentecostals were on the Biblical base,
though unfortunately, they did not seem to discern their
role in taking a full stand against Formalism, Liberalism,
and Modernism. It was in this climate that Fundamentalism stood in its greatest hour.

Fundamentalists acknowledged the liberty of the
Biblical distinctives of the individual Christian, but
shared affinities for those distinctives only as they were
claimed from the Word of God, with a militant, separated
position. The plea of the Fundamentalist was for
centrality of truth—and rightly so, for the Christian must
always maintain integrity in this matter of central and
essential faith and truth as presented through the Gospel
of the Lord Jesus Christ.

Although beset by many foes and often misunderstood in their aggressive and militant manner, Fundamentalists have panoplied themselves for the warfare
that plagues modern church history. They are strong for
the inerrancy and authority of the Scriptures, as well as
for the preservation of Biblical inspiration. They affirm,
espouse, and defend—vehemently at times— the doctrine
of the Trinity, the incarnation and Virgin Birth of the
Lord Jesus, the substitutionary atonement, the Bodily
resurrection, the ascension, the Second Coming of Christ,
the New Birth, and the resurrection of both the saints and

the wicked; and they expose, and separate from, all ecclesiastical or other denials of the Faith. They are a hearty group of soldiers, though not free of problems from within as from foes without. We need to earnestly pray that all Fundamentalists will have an awakening of spiritual discernment to the need of the hour. Because they are undergoing certain weaknesses and internal change, we need to discern among the Fundamentalists those who with this change will lose the spirit and power of Christ.

Pertinent to this discussion are some remarks which Dr. Bob Jones III, president of Bob Jones University, made at the University's fiftieth anniversary. In essence, Dr. Bob III, said:

> From within Fundamentalism there is taking place a restructuring which I feel is harmful to the cause. This departure will lead to doctrinal and directional errors in Christ's Church, for it will be a departure from Biblical Fundamentalism. I think the pressures of the age—the commercialism of the age—are largely responsible for this condition. There is the idea that as long as soulwinning is taking place, it does not matter what methods we use to arrive at success. I fear that if the Lord tarries, the prevailing idea that the end justifies the means will destroy Fundamentalism as we know it. I assume that the practice stems from good motives on the part of men who want to see souls saved; but they have weakened the structure of Bible allegiance. They have made soulwinning the ultimate criterion for all our labors, when actually the bringing of glory to Jesus Christ is the main objective of our labors. If we obey Him in witnessing but disobey Him in the method, we have dishonored Him.[126]

Dr. Bob III, further commented on the foes without, and the need of certain Biblical distinctives within the people of God:

> Then, of course, there are winds blowing from outside Bible Christianity that could very easily get this school off course. There is the fierce opposition of a hostile government. When this school was given birth by God, the government was friendly to Bible Christianity. That is no

longer true. Today we are persecuted by a socialistic, humanistic, secularistic government that has no place for a school of this type. This does not mean that we are slaves to tradition. It means that we are slaves to Bible authority and completely subject to what we know to be the will of God. Beyond this, there is plenty of room for advancement and changes—academic changes, or whatever, but not foundational changes. Fidelity, not originality, is the purpose to which I believe I have been called.

Each man's ministry—his preparation for it, his actual work, and his particular wisdom in carrying it out—is individualistic. To one was committed the founding, to the next the burden of culturally establishing the school, and to the present president the task of continuing the University on course. But the three ministries marvelously combine and overlap to make one continuous contribution stretching over half a century... Each man, ruled over by an all-wise Creator as to his natural inclinations, was given a larger task than anyone could do without divine enabling.[127]

Early Pentecostalism and Fundamentalism

Not all Pentecostals will acknowledge a relationship with Fundamentalism at the beginning of this century. As we have already commented, first-generation Pentecostals at the beginning of this century often stood upon the Biblical base in a minority, but they identified with the Biblical fundamentals.

Charles W. Conn, historian of the Church of God, Cleveland, Tennessee, sets forth this fact in his newly revised and updated history of his denomination. Describing the immediate condition surrounding the birth of his Pentecostal denomination, which is the oldest Pentecostal denomination in the world, he says:

Everywhere the Church became the scene of a struggle. Darwin's theory of evolution became one of the most divisive lines of combat. Sophistry replaced theology. The thought of Kant, Emerson, Newman, Voltaire, Schleiermacher, Carlyle, and a confusion of theologians, philosophies, and poets came to exert a greater influence on many a fashionable pulpit than did the Word of God.

The Bible was largely forgotten. This hastened a deterioration of the evangelical life of the Church.[128]

This worsening of religion distressed many earnest Christians who found the new liberalism unpalatable. They withdrew from the churches and worshiped in small groups of kindred believers. A revival of modest proportions was born. Holiness groups—more than a score of them—gradually appeared on the American scene.[129]

Splinterings, separations, and schisms were very evident in Protestantism between 1865 to 1925. They should be, in many cases, known as separatists, biblicists, or nonconformists rather than understood that early as pentecostals ... The Church of God dates back to 1884-86, known then as the Christian Union, organized in Monroe County, Tennessee, led by Richard G. Spurling, with eight members; later, in 1896, joining a group under the leadership of W. F. Bryant, in Cherokee County, North Carolina.[130]

Mr. Conn should be identified as a *second-generation* Pentecostal and although he associates his denomination with Fundamentalism sympathies, we must admit that he, personally, implies affinity for the Charismatic movement:

If the Pentecostal Movement was born in a time of theological tempest—Modernism versus Fundamentalism—it has thrived in the midst of an ascending apostasy . . . .

At no time have the Pentecostal people regarded themselves as other than simple orthodox Christian believers. Their experience is merely a deeper blessing in their Christian lives; it does not supplant or supercede the gospel of Jesus Christ as the Son of God. The Pentecostal claim of being Christian is no hollow pretense, for Christ is accepted literally as He is represented in the Word of God; He is sovereign Lord, Saviour, Redeemer and King of all the earth. . . .

Despite the sincere and simplistic faith of Pentecostals, until about mid-century they were widely disdained and derided. At mid-century, however, the Pentecostal Movement gained a belated intellectual respectability. An article by Dr. Henry P. Van Dusen in the *Christian Century* in 1955 was typical of this new ice-breaking respect and acceptance.

As if on cue, other writers began to give credence to, and other periodicals, both religious and secular, focused attention upon, the Pentecostal Movement. Another dramatic development of the 1950's, encouraged by the newly hospitable climate and a Pentecostal persistence, was an acceptance of the Pentecostal experience in numerous older denominations. Among Baptists, Methodists, Presbyterians, and even Episcopalians and Catholics, there was a sudden awareness that the experience claimed by the Pentecostals had been true all along. These Spirit-filled believers, called "Charismatics" because the Greek word for spiritual gifts is *charisma,* constituted a parallel body of Pentecostal believers.

With this, the Pentecostal purpose came full circle; the place of the Pentecostal Movement was as permanent in the Christian world as its impact had been vital to it.

From the outset the Church of God was on the cutting edge of the Pentecostal Awakening.[131]

I know of no denominational leader of any Pentecostal denomination of any consequence that has taken an open and definite stand *against* the Classical Pentecostal, Neo-Pentecostal, or Roman Catholic Charismatic positions. Neither do I know of any independent Pentecostal evangelist, or personality of any consequence, who has denounced the heresy and the apostasy of these movements. To me, this is a sad commentary of the departure of Pentecostal leaderships away from the Biblical base, and they do not seem to discern what is happening to their churches in the apostasy.

The Panoply of Scripture

In this twentieth century, each of us must remember his role as a fortified defender of the Faith. We are obligated to restrain that which does not exalt Jesus Christ, and we are to perform this in the Truth of the Holy Spirit and in the Spirit of the Truth.

There are at least seven principles which often are forgotten or ignored in our day, but which must be revived and remembered in mind and heart as we proceed through this apostasy.

First, there is the Trinity. We must not forget the importance of the triune God. Nowhere in the Bible is God the Father commanded to do anything. He is the Commander. Even the Christ of God and the Holy Spirit of God proceed from the Father. Jesus brings the Gospel into the world like a gunshot and bomb to explode the preponderance of sin and Satan. The Holy Spirit ignites this ammunition in the strongholds of Satan and sin and error. In our understanding of this matter, we must maintain a consistency. We cannot afford a schizophrenic attitude with regard to the Trinity; we must keep our hearts right with God in the Third Heaven; we must arm our hearts and minds with the Gospel Message of the Word of God, and we must go forth in the power and demonstration of the Holy Spirit to attack the center of the target in the camps of the enemy.

Second, each of us has an appointment in the will of God. Like Job, some of us will be called upon by God to actually become a *battlefield,* and suffer special controversy as a man of contention in the earth. We must accept this appointment as a privilege and must fight in good spirit and with dignity. There must be no moaning or groaning, or feeling sorry for ourselves. If we lose our lives in the battle, it will not be the church, the enemy, or the movement that is killing us; we will be dying to the glory of the Name of Jesus. Few Christians will allow God to take such complete charge of them that the entire life becomes a battlefield for the enemy in special sufferings, reproaches, and controversies. But thank God, certain men in our time are being used of God in this special place of contention; and when the Sovereign Father places men in this position, they should stand grandly—without fear, favor, compromise, or conformity—and lean solely on the authority of the Word of God, regardless of personal cost. Jeremiah was a man of "contention" in the earth (Jeremiah 15:10). God, the Commander, may not inform you that you have been appointed as a battlefield, any more than He informed Job; but you must stand without fear or further need of knowledge simply because your life is under the authority and will of God through His Word.

Third, you may be called to be a warrior. If you are not a battlefield, you may be selected as a *warrior,* which means that you will be placed on the front line of the battlefield. No longer do you serve coffee and doughnuts behind the lines, as a Red Cross aide would do. Too many Christians *know* where they ought to be in this warfare of the twentieth century, but they deliberately seek the pleasure resorts in retreats away from prayer and Bible study, soulwinning, and militant action against sin and error. If the Commander has not set you forth as a battlefield, be willing to stand at His appointed place on His battlefield and for His Word.

Fourth, you must be a weapon. If you are not a battlefield or a warrior, you must be a *weapon.* There is no other position open. To you it is given to support the means, the methods, the missions, and the faithful men who are the Lord's battlefield and warriors.

No one can afford to watch this battle from the bleachers or from a tree. Even our children, by their obedience and training in the home, must share in this warfare. Some of you will be chosen to occupy unique positions of influence and stewardship of money for the warfare against the enemy. Though sometimes hard to find, there are evangelists, schools, churches, and organizations, which we must support with our prayers and our means. You *must* be a weapon; you *must* seek out the warriors; you *must* support the cause of the battle and know where the battlefields are.

As time passes, more and more suspicion and scandal will be directed against Godly men. Do not believe these false accusations. Observe the true people of God. Seek them out! Do not allow anyone to "talk you out of" a Bible preacher and friend. Let their enemies be your enemies. Make it clear that you stand *with* them. Follow the man who is following God in truth. He is recognizable by his message and his daily character.

When men follow such men as Pike, Graham, Roberts, or others of that fellowship, the world commends them; but let a solid Christian follow a name identified against the apostasy, and he is declared a fool. This age is brainwashed by a neo-leader, new ecumenism, a renewal, or an "awakening"; and they call it unity. But let a man dare to be different and gain a group to assist in that difference, and they call it brainwashing. They forget that brainwashing is usually a majority matter, and that the person who *really thinks* and *touches* God, individually, is a minority matter. Paul spoke of being delivered from "people" as well as from sin (Acts 26:17-18).

Allow yourself to become totally identified with the battlefield, the warrior, and the weapon. Make your fellowships and friendships according to the Army of the Lord; do not patronize the enemy and his strongholds. Give yourself to prayer, Bible study, witnessing, and the assembly of the saints who live on the Biblical base. Seek sinners to accept the free gift of eternal life in Christ Jesus, and enlist them in the cause of Christ. Do not become entangled with the world; but do not be an isolationist, either. In your service to the King you must be free of unholy entanglements. Do not be afraid to be identified with the war and the warrior of the Lord. Find yourself in the Whole Vision. Are you presently in the place of the *prime* vision, are you *preparing* for the prime vision, are you a part of the *potential* vision, or are you in the *past* vision? God needs the *whole* vision!

Fifth, you must remember what fundamentals are necessary in this warfare. We must give priority to the Blood of the Lord Jesus, and to the inerrancy and authority of the Bible. We must have the Holy Spirit in our lives—yea, not just one baptism, but many, many infillings of the Holy Spirit. We are like people from another world who, in a holy way, have invaded the earth to establish beachheads and strongholds against the enemy. We cannot do this in our own strength. We must have the abiding presence of the Holy Spirit in all battles.

In spite of the fact that the Neo-Pentecostals have abused and exceeded the true works and workings of the Holy Spirit, we must not abuse Him. They do not have the Spirit of God; they have the spirit of error. This condition will increase in the coming days, for there is no way to save the world. Individual souls are important. We must not forget the individual—even the Pentecostal individual, for some Pentecostals are really *hungering* for truth.

Sixth, we must be sure that we identify the enemy in these days. There are *human personalities* that must be identified and separated from in crusades, conferences, dialogue, and public witness. But the enemy is more than a human personality. Forces greater than man are inspiring and empowering the various personalities of the apostasy. In Ephesians 6:12 the Apostle Paul identifies our enemies as more than "flesh and blood." He labels them spiritual forces.

We wrestle against *principalities.* In Satan's kingdom princes preside over certain provinces. There are evil spirits whose special work is to influence the entire range of men and things connected with earthly governments.

We wrestle against *powers.* There exists a Satanic power that is different or separate from principalities. This power involves evil spirits of energy and force that attack feelings and imagination. They stir people in an excited way to commit terrible sins, as well as inspire deceptive errors; to bring hate while speaking of love; to betray and quarrel; and to be fraudulent or dishonest or slanderous. Often these powers conceal themselves in the midst of would-be spiritual claims and erroneous claims of supernatural powers above the promise of the Word of God. At the root, of course, is the flesh; but it is under the guise of *deeper* things claimed from the Lord.

Again, we wrestle with *rulers of darkness of this age.* The Greek word emphasizes *age* rather than *world.* These rulers of darkness manage superstition, witchcraft, fortune-telling, heresy, ignorance, and all sorts of stupidity, self conceit, and spiritual blindness. There are many brands and breeds of this force, and there is a common bond in parallel areas such as signs, foolish dreams, voices, whimsical impressions, and visionary but Satanic insights.

Finally, we wrestle with *wicked spirits in heavenly places*. "High places" or "heavenly places" and "spiritual wickedness" or "wicked spirits" seem impersonal; but these wicked spirits are personalities who can and do act upon other persons. They are dangerous, and should be regarded as spiritual wickedness. There are religious demons whose special work is from "heavenly places." These demons intrude into the highest religious experiences and deal with deep spiritual truth, in counterfeit, seeking, through fleshly and carnal claims, to pervert truth into error. They change themselves into angels of light (II Corinthians 11:13-15), hoping to trap people into following their suggestions under the impression that they are following the Holy Spirit. There are demons who could have joined the church, professed religion and holiness, and could have received marvelous dreams, visions, ecstasies, prophecies, gifts, demonstrations; yet their whole aim is to attack the most lofty and spiritual hopes of a person by counterfeiting a genuine truth. If some demons fail to make a man entirely unholy, others try to make him feel that he is super-holy. Men are puffed up with self-righteous fancy of being great saints beyond the authority of the Word of God, believing that they are prophets of a new order, ordained of the Lord. They regard themselves as "special pets and partners of God" who have been sent to touch an age and the mass through psychic and spiritual means. They almost always believe that the world is theirs to exploit and use; but they are void of that separation from the age that results from the true sanctification of the Blood of Jesus to deliver a soul from destruction.

Seventh, the Christian will receive wounds. We must learn to live gracefully with our wounds. Bitterness in the soul short-circuits effective warfare. We must fight joyously! We must live with a sword in our hand, a dream in our eye, a word in our ear, and a song in our heart. Our wounds must be badges of valor, not marks of disgrace or overzealous heroism.

The Shulamite in the Song of Solomon reveals certain scars: She was black from her life in the sun, she faced the angry faces of the daughters of Jerusalem, and she lived among thorns (cf. 1:5-6 and 2:2). She lived in the cracks of the rocks (2:14). She suffered sleepless nights for her Solomon (3:1). She fought in the chariot of her Warrior (3:7-8). She knew the suffering of the mountain of myrrh and the hill of frankincense (4:6). She faced the lions' dens and the mountains of the leopards (4:8). She allowed the north wind to break up her garden (4:16). She arose to serve her King, although the myrrh of suffering came upon her hand from the handles of the lock (5:4-6). The false watchman of ecclesiastical leaderships smote her, wounded her, and tore away the sacred veil of her face (5:7). She is portrayed as beautiful as Tirzah and as comely as Jerusalem, but also as terrible as an "army with banners" (6:4).

Charismatics and Their Compartments

There is another aspect of the Charismatic emphasis that should disturb the Christian. Emphasis upon the glossolalia and the gifts of the Holy Spirit compartmentalize the Christian into thinking that "spiritual experience" is the greatest experience of life. This truncates the Christian's life away from other equal areas where Christ desires to manifest Himself. This is an important observation. As we have mentioned earlier, Dr. Bob Jones, Sr., founder of Bob Jones University, emphasized that there is no difference between the sacred and secular parts of a Christian's life.

One of the main errors among the Charismatics involves this very issue. The Bible does not teach that the "spiritual" phenomenon of the "glossolalia" and the "gifts" are more sacred or spiritual than other areas of a Christian's life. It is a fallacy to believe that an entire life of praying or singing or praising would be greater than a life of witnessing, Bible reading, or working. The

Christian is to know Christ in every area of life. The *manifestations* of the Holy Spirit are not greater than the *abiding presence* of the Holy Spirit. The presence of God is the presence of God, whether it is simply abiding or manifesting itself. We should not make a distinction between the blessedness of the Christian experience in the closet of spiritual benefits and the necessity of the Christian experience in the public concourse of life.

Throughout my life I have observed this principle: Most Pentecostals of every generation in this century tend to regard themselves as more spiritual when at an altar they are experiencing some manifestation of a supernatural nature, than when they are standing in the vestibule of the church after the prayer is over. Many persons have been observed as "under the power"; yet when someone would touch them on the shoulder and say, "Here is your coke from the church canteen," the "power" would quickly subside and the coke would be consumed. I contend that persons who earnestly pray before God do not experience such shallow thought; and I have heard many "old timers" decry this surface attitude.

In connection with the compartments of our lives, I present these Biblical principles:

> Hear, O Israel: The Lord our God is one Lord: And thou shalt love the Lord thy God with all thine heart, and with all thy soul, and with all thy might (Deuteronomy 6:4, 5).

> And whatsoever ye do in word or deed, do all in the name of the Lord Jesus, giving thanks to God and the Father by him (Colossians 3:17).

> Finally, brethren, whatsoever things are true, whatsoever things are honest, whatsoever things are just, whatsoever things are pure, whatsoever things are lovely, whatsoever things are of good report; if there be any virtue, and if there be any praise, think on these things (Philippians 4:8).

This principle could be extended into many other Scriptures which clearly set forth the fact that the Lord Jesus should fill every area of our lives—soul, mind, body, heart, might, art, science, occupation, recreation, study, prayer, home, community, church, nation, and all things that Christ has given to us to enjoy (I Timothy 6:17).

The entire life of the Christian should be spiritual. The Holy Spirit touches man's hands at the workman's bench just as wonderfully as He touches man's tongue of praise. The *grit* of life and the *gifts* of the Spirit are equally important. The Charismatic lives on a narrow edge.

This reminds me of the rather strange text of Isaiah 28:20: "For the bed is shorter than that a man can stretch himself on it: and the covering narrower than that he can wrap himself in it." These words were spoken to Ephraim in a warning to Judah in the matter of Israel's impending captivity by the Assyrians. God intended to put it in the language of this text that man should have a longer bed and a wider blanket. It is the overhang of the blanket that secures the warmth of the sleeper. God could give to a man an extra cushion to life through a sanctified sense of humor without its deteriorating into frivolity; He could also give him the strength of anger without its becoming wrath. To the Christian on the Biblical base, all of life is sacred and spiritual.

When as a young Christian I would read the Bible, the Devil would suggest that I should be praying. As I prayed, he would suggest that I should be reading the Bible. He wanted to hinder my Bible reading and prayer by getting me torn between them so that I would not accomplish either. Also the Devil was hindering my arising from the reading-seat and the praying-knees to go out into a world and witness with my walking-feet.

We need to exalt the Lord Jesus Christ in *all* that we do, whatever it might be. The Charismatics get stuck in the "sticky" error of the gifts, causing the harmony of the entire life to be aborted by the "stuck-song-note" of their glossolalia. They truncate the Christian life to a narrow and somewhat selfish subjectivism of emotional experience. Once again, the problem is that they do not build on the Bible base.

I know of nothing that better illustrates this compartmentalizing by the Charismatics than the fact that they leave Christ out of their music. There is that background accompaniment of the contemporary beat of "rock" and "gospel rock." There is an apparent lack of consecration and spirituality, speaking from a Biblical sense, in their art, in their manner of dress, and in other areas of Christian culture. Lifestyles and carnal identities are obvious among them. I think that it is necessary to say that when you see the Oral Roberts' Show on television, it is not a presentation of the Lord Jesus upon the Biblical base; it is a worldly product of modern dress and song. There simply is not the manifestation of the Holy Spirit in these things; and it amazes me that the Charismatics speak so loftily of the gifts and the glossolalia and super-spiritualities and yet present such a cheap manifestation of the Holy Spirit in their contemporary culture and lifestyles. Being "loose," they present a worldly gospel.

In my opinion, Dr. Frank Garlock presents a more Biblical presentation of Christian music on the Biblical base than any Christian musician and teacher in this generation. It would be profitable for everyone to read his writings, attend his seminars, and prayerfully consider what he is saying to us at this time with regard to church music versus rock music.[132] Dr. Garlock is from an early Pentecostal background, which makes his presentation of Christian music more meaningful to me; for in the early Pentecostal days, the Stamps-Baxter type of music was almost the trademark of Pentecostal music. (To be fair, I must admit that some groups used the Rodeheaver Hymnal and other pieces of music more in keeping with the Biblical spirit.) But even the old Stamps-Baxter songs, which were sung better by some people than by others, have mutated further into the rock beat; and the Charismatics carry this sound wherever they go. Most of them do not consider the matter of culture as important. This is the point: the compartmentalizing of the Holy Spirit in the so-called *spirit-realm* of the Christian and the absence of the Holy Spirit in the *art-music-realm* is really ridiculous. It would be like having the Holy Spirit in your prayer life, but not in your married life, or whatever. He desires to be in the whole life—in everything we are and in everything we do. I have heard many persons claim that the Holy Spirit taught them to play the piano or guitar, or taught them to sing. I listened to the music and concluded that it was an insult to the Holy Spirit to say that He had taught them. If we learn to play the piano or sing, we will have to take the long, hard way—instruction and practice. The Holy Spirit is the Custodian of the laws of music in the universe, and He will assist us in our instruction and practice. But far too much emphasis has been given to the Holy Spirit in the Charismatic manner and less emphasis to Christ in other compartments of the Christian life. We do not mean to imply that the Holy Spirit is not urgently needed in these areas; we are simply stating that He does not desire that we elevate His work in one area of life over His work in another.

I must gratefully acknowledge Dr. Francis A. Schaeffer who, in his many volumes, and as much as anyone in this century, has emphasized Christ in our culture. His most recent work has been a special blessing to me. Entitled *How Should We Then Live?* it represents the largest and strongest of his writings with regard to this particular emphasis. I must admit that as I have read his voluminous works and attended his seminar, I have been amazed at his failure to point out the positive and personal need of Biblical separation as his many premises demand. To me, Dr. Schaeffer assumes that all in his audience are Christians. He seems to have the usual Neo-Evangelical approach to the practical outworking of the Biblical orthodoxy without Biblical orthopraxy. Judging from his seminars there is ample room for this criticism. His son, Franky, Jr., adopts an even less practical approach of Biblical separation than does his father.[133]

Richard S. Taylor, in *A Return to Christian Culture*, equally presents "the cult of the slob."[134] There is much that needs to be said concerning the power of the Holy Spirit's manifesting Himself in music, dress, and the matter of ethics. Actually our society needs a total revival of Christ, character, and culture.

It seems imperative that we recognize the three greatest needs of spiritual discernment and the three matters that will determine much of the future outcome of public evangelicalism. They are these: (1) The discernment of the need for a totalitarian authority on the Biblical base; (2) the discernment of the need for a sound Biblical separation of practical Christian living on that Biblical base; and (3) the discernment of the condition of our time, as it involves the Biblical announcement of the Apostasy, rather than a so-called Holy Ghost Awakening, as the Charismatics claim.

Without doubt, the future will be filled with the need of these spiritual discernments; and if the future outcome is to be true repentance and Godliness, much depends on the Christian's attitude and understanding of these three areas.

10

Theology of the Deeper Life

There remains a singular obligation to our subject. It could be abbreviated in one sentence: *God intended Christian character, not Pentecostal Charismatics.* This concerns the deeper life of the Christian and has nothing at all to do with the meaning of the Deeper Life Movement associated with Robert Pearsall Smith and his wife, Hannah Whitall Smith, which appeared on the religious scene between 1851 and 1911. We are simply urging the Scriptural injunctions to "take root downward, and bear fruit upward" (Isaiah 37:31), to glorify and exalt the Name of Jesus. Our use of the phrase is synonymous with Christian character.

The search for spiritual Charismatics leads a person on a different road than does the search for Christian and Godly character. No matter whether you pursue the search into the future or into the past, Charismatics and character are on different roads.

Pentecostal historians have searched through history to give credence to their present, experiential search for Charismatics.

Some Pentecostals view the modern Charismatic movement as linked in the past to the Methodist movement and Aldersgate; racial movements and Azusa Street; Europe, North America, and members of the Catholic Apostolic Church; "Irvingism"; Mary Campbell in Fernicarry, Scotland; Agnes Ozman, a student at Bethel Bible School, Topeka, Kansas; Emil Brunner and his "pneumatic factor"; Timothy Merritt, Phoebe Palmer, Sarah Lankford, Charles G. Finney, and Asa Mahan, of the Oberlin School; A. J. Gordon; D. L. Moody, Keswick and Northfield; Dr. Charles Cullis, an Episcopalian; Arthur T. Pierson, a Presbyterian; S. B. Shaw, C. W. Ruth, Dr. Asbury Lowrey, Ralph C. Horner, R. A. Torrey, Phineas Bresee; "some evidence of influence from early Fundamentalism in the forming of the Pentecostal tradition"; and a host of other influences from Unitarian, Calvinistic, and Arminian background.[135]

The above variety of speculations presupposes that God was endeavoring to bring to the world the Charismatic phenomena and that all these individuals and movements were a part of His final plan in bringing the present Charismatic movement.

This presupposition and conclusion is presumptuous and erroneous. Any true longing in the heart of God's people during these periods of history—longing which was Scriptural and Holy Spirit inspired—was simply the honorable hungering of a deeper life in Christ Jesus, not the hunger for a deeper life in the supernatural phenomena of the error of the Charismatics. The quest of the true believer has always been that of a basic Christian purity and piety in the Lord and in His Word. The Holy Spirit has always desired to do a work of glorifying Christ in the Christian's life, and all of God's true saints in church history have been a part of that search which is presented in the Bible, God's Holy Word.

Theological Shifts

We have already observed that during the Protestant Reformation there was an exegetical and expositional shift in the interpretation of Scripture to the *Biblical fundamentals*. John Calvin is recognized as the father of Biblical exegesis as we know it today, and these Biblical fundamentals centered on the authority of Scripture and the work of Jesus Christ in the doctrine of justification by faith. The Reformation cleared the air, bringing the greatest—though not perfect—demonstration of the influence of Christian Faith that we have in church history. Biblical fundamentals, on the Biblical base, were set forth in both the secular and the sacred world, and for a number of years we observed a tremendous force throughout the world. Like a great light and hope, evangelical evangelism was born and shed abroad in the land. Biblical fundamentals were proclaimed and settled as the foundation touchstone of the Christian Faith, and that influence remains until this very hour.

Biblical fundamentals brought a second search of soul for *Biblical distinctives* of a truly deeper life in Christ Jesus, our Lord. There was nothing wrong with this. Jesus had saved; but He was also Lord. There are not two different kinds of Christians—one under Christ as *Saviour*, and the other under Christ as *Lord*; both are under Christ the Lord. This opened up the lofty search for not only the work of Christ *for* us, but also the work of the Holy Spirit *in* us. This was not wrong; it was right and spiritual.

This *second* exegetical and theological shift came to a deep concern in John Wesley; or, to say the least, in Wesley we see the struggle not only for the fundamental of justification by faith in the essential of the New Birth, but also the *distinctive* which involved "holiness," "Christian perfection" and "perfect love,"—or in a more intimate phrase, the "burning heart experience." Many have concluded that Wesley saw only the New Birth; others feel that his hunger was so intense for the deeper life that his record emphasizes deeper life more than it emphasizes the time and place of conversion. No matter how it might be appraised, Wesley sought a deeper life in Christ Jesus, and he sought it on the basis of grace and the Biblical base.

This is not to say that Luther, Calvin, and others had not dealt with the deeper life of a Christian, but that a definite theological shift had not come about in the public and preached Gospel as it did during the days of Wesley.

The Wesley movement definitely crystallized this Biblical shift to a great awareness of the deeper life theology of the Bible, and it affected the music as well as the message.

When we look back across history, we observe in this matter of a practical, deeper life theology a mass of all-inclusive subjects. It involved so much that it would be impossible to discuss all the facets of the observation. It would involve law and grace, antinomianism and perfectionism, positional and experiential sanctification, the finished work and the second work, liberty and legalism, Christian perfection and sinless perfection, piety and self-righteousness, purity and power, prayer and service, praise and discouragement, temptation and sin, purity and maturity, salvation and rewards, faith and assurance, peace of heart and peace of mind, faith and works, theology and practice, virtue and fruit, being and doing, charity and character, and literally hundreds of other comparisons and contrasts.

The conclusion to this matter involves a final question: "Why has there been another shift, and this time to Charismatics?" The answer must first be simply stated. There has been a move away from the Biblical base, and an influence of apostasy. There has been a departure from the Biblical fundamentals, leaving in its wake an apostasy in the land.

The love for Biblical fundamentals having ceased in many churches, pulpits, and seminaries, there can be no honorable search for Biblical distinctives. Modern Pentecostal movements are endeavoring to talk about Biblical distinctives of certain ideas of spirituality and spiritualities without being devoted to the inerrant authority of the Word of God. First, their departure was *from* the Bible. Today they are hanging their distinctives on skyhooks that are attached to nebulous clouds. They are building the one-hundredth story of their building while omitting the foundation and the first ninety-nine stories. This *sounds* lofty and spiritual. It is untenable, however, for it does not stand on the Bible! Therefore, it cannot meet the need and hunger of that which effected

previous revivals in history and that led to a deeper life
under the Lordship of Christ.

Working Out the Theology of the Deeper Life

It may well be that we have not worked out the Biblical
distinctives upon the Biblical base as we should have
done in history and during this twentieth century. We
who are anchored in the inerrancy and authority of the
Scriptures have had to spend so much time and concern
with evangelism and apologetics that we may have
neglected to follow through, personally, as witnesses,
evangelists, ministers, and teachers—leaving a dearth in
our time of genuine Godliness and spirituality. In some
quarters evangelism is suffering under a cheap "decision" that is urged without cost of discipleship. I have
deep concern in my own life about deep spirituality in a
time of dead orthodoxy. I need wisdom in a time of unwise
zeals. I need Godliness in a time of ungodliness, and
character in a time of Charismatics.

It is often my prayer that I might be adequately
prepared to proclaim the true spirituality of the Christian
life. Evangelism needs deeper life. Stewardship needs a
more pious attitude toward the Master. And ministers
need a stronger soul and spirit in their ministries. We
cannot afford to take the attitude that because the
Charismatics have dared to announce a deeper life
without the Biblical base, we shall ignore the deeper life
on the Biblical base. I do not make an unreserved
appropriation of Wesley, for his influence brought the
dreaded doctrine of eradication. But I do appreciate and
share his desire for a burning heart and an experiential
outworking of sanctification subsequent to the New
Birth, when assurance of salvation and the power of the
Holy Spirit effect victory over sin and anointing for
soulwinning that I need. At this point, there is a sense in
which it is impossible to go back to find the answer to our
present need and the error of the time.

Character, Not Charismatics

A term meets the need of the times and announces the hope of the lofty desires based on the Bible. That term is *Christian character.*

Everyone is born with a *disposition* mixed with the heredity of moral pollution and family distinctiveness. After the child is born, the age in which he lives endeavors to weave around him a certain *personality.* This comes about when the individual conforms to an age. Frequently the uniqueness of his depraved disposition is swallowed up in the current vogue of the personality, style, mood, error, and spirit of the age.

God has an entirely different purpose in His will for the Christian. The pollution of Adam, the heredity of disposition, and the personality of an age are to give way to the transforming power of the New Birth in separation, purity, power, prayer, Godliness, and maturity that reaches fruition in Christian character. One of the greatest needs of the twentieth century is character. Too many professing Christians fail to manifest consistency, loyalty, trustworthiness, love, determination, ethics, prayer, honesty, purity, humility, obedience, assurance, victory, honor, integrity, boldness, strength, or character.

What would be a workable definition of Christian character? To me Christian character is a life of thoughts, attitudes, acts, habits, and practices which are dominated by the principles of the Word of God, which are brought into the life through the miracle of the New Birth, and which seek to exalt the Lord Jesus Christ in all things.

One of the most important words to be associated with character is the word *separation.* We are surprised to see in the twentieth century one who is really living on the Biblical base with Biblical separation. We are not talking about isolation; that is total separation. We are not talking about synthesis and dialogue; that is total integration. We are talking about Biblical separation: *in* the world without being *of* the world; winning souls without sacrificing principle; evangelistic outreach

without backsliding inroads; successful increase without
spiritual decrease; steadfast orthodoxy without inconsistent orthopraxy; statistics with honor rather than a
mere bus ministry with grandeur; crusades to reach all
sinners, but without compromise with error; progress
without compromise; change without conformity; and
character without hypocrisy.

The etymology of *holiness* and *sanctification* in the
Hebrew and the Greek is rooted in *separation*. It involves
more than separation; there are positive overtones of
cleansing and consecration. Nevertheless, one cannot
build cleansing and consecration without the foundational truth of separation.

One of the largest groups of words in the Old
Testament is the Hebrew root of three radicals KDSH.
This word and its accompanying cognates are most
commonly translated "holiness." The fact that it occurs
more than 830 times signifies importance. Note its
relationships:

1. The word is believed to be rooted in an Assyrian
word, *kuddusu,* meaning "bright," or "clear."

2. It is believed that it is clearly rooted in a Semitic
word (QDSH), meaning "to cut off," or "separate."

3. It is also similar in meaning to the term *kabod,*
meaning "glory," "honor," and "weight," and is the
opposite of *chol,* meaning "common," or "profane."

4. It is linked with "purity," "new," "fresh," and
"pure."

In the New Testament, the Greek *hagios* seems to
indicate "to hallow" (Matthew 6:9; I Peter 3:15; Luke 11:2);
to separate or dedicate to God (I Corinthians 1:2; I
Timothy 4:5; Hebrews 2:11; 10:29); to consecrate (John
10:36; 17:19); sanctification (Matthew 23:17; I Thessalonians 4:3); or, cleanse (John 17:17; Ephesians 5:26; I
Thessalonians 5:23). Its etymology is hard to find,
though it seems to come from *hagei,* meaning, "no
ground"; therefore, separation from the ground is
indicated. But the great root of the words lies in the singular meaning of separation, without which there can

be no hope of cleansing, consecration, and holiness.

Another important word in Christian character is *discernment.* Equal to lack of separation among Christians is the lack of spiritual discernment. We have mentioned this before and repeat it only for emphasis. People who are filled with the Holy Spirit must *see.* People with Christian character must have a spiritual discernment of the Bible and of the times in which they live. Christ will be truly exalted only when we follow Biblical separation and realize a keen sense of spiritual discernment.

A Line of Demarcation is Being Drawn

In our time we can expect to see the Lord draw a line of demarcation between the counterfeit and the genuine with regard to the Christian and the deeper life. This line will be a work of the sovereign God. Of course, we must see the matter and yield to the Holy Spirit, but it will be a work of God as well.

There are at least seven areas, seven priority emphases, in which a work is already being done by the Holy Spirit in this matter:

1. A total emphasis upon the authority of the Bible.

2. A loyalty to the fundamentals of the Bible above other claims.

3. A practice of Biblical separation in the matter of crusades and Christian living.

4. A manifested difference in the music used in worship and evangelism.

5. An obvious distinction in the appearance and dress of the Christian.

6. A more private and less conspicuous demonstration of prayer, worship, and communion with God.

7. A more careful manifestation of Biblical praise in view of the erroneous glossolalia, with a greater emphasis upon preaching.

We should not be surprised if the Holy Spirit furthers His manifestation of wisdom to us as more and more we

need to know what would exalt Christ during this time of
Apostasy. There will be a definite difference between the
true people of God and the growing masses toward Neo-
Christianity.

Principles That Bring the Deeper Life

There are certain principles without which there can
be no deeper life in Christ. These, of course, presuppose
the reality of Biblical authority and the New Birth in the
heart (I Corinthians 2:14). We shall enumerate twelve of
them:

First, note the centrality of the Christ.   Seven items
in the Old Testament were extremely precious to the Jew.
They were the *name* of God (Exodus 20:7; Leviticus 24:11);
the *law* of God (Exodus 20:18-20; Numbers 15:32-36); the
high priest of God (II Chronicles 26:14-21); the *day* of
Atonement (Leviticus 16:2); the *ark* (II Samuel 6:6); the
candlestick (Daniel 5:5); and the *incense* (Numbers 16:6,
17-19, 35-40).

All of these items find their greatest manifestation in
the centrality of Jesus Christ. The typology of the Bible is
set forth in abundance in order that in this century we
might see the great centrality of Christ from which
salvation and character must come. No subject in the
Bible approximates the material expended and lavished
upon the Lord Jesus. He is still Scripture's greatest
Treasure.

When we contemplate the Mosaic Tabernacle, the
Solomonic Temple, or the Temple of Ezekiel, we are
overwhelmed with the type and shadow of the truths
involved. The study of the Charismatics was never to be
greater than the Lord. The Giver and the Saviour is
greater than all His gifts.

The moral and spiritual implications which flow from
the centrality of Christ capture our attention without
measure. When we contrast the Charismatics with the
Ten Commandments (Exodus 20:1-7; Deuteronomy 5:1-
21), the nine Beatitudes (Matthew 5:3-12), the nine
ingredients in the fruit of the Spirit (Galatians 5:22-23),

the seven pieces of the Christian's armor (Ephesians 6:14-18), the seven pieces of the Christian's daily wardrobe (II Peter 1:5-7), and the Christian character of the Sermon on the Mount (usually thought of in ten divisions; Matthew 5-7), we realize that God knew our need and revealed the more excellent way for the Christian life.

Second, consider the superiority of the cleansing Blood of Christ. If we were to undertake the multiplicity of times, ways, and types of blood as used in the Bible it would exhaust quite a number of volumes. We cannot afford to emphasize the Charismatics above the Blood of Jesus.

Third, note the meticulous details and the larger amount of material on the Cross of Calvary.

In the first eleven chapters of the Old Testament 2,000 years are passed over rather quickly to come to Abraham and the Messianic Seed. In the Four Gospels of the New Testament there are 89 chapters; only four chapters are devoted to the first thirty years in the life of the Lord; 85 chapters for the last three-and-a-half years of the Lord, with 27 of these chapters describing the last eight days of the Lord. It is obvious, therefore, that the death of Jesus Christ on the Cross of Calvary gains prominent attention.

Fourth, consider the rich meanings of the Atonement. The typology of the Holy Spirit in the Old Testament may be viewed in the cleansing of the leper (Leviticus 13 & 14) and the ingredients of the holy anointing oil (Exodus 30). In the cleansing of the leper we see the priority of the blood being applied first upon the right ear, the right thumb, and the big toe of the right foot before the anointing oil is poured there. The pattern is first, the blood, then the oil. In the Atonement are these riches: first the cleansing and forgiveness through the atoning sacrifice of Jesus Christ; then the anointing and empowering typified in the oil—of the Holy Spirit.

In the ingredients of the anointing oil itself we see a similar pattern as well as richer implications from the nature of the oil. The silver shekel and the brazen laver are interposed and presupposed before there can be the rich and wonderful manifestation of the oil poured into our lives (Exodus 30:11-33).

And the balance in the oil's formula is important. It was not to be poured on the flesh or on a stranger, and it was to be made according to the art of the apothecary. The ingredients consisted of 500 shekels of myrrh, 250 shekels of sweet cinnamon, 250 shekels of sweet calamus, and 500 shekels of cassia, with an *hin* of olive oil. Note the balance of the riches of these things involved and provided, in type, from the Atonement given to mankind by Jesus Christ. Lesser emphasis is placed upon cinnamon and greater emphasis upon myrrh. These are somewhat opposites, yet both are in the formula. The Charismatics of our time would have us overemphasize the cinnamon to the neglect of the Biblical formula and Biblical balance.

Fifth, observe the emphasis of types in Scripture. Here again we can see the greater importance of Scriptural types and shadows centering on the exaltation and emphasis of Jesus Christ. Wherever typology deals with the Holy Spirit, there is continued respect to the Son and the Sacrifice. This is not to say that the Holy Spirit is inferior to the Saviour; it simply means that the types agree with the principles—that the Trinity has set the Son in the midst of the Christian Faith, with supporting types teaching us of Biblical character.

Sixth, mark the spirituality of the Scriptures. Spiritual implications abound in the Bible. Extended commentations on the Law, principles of the Sermon on the Mount, and a large number of spiritual precepts, proverbs, and parables capture our hearts from beginning to end in Scripture. Every sacred page has on it some spiritual truth for us to glean, some lesson for us to learn.

Seventh, we view the pilgrimage of the saints. This world is not our home. We are pilgrims and strangers, seeking a City, an Age, and a World to come. Oh, the journeys of Abraham, Isaac, and Jacob! And the journeyings of Israel from Egypt to Canaan, as well as the flights of David from King Saul, inspire our own journey. Whether we wander in a wilderness, sojourn in a strange land, or flee into another land—all of these examples instruct us to pilgrim and journey in good spirit. But the Charismatics center their joys, their delights, their glossolalia, their prosperity, and their pleasures too much in this age. The Christian's attraction is the Holy Spirit.

Eighth, is the beauty of the Bride of Christ. Many people spend their time arguing about who Cain's wife was, and never see the greater revelation of who Christ's bride will be. Yet Scripture is filled with pictures, principles, and presentations of the bride of Christ. The brides of Abraham, Isaac, Jacob, Joseph, and Solomon—none of these can be compared with the teachings concerning the bride of Christ; yet all of them have a pointing finger, contributing some detail to the final picture of the Lamb's Wife.

Ninth, notice the preponderance of sin and error in the world. This is not a popular subject, but it needs to be discussed. We cannot preach *positive* platitudes about Christ without considering the *negatives* against sin. The Ten Commandments include many negatives, for man is first found in sin, doing what he should *not* do. We must give Biblical consideration to sin and error, and we must take a firm stand against sin and error. Apostasy demands a militant stand in favor of God's cause, and Scripture supports our warfare.

Tenth, is the wonder of God's providence. When there are no miracles or Charismatics to be seen in our lives, God's providence remains. How many there are in our time who are feverishly begging for signs, wonders, miracles, and works without recognizing that they are standing in the midst of a million providences. It takes character to see God working behind the scenes; but He is there.

Eleventh, ponder the greatness of the coming judgment. No matter what our eschatological position may be, there is a coming judgment. We are moving, with accelerated speed, to a time of judgment in the land—the Bema Judgment of the saints in the heavens, as well as the final White Throne Judgment at the end. God will come from behind His silence and providence and speak and act openly to man; and every man will have to meet God. This should give impetus for a deeper life in Christ.

Twelfth, let us mark the blessedness of our future, Heavenly Home. We must never lose sight of the fact that after all earthly things end; after the four curses placed upon the serpent, the woman, the man, and the land have been lifted; after the judgments placed against Pharaoh and the exodus of Israel from Egypt; after the four stages of locusts in the land during the days of Joel, and the four sore judgments of Ezekiel, involving sword, famine, noisome beast, and pestilence; after the four horns of Zechariah, representing four empires, and the four carpenters of Zechariah, representing four judgments; after the Olivet Discourse by Jesus and the Four Horsemen, the seals, the trumpets, the vials of wrath, in the Book of Revelation; after the 120 years of the Holy Spirit striving with man, and the Flood which followed; after the 430 years of Israel's waiting from Abraham to the Exodus; after forty years of Israel's wanderings in the Wilderness; after the agony of Judah's seventy years in the Babylonian Captivity; after the "seventy weeks" of years to the fulfillment of Daniel's prophecy of Christ and Antichrist; and after the sun has grown old and the moon has grown cold—there is our Heavenly Home!

Foretastes of Glory and Tokens of Perdition

Some of you may accuse us of ignoring Biblical insights which teach certain foretastes of glory, and which at times have been received by Christians in this present history. Therefore, we must exercise care in this closing subject. But we genuinely believe that Scripture sets forth certain foretastes of the age to come, which, according to the Scriptures and the sovereignty of God, have been witnessed and experienced by some in this present age. There is a vast difference between erroneous

Charismatics and Biblical foretastes. In fact, there are certain tokens of perdition, as well, which sometimes are viewed from this world and age by certain sinners (cf. Romans 8:23, "firstfruits"; Philippians 1:28, "tokens of perdition").

In anticipation of the Heavenly glory, and if He wills it, God may manifest Himself to someone—even in New Testament time—concerning the foretastes of Heaven; and if God permits, a sinner may anticipate certain aspects of Hell, in a spiritual way, through "evident tokens of perdition" here in this age.

We could present this another way with the hope that you readers will be aware of our desire to preserve certain Biblical aspects of God's dealings with man. Gifts, as revealed in Scripture, should be understood in at least four ways: (1) The gifts of God Himself to man; (2) the gifts of grace; (3) the gifts of the Holy Spirit; and (4) the gifts or foretastes of the Age to come.

According to James 1:17, every good and every perfect gift comes down from God and is dispensed in numerous ways.

The word *gift,* as used in Scripture, comes from at least ten Hebrew words in the Old Testament and at least nine words in the New Testament Greek, including cognates from four distinct words. Altogether we view the word in our King James version about 105 times.

Sometimes we may think of the word "gift" as any endowment that comes through the grace of God (Romans 1:11); gifts that make possible good works (Ephesians 2:10); enduements given for special tasks (II Corinthians 1:11); representative of all the gifts that we may have received in life (I Corinthians 4:7); claims tested by doctrine (I Corinthians 12:2, 3) and morals (Matthew 7:15; Romans 8:9); or the ability in preaching as through a gift (I Corinthians 2:4; II Timothy 1:6).

The gifts of the Godhead are very prominent: the Father (Romans 6:23); the Son (Romans 5:15, grace; 5:17, righteousness; II Corinthians 9:15, unspeakable gift; Ephesians 4:7, gift of Christ; Hebrews 6:4, heavenly gift;

Romans 5:16, free gift); and the Holy Spirit (Acts 2:38; 10:45; Hebrews 2:4).

The free and rich gifts of grace, or gifts given because of grace, are indeed abundant in the Word of God (on sinners, Romans 5:15, 16; 6:23; 11:29; on believers, Romans 12:6; I Corinthians 1:7; 12:4, 9, 28, 30, 31; I Timothy 4:14; II Timothy 1:6; I Peter 4:10).

The gifts of the Holy Spirit to the body of Christ are also set forth in Scripture (Ephesians 4:8; Romans 12:4-5; I Corinthians 12:8-10 and 28-29).

The foretastes or gifts of the age to come occupy still another part of the revelation through God's Word, including illumination, insights, foretastes (I Corinthians 2:11-16; II Corinthians 1:8-11; Hebrews 6:4-5).

Those who have become "the firstfruits of the Spirit" (Romans 8:23) through Jesus Christ are the highest and dearest to the heart of God, though being participants in the "firstfruits" does not exempt believers from the groaning of their pilgrimage on earth. We need to distinguish between "firstfruits of the Spirit" and "gifts" of the Holy Spirit. The gifts of the Holy Spirit are temporary—for the needs of the Body of Christ on earth—whereas the firstfruits are in anticipation of our glorified life in Heaven. Therefore, we anticipate that our firstfruits are our employments and enjoyments freely given to us here in this world to prepare us for a better world. The "firstfruits of the Spirit," in their fulness, are from the other side of the resurrection of believers, but given to a small degree in a foretaste here on earth.

Perhaps many of these foretastes of Heaven do not belong to and are not experienced by all Christians. They should not be confused with the general blessings which by the grace of God are given to every Christian. Apparently, however, there are special favors, dispensed by sovereignty and grace, which are bestowed on some particular persons by the special will of God. Let us consider three kinds of individuals who may be identified with such special foretastes: (1) God chooses some who are strong and eminent in faith and purpose to receive certain foretastes in their lives. (2) There are others who are weak both in reason and faith; but they are definitely justified and regenerated, and God might bestow foretastes upon them under their present temptation or trial. (3) There are still others who sometimes, because they are called by God's great providence and purpose to accomplish a large task through trials and sufferings, will be given added foretastes to build courage, power, and defense against overwhelming odds.

These foretastes are solely in the hands of a sovereign God; He alone wills them through His purpose and grace.

Also, if any of us should ever be favored to receive these foretastes, we must keep in mind that they must be received as from the source of grace, and not necessarily to remain resident within us as a franchise, monopoly, or perpetual power. In fine, the *gifts* of the Holy Spirit are in the mystical Body of Christ, rather than in the physical body and monopoly of the individual; the *foretastes* of Heaven are given from the sovereignty of God and may be withdrawn by that same sovereign will. However great the gifts and foretastes, let us not depend on them to the neglect of the more central and fundamental evidences which we have been given freely by God's grace and which come through God's Word, prayer, and the Holy Spirit in our lives.

Those who "have tasted" of "the powers of the world to come" are strangely connected with certain warnings of the apostasy. Eminent dangers are connected with all of these matters, and we must walk with softness before the Lord. It is necessary that we acknowledge these dangers, and I am doing it so that no one will accuse us of slighting this certain, Biblical presentation. These dangers are real and they are set by sovereign appointment alone. It is wonderful to have God set such appointment upon a finite creature; but it is dangerous to set oneself upon the foretaste without divine appointment.

The Stars in Their Courses Fought

Two terms resolve our subject: *institutional* church

and Biblical *apostasy*. Unfortunately, we have come to
the time of the institutional church. In history a variety of
descriptions has been manifested in the visible and
earthly demonstration of the church. Several outlines
could illustrate this matter, but we offer a typical outline
for the purpose at hand.

We have seen the Apostolic Church (30-100 A.D.), the
Persecuted Church (100-313 A.D.), the State or Worldly
Church (313-590 A.D.), the Roman Catholic Church (590-
1517 A.D.), the Reformed Church (1517-1750 A.D.), the
Missionary or Brotherly Love Church (1750-1900 A.D.),
and the Apostate Church (1900- A.D.). Now we come to the
ecumenism of Modernism, Neo-Pentecostalism, and the
Apostate Church.

The *institutional* church has played a great part in
producing the Apostate Church, and we agree with the
following:

> The tragedy of the Christian churches today is that they
> can continue to exist as *institutions* when the spiritual life
> has gone out of them. The institutional life of a church
> does not appear to depend on its spiritual vitality. Over the
> centuries, all the major churches have developed a number
> of secondary functions and resources which enable them
> to continue to exist, and in some cases to appear to prosper,
> without in the least fulfilling the task that Christ assigned
> to them.[136]

The institutional church has become somewhat of a
halfway house for the assistance of the modern message
of Neo-Christianity—that it might become successful in
our time (as the world speaks of success).

The product of this movement will be the apostasy.
Two prominent passages of Scripture will dispel the
misunderstanding which is suffered by some persons in
our time over the word "apostasy." In the King James
Version, in Luke's Book of The Acts, the word is
translated "forsake" (Greek; *apostasian*) and Paul, in his
Epistle to the Thessalonians, uses the phrase "a falling
away" (Greek; *apostasia*).

And they are informed of thee, that thou teachest all the Jews which are among the Gentiles to forsake Moses, saying that they ought not to circumcise their children, neither to walk after the customs (Acts 21:21).

Let no man deceive you by any means: for that day shall not come, except there come a falling away first...
(II Thessalonians 2:3).

The Song of Deborah, at the defeat of Sisera and the Canaanites, declares that victory was achieved from a prophetess and the stars. This is not the language of the occult, however; it is victory through the Word of God by a prophetess and the powers of God through nature. The Book of Judges declares: "They fought from heaven; the stars in their courses fought against Sisera" (Judges 5:20). From Heaven came the Word of God and the stars to assist the fight.

In the present apostasy being witnessed across the land there is need of spiritual victories through the Word of God and the combined work of God's providences.

When God created the world, He set in the heavens certain luminaries—sun, moon, and stars (Genesis 1:14-16). These luminaries were fixed by God, and they continue in their orbits as a testimony to God's faithfulness to man. Even when Joshua witnessed the miracle of the extra twenty-four hour solar day in his victory at Gibeon and Hezekiah received the sign of assurance via the miracle of the sun's turning backward ten degrees and its being confirmed by the sundial of Ahaz, it was not to be understood that the heavens were falling and the sun and the stars were leaving their orbits to burn out in the night. No; the stars are fixed by the Hand of God, and to this day they serve in orderly orbits. Even a miracle does not change the blessedness of the order and design that God has established for mankind.

Jude tells us that a time will come when false teachers and preachers and prophets will come to the world; and he characterizes these apostates as "wandering stars" (Jude 13) who have left their orderly orbits of the Word of God. In the Greek New Testament this word is also translated "delusion." A false teacher is a "wandering star" and a "delusion." Christians are fixed stars, remaining in a posture of stable consistency to the Word of God.

In our day we need a great revival among the true people of God on the Bible base. We need Christ in all compartments of life. We need Him in the luminaries of business administration, art, music, science, worship, home, recreation—everywhere! We must fight the dishonesty of business with honorable Christian business. We must take a firm stand against the rock music and rock Gospel; against the perverted sexuality of TV drama and speech; and against the fallacies, limitations, and false scholarship of science, so-called. It is our prayer that not only shall we fight the evils of apostasy with all the skills and crafts of these intellectual luminaries, but also that we shall proceed in these things upon the infallible and inerrant Biblical base of the Word of God and in the manifested power of the Holy Spirit. We know our enemies, but we also know our God; and He is greater than all our enemies. In a day when wandering stars have left their fixed positions to follow their heretical tendencies, tangents, and heresies, and are falling into the apostasy of Neo-Christianity, we shall be sustained by the Word of God and by the providential order of things from the very hand of God.

It will not be long before our Lord Jesus will return; and with His return the sun, moon, and stars will work for Him again, and the powers of the heavens will be shaken (cf. Matthew 24:29; Revelation 8:12, 13). Then the Prince of Peace will return to the earth to reign in equity and power, and forever we shall enjoy the gifts of God, of grace, and of the Holy Spirit. Forever we shall know that which now is only a foretaste. Instead of the sirens which confuse men at the noon hour, as they broadcast temporary refreshment and criminal alarm, there will be the everlasting refreshment in a glorified state. And the Christian character which has been given so graciously of God and which has withstood the songs from the island of the Sirens, will be drawn no more to fail. On that imaginary island of the Sirens, believed to be somewhere near the West coast of Italy, there was a strong resistance to the power of the charming songs that sought to lure the crew and captain of the ship of Ulysses. To dispel the effect of the songs, the ears of the crew were filled with wax and Ulysses remained tied to the mast until the ship was out of earshot of the Sirens' song. Standing in sharp contrast is the example of Jason. When the mythological Argonauts, in pursuit of the golden fleece, passed by the Sirens' island, Jason, instead of binding himself to the mast and stuffing the ears of his men with wax, commanded Orpheus to strike his lyre. "His song so surpassed in sweetness that of the charmers, that their music seemed harsh discord. The Sirens, seeing them sail by unmoved, threw themselves into the sea and were metamorphosed into rocks. They had been conquered with their own weapons. Melody had surpassed melody."

Whether by the character of Biblical discipline and moderation we overcome earthly temptations pictured in the first with Ulysses, or the character of Biblical delight in the music of the soul signified in the second with Jason, we know that soon the sounds of the Second Coming will lift us to our Lord and Saviour and a new song in glory!

For the Lord himself shall descend from heaven with a shout, with the voice of the archangel, and with the trump of God: and the dead in Christ shall rise first: Then we which are alive and remain shall be caught up together with them in the clouds, to meet the Lord in the air: and so shall we ever be with the Lord. Wherefore comfort one another with these words (I Thessalonians 4:16-18).

Footnotes

[1]George E. Gardiner, *The Corinthian Catastrophe* (Grand Rapids: Kregel Publishing Co., 1974).

[2]Donald T. Kauffman, *The Dictionary of Religious Terms,* p. 228.

[3]Carl F. H. Henry, *Frontiers in Modern Theology* (Chicago: Moody Press, 1965), p. 109.

[4]Ibid., p. 17.

[5]William H. Turpie, Jr., *Catalyst Tape Talk* (Waco: Word Publisher, 1977), p. 1.

[6]Frank Garlock, Bob Jones University Faculty, oral lecture.

[7]N. J. Holmes, *Life and Sketches and Sermons* (Royston: Pentecostal Holiness Church Press, 1920), pp. 68-69.

[8]Ibid., p. 69.

[9]Ibid., p. 71.

[10]Ibid.

[11]H. P. Robinson, *Heaven's Quest for a Man Like God* (Franklin Springs, Ga.: Advocate Press), pp. 144-181.

[12]Ibid., p. 156.

[13]Ibid., pp. 156-157.

[14]Ibid., p. 159.

[15]Ibid., p. 163.

[16]Vinson Synan, *The Old-Time Power* (Franklin Springs, Ga.: Advocate Press), p. 234.

[17]Ibid., p. 274.

[18]W. R. Corvin, "Let the Bible Speak," *The Pentecostal Holiness Advocate,* 18 May 1977, p. 9.

[19]Vinson Synan, *The Holiness-Pentecostal Movement* (Grand Rapids: Eerdmans Publishing Co., 1971), p. 161.

[20]Vinson Synan, *Aspects of Pentecostal-Charismatic Origins* (Plainfield, N.J.: Logos International, 1975), p. 41.

[21]Ibid., p. 47.

[22]Ibid., p. 41.

[23]Ibid., pp. 41-42.

[24]Vinson Synan, *Charismatics Bridges* (Ann Arbor, Mich.: Word of Life, 1974), pp. 23-24.

[25]Ibid., pp. 24-25.

[26]Vinson Synan, "Pentecostal Catholics at Notre Dame," *Pentecostal Holiness Advocate,* 15 July 1972, pp. 3-4.

[27]Vinson Synan, *Pentecostal Holiness Advocate,* pp. 26-28.

[28]Ibid., p. 48.

[29]H. P. Robinson, p. 163.

[30]Synan, *The Holiness-Pentecostal Movement,* p. 53.

[31]Philip Schaff, *Creeds of Christendom* (New York: Harper, 1919), Volume II, p. 4.

[32]Ibid., pp. 66-68.

[33]Bernard L. Ramm, *Rapping About the Spirit* (Waco: Word Books Publisher, 1974), p. 37.

[34]Charles R. Smith, *Tongues in Biblical Perspective* (Winona Lake: B.M.H. Books, 1972), pp. 13-14.

[35]Ibid., p. 20.

[36]Ibid., pp. 88-89.

[37]Ibid., p. 17.

[38]Ibid.

[39]Ibid.

[40]Ibid., pp. 17-18.

[41]Ibid., p. 18.

[42]Ibid.

[43]Ibid., p. 19.

[44]Philip Schaff, *Creeds of Christendom,* pp. 333-334.

[45]Ibid., p. 334.

[46]Ibid.

[47]Ibid., pp. 334-335.

[48]Synan, *Charismatics Bridges,* pp. 10, 14.

[49]David Wilkerson, "The Charismatic Itch," a tape recorded sermon.

[50]The Fayetteville *Times:*Fayetteville, North Carolina.

[51]Erling Jorstad, *A Charismatic Reader* (New York: Evangelical Book Club, 1974), p. 16.

[52]Ibid., p. 17.

[53]Ibid.

[54]Ibid., pp. 18-19.

[55]Ibid., p. 20.

[56]J. S. Murray, "What We Can Learn from the Pentecostal Churches," *Christianity Today*, June 9, 1967, p. 10.

[57]James W. L. Hills, *The New Wave of Pentecostalism* (Evangelical Foundations, Inc., 1973), pp. 20-29.

[58]The Committee on the Definition of Fundamentalism, passed in open session, World Congress of Fundamentalists, Usher Hall, Edinburgh, Scotland, June 15-22, 1976, printed by Bob Jones University Press.

[59]Wayne A. Robinson, *Oral: The Warm, Intimate, Unauthorized Portrait of a Man of God*, pp. 94-95.

[60]Merrill Unger, *The Haunting of Bishop Pike* (Wheaton: Tyndale House Publishers, 1971), p. 57.

[61]Oral Roberts, *America's Healing Magazine*, October 1954, pp. 4-5.

[62]Ibid., September 1954, pp. 2-3.

[63]T. L. Osborn, *Healing*, pp. 99-100.

[64]Oral Roberts, "New Delivery System," Letter, 1976.

[65]T. L. Osborn, Open Letter, 1976.

[66]Kauffman, pp. 39-40.

[67]Ibid., p. 306.

[68]Peter J. Foxx, *The Projector*, September 1977, p. 3.

[69]Ibid.

[70]Dr. Baldwin, Troy, New York. (Sermon)

[71]*Britannica Book of the Year*, 1973, pp. 592-593.

[72]World Congress on Evangelism in Berlin Correspondence Material, 1966.

[73]*Abundant Life*, January-February 1967.

[74]*Sword of the Lord*, 6 Nov. 1964, p. 6.

[75]Ibid.

[76]Ibid.

[77]*Logos Journal* (Plainfield, N. J., Logos International 1974), p. 68.

[78]*Charisma Digest*, Volume I, 1968.

[79]*Pentecostal Evangel*, October 1975; p. 15.

[80]Ibid., p. 16.

[81]Arthur Meacham, *The Charismatics*, An Unpublished Research Paper, April 1975, p. 9.

[82]Henry Pitney van Dusen, *The Christian Century*, August 17, 1955.

[83]Charles W. Conn, *Like A Mighty Army* (Cleveland: Pathway Press, 1977), p. xxvii.

[84]"The Living Church," September 6, 1964 (*Sword of the Lord*; Nov. 6, 1964) p. 6.

[85]*The Christian Century*, 21 Dec., 1960.

[86]Unger, p. 57.

[87]*Sword of the Lord*, November 6, 1964; p. 6.

[88]Ibid.

[89]*The Christian Century*, April 3, 1963.

[90]Smith, pp. 13-14.

[91]Hills, p. 26.

[92]Synan, pp. 26-28.

[93]Harold Lindsell, "Tests for the Tongues Movement," *Christianity Today* Reprint, 1972.

[94]Synan, "Pentecostal Catholics at Notre Dame," *Pentecostal Holiness Advocate*, July 15, 1972.

[95]Hills, p. 21.

[96]Ibid.

[97]Schaff, Volume II, p. 4.

[98]Ibid., p. 34.

[99]R. C. Trench, *Synonyms of the New Testament* (Grand Rapids: Eerdmans Publishing Co., 1948), pp. 219-221.

[100]*Webster's Seventh New Collegiate Dictionary*.

[101]Oral Roberts, "Samson and Delilah," Tape Sermon (Washington, D.C.), 1952.

[102]*Encyclopedia Britannica*, 1973.

[103]*The Nestle Greek Text of the New Testament*, Luke 1:37.

[104]M. Adler, *The Great Conversation*, Volume I, *Great Books of the Western World*.

[105]Soren Kierkegaard, *Concluding Unscientific Postscript* (Princeton: Princeton University Press, 1941), pp. 21-22.

[106]Kierkegaard, p. 178.

[107]The Oklahoma *Times*, April 5, 1968, by Robert Allen.

[108]Trench, pp. 217-218.

[109]Martin Luther.

[110]Bud Bierman, "Ecstasy and Emptiness: The 1977 Charismatic Conferences," *Faith for the Family*, Nov. 1977, p. 14.

[111]Ibid., p. 13.

[112]Bob Slosser, *A Man Called Mr. Pentecost* (Plainfield: Logos International, 1977), pp. 2-3.

[113]Ibid., p. 92.

[114]Ibid., pp. 191-192.

[115]Ibid., p. 195.

[116]Ibid., p. 233.

[117]Ibid., p. 234.

[118]"Charismatic Study Report;" The Assembly of God Church, August 14, 1972.

[119]B. E. Underwood, "What About the Charismatics," *Pentecostal Holiness Advocate.*

[120]G. F. Taylor, *The Rainbow* (Franklin Springs, Ga.: Publishing House of the Pentecostal Holiness Church, 1924), pp. 103-107.

[121]A. E. Robinson, *A Layman and the Book* (Washington, D.C.: North Washington Press), p. 151.

[122]*World Congress of Fundamentalists*, General Publicity.

[123]Perry Miller, *Religion and Freedom of Thought*, p. 18.

[124]Albert Hyma, *World History: A Christian Interpretation*, p. 355.

[125]George W. Dollar, *A History of Fundamentalism in America* (Greenville, S.C.: Bob Jones University Press, 1974).

[126]Bob Jones III, *Bob Jones University/Fifty Years Under God.*

[127]Ibid.

[128]Conn, pp. xxiv-v.

[129]Ibid., p. xxv.

[130]Ibid., p. xxix.

[131]Ibid., p. xxviii.

[132]Frank Garlock.

[133]Francis A. Schaeffer, Seminar, Atlanta, Georgia.

[134]Richard S. Taylor, *A Return To Christian Culture*, Dimension Books.

[135]Synan, *Aspects of Pentecostal Charismatic Origins.*

[136]Harold O. J. Brown, *The Protest of a Troubled Protestant* (New York: Arlington House, 1969), p. 111.

Bibliography

Beecher, Willis J. *The Prophets and the Promise.* Grand Rapids: Baker Book House, 1963.

Bierman, Bud. "Ecstasy and Emptiness: The 1977 Charismatic Conferences," *Faith for the Family*, Nov. 1977, p. 14.

Boettner, Loraine. *Roman Catholicism.* Philadelphia: Presbyterian and Reformed Publishing Company, 1962.

Brown, Harold O. J. *The Protest of a Troubled Protestant.* New York: Arlington House, 1969.

Carnell, Edward John. *The Burden of Soren Kierkegaard.* Grand Rapids: Eerdmans Publishing Co., 1965.

Conn, Charles W. *Like a Mighty Army.* Cleveland: Pathway Press, 1977.

Dollar, George W. *A History of Fundamentalism in America.* Greenville: Bob Jones University Press, 1974.

Enroth, Ronald M. and Gerald Jamison. *The Gay Church.* Grand Rapids: Eerdmans Publishing Co., 1974.

Gardiner, George E. *The Corinthian Catastrophe.* Grand Rapids: Kregel Publishing Co., 1974.

Girdlestone, Robert Baker. *Synonyms of the Old Testament.* Grand Rapids: Eerdmans Publishing Co., 1977.

Henry, Carl F. H. *Frontiers in Modern Theology.* Chicago: Moody Press, 1965.

Hills, James W. L. *The New Wave of Pentecostalism.* Evangelical Foundations, Inc., 1973.

Holmes, N. J. *Life Sketches and Sermons.* Royston: Pentecostal Holiness Church Press, 1920.

Hyma, Albert. *World History: A Christian Interpretation.* Grand Rapids: Eerdmans Publishing Co., 1942.

Jorstad, Erling. *A Charismatic Reader.* New York: Evangelical Book Club, 1974.

Kauffman, Donald T. *The Dictionary of Religious Terms.* Westwood, N.J.: Revell Co., 1967.

Kierkegaard, Soren. *Concluding Unscientific Postscript.* Princeton: Princeton University Press, 1941.

Lindsell, Harold. "Tests for the Tongues Movement," *Christianity Today,* 1972.

Murray, J. S. "What We Can Learn from the Pentecostal Churches," *Christianity Today,* 9 June 1967, p. 10.

Novak, Al. *Hebrew Honey.* New York: Vantage Press, 1965.

Orr, J. Edwin. *The Flaming Tongue.* Chicago: Moody Press, 1973.

Ramm, Bernard. *Rapping About the Spirit.* Waco: Word Books Publisher, 1974.

Robinson, A. E. *A Layman and the Book.* Washington, D.C.: North Washington Press.

Robinson, H. P. *Heaven's Quest for a Man Like God.* Franklin Springs, Ga.: Advocate Press, 1969.

Robinson, Wayne A. *The Warm, Intimate, Unauthorized Portrait of a Man of God.* Los Angeles: Acton House, Inc., 1976.

Schaeffer, Francis August. *How Should We Then Live?* Old Tappan, N.J.: Revell Publishing Co., 1976.

Schaff, Philip. *Creeds of Christendom.* New York: Harper, 1919.

Schaff, Philip. *History of the Christian Church.* Grand Rapids: Eerdmans Publishing Co., 1971.

Slosser, Bob. *A Man Called Mr. Pentecost.* Plainfield, N.J.: Logos International, 1977.

Smith, Charles R. *Tongues in Biblical Perspective.* Winona Lake: B.M.H. books, 1972.

Synan, Vinson. *Aspects of Pentecostal-Charismatic Origins.* Plainfield, N. J.: Logos International, 1975.

Synan, Vinson. *The Holiness-Pentecostal Movement.* Grand Rapids: Eerdmans Publishing Co., 1971.

Synan, Vinson. *Charismatic Bridges.* Ann Arbor, Michigan: Word of Life, 1974.

Synan, Vinson. *The Old-Time Power.* Franklin Springs, Ga.: Advocate Press.

Taylor, G. F. *The Rainbow.* Franklin Springs, Ga.: Publishing House of the Pentecostal Holiness Church, 1924.

Thayer's Greek English Lexicon of the New Testament. New York: Harper, 1897.

Trench, R. C. *Synonyms of the New Testament.* Grand Rapids: Eerdmans Publishing Co., 1948.

Turpie, William H., Jr. *Catalyst Tape Talk.* Waco: Word Publisher, 1977.

Unger, Merrill. *The Haunting of Bishop Pike.* Wheaton: Tyndale House Publishers, 1971.

Van Baalen, Jan Karel. *The Chaos of Cults.* Grand Rapids: Eerdmans Publishing Co., 1953.

Vine, W. E. *Expository Dictionary of New Testament Words.* Westwood, N.J.: Revell Co., 1966.

Watts, J. Wash. *A Survey of Syntax* in the Hebrew Old Testament. Grand Rapids: Eerdmans Publishing Company, 1964.

Westcott, B. F. *The Canon of the New Testament.* Cambridge: Macmillan, 1855.

Williams, Pat and Douglas Hill. *The Supernatural.* New York: Hawthorn Book Publishers, 1965.

Young, Robert. *Young's Analytical Concordance to the Bible.* Grand Rapids: Eerdmans, 1969.